CREATIVE

CLOWNING

Bruce Fife • Tony Blanco •
Bruce Johnson • Ralph Dewey
Jack Wiley • Gene

Illustrated by
Ed Harris

JAVA PUBLISHING COMPANY
COLORADO SPRINGS, CO.

Library of Congress Cataloging-in-Publication Data

Creative Clowning.

    1. Clowns.   I. Fife, Bruce, 1952-
GV1828.C74   1987   791.3'3   87-22638

ISBN 0-941599-03-5

ACKNOWLEDGMENTS

Grateful acknowledgment is made for permission to reprint excerpts from the following:

The Wonderful Father Book, 1985, published by Turnbull & Willoughby Publishers, Inc. *Tannen's Magic Manuscript*, published by Tannen's Magic Manuscript, Ltd. *Laughing Matters*, published and edited by Dr. Joel Goodman.

The publisher expresses thanks and indebtedness to the following people and organizations who have helped in the preparation of this book:

Library of Congress, National Archives, Times-Herald, Bettmann Archives, Circus World Museum, Dixon and Turner Research Associates, Hertzberg Circus Museum, Juggler's World, and the many individuals who graciously contributed photographs from personal collections.

Front Cover: Photo of Tony Blanco by Paul Bernstein.
Back Cover: Auguste and Grimaldi clown photographs courtesy of Masters Costumes, 5845 Leesburg Pike, Bailey's Crossroads, Virginia 22041

TABLE OF CONTENTS

FOREWORD

Clowning is beginning to come-of-age. "What are you talking about?" you may ask. "We've had clowning for centuries." Actually what I am talking about is the body of knowledge and information on clowning that is finally coming-of-age. If you were to travel back to 1960 and examine the materials available, in print or on various visual media at that time, you'd find a dismal situation indeed. At that point in our history, clowning was a very secretive art form. This situation further compounded the demise of clowning, as fewer and fewer clowns remained. Clown associations, clown conventions, clown schools, clown museums, clown classes, and clown newspapers or magazines did not exist. Clowning was becoming a vanishing art. Since that time however, all of the above have come about. Major strides have been made, but we still have a somewhat elementary level of written materials available for those seriously interested in learning more about the multiple aspects of clowning. A single source omnibus of clowning techniques and information has not been available—until now.

Creative Clowning is what I consider to be the first one volume encyclopedia of clowning ever published. Its release comes at a most opportune time in the development and growth of clowning in North America. It is the right product at the right time. Within the pages of this volume you will find an amazing collec-tion of information on nearly every aspect of clowning. Often an anthology or collection of different writers' works is loosely organized or poorly structured, but that is not the case with this book. You will be pleasantly surprised at how well the editors have integrated the writings of so many authors into such a smooth flowing volume on the pleasure and business of being funny.

This book should not be read in one or two sittings. It can be of maximum benefit to readers seriously interested in learning about clowning, if they will become "active" in their reading. Put another way, you will learn more, and appreciate just what the authors are saying, if you will do what the book suggests. Don't be a passive reader; participate in the activities outlined for you when you read through the pages. For example, there are several paper and pencil activities which will help you write comedy routines or create a better concept of your clown character. Consider the book a personal tutor as you follow its guidance and suggestions. But, do the exercises immediately. In this way you will achieve the maximum benefits. Believe me, this should not be a book read as a speed reading exercise. It is a "workbook".

The chapter entitled **Creating Your Own Comedy Act** offers value to both the beginner and the experienced joey. Here you will find techniques which will assist you in creating humorous skits and routines. The authors are generous with ideas which are very specific. Try the techniques and you will be reading and smiling at the same time. This is a fun book to experience.

For whom is this book really intended? Is it for beginner or advanced performer? Frankly, it is a book suitable and desirable for both. As with most "encyclopedias," this work contains such a breadth of information, that few performers will be adept in all of the areas covered. Even the experienced clowns who turn the pages of this book will find new and creative techniques that they can employ in strengthening their acts. As for the newer clowns, here you will find the meat of all the areas necessary for becoming a well rounded clown.

As the current president of the World Clown Association and director of a large clown training program, I see this book as a major stepping stone in our quest for improving the field of clowning. Take this practical, techniques oriented workbook and put it to the test. See if you do not agree that it will improve your techniques and skills at being the *best clown possible!*

Richard Snowberg
President, World Clown Association

INTRODUCTION

"All the world loves a clown," so the saying goes. That statement is true today more than ever before. Children everywhere giggle and leap with wide-eyed excitement at the very sight of these mirthmakers. Parents too, share the thrill that clowns create. Why are clowns so popular? Because they are fun! And clowning too is fun. Thousands of ordinary people are discovering the truth of this statement as they step into the fascinating and rewarding world of clowning. Amateur and professional entertainers, teachers, youth leaders, recreation enthusiasts, and other fun-loving folks are finding the art of clowning a great benefit as a form of recreation, instruction, and entertainment, as well as a pleasant source of income. Experience the thrill yourself of bringing laughter and smiles to people's faces only once, and you'll be hooked—it's exciting!

In this book you will learn everything you need to know to share in the joy of clowning. Topics include the basics of applying makeup, designing a wardrobe, and discovering the clown personality hidden inside you, as well as learning how to juggle, work with puppets, ride a unicycle, and other clown skills. It also provides information on a variety of jobs available for clowns and how to get these jobs, including complete details for setting up and operating your own home based birthday party business.

Although it contains all the how-to information, this is more than just a how-to book. It would be described better as a "how-to-do-it-funny" book. Performing a clever trick is one thing, but doing it in a way that makes it comical is something else.

Bettmann Archive

Some years ago a father approached me and said, "I'm really impressed with your show. How do you do it?"

I looked at him inquisitively. "How do I do what?"

"How do you get kids to laugh at your tricks? Whenever I try some of those same stunts my kids look at me as if I'm dumb. But when you do it, they can't stop laughing. What's your secret?"

What is my secret? What is it that makes a simple trick, such as pretending to remove your thumb, hilariously funny when one person does it, but a bore when performed by another? This so-called secret is simply the creative use of a buildup or story to accompany the trick. Tricks by themselves may be interesting, but have limited entertainment value. Silly stunts, that even kids can do, appear corny unless accompanied by a creative story that transforms the trick into a humorous event.

This book, *Creative Clowning*, is directed toward teaching the reader not just how to perform clown type-skills, but how to perform them in a funny and entertaining way.

Given a little time, anybody can learn to juggle, do magic, or perform balancing tricks, but to make these skills humorously entertaining requires creative innovation. If you have a desire to learn about clowning, you no doubt possess a good sense of humor. A sense of humor is the basic ingredient you need to make any stunt delightfully amusing.

Eight authors pooled their thoughts and experience in creating this unique book. The editor and compiler, Bruce Fife, participated in the writing of almost every chapter but made significant contributions in Chapters 1, 2, 3, 5, 6, 8, 10 through 14, and 16 through 19. The following authors contributed in whole or in part to the chapters indicated: Tony Blanco Chapters 3, 4, and 10; Ralph Dewey Chapter 9 (including illustrations); Hal Diamond Chapter 20; Bruce Johnson Chapters 2, 7, 11, and 18; Steve Kissell Chapters 5, 8, and 17; Gene Lee Chapters 2, 6, and 7; Jack Wiley Chapter 15.

CHAPTER 1

THE ART OF CLOWNING

WHAT IS A CLOWN?

We hear the term "clown" often, but what is a clown? Are clowns just silly comedians who dress up in outlandish costumes and makeup to entertain kids?

Clowns have been called by a variety of names: pranksters, mirthmakers, jesters, comics, jokers, buffoons, harlequins, merry-andrews, fools, mimes, and joeys. They are described as preposterous, ridiculous, clever, odd, bizarre, clumsy, eccentric, foolish, extravagant, funny, and zany. Clowns are all this and more. For some, a clown is a treasured memory from childhood; for others, a relaxing moment away from daily activities, a brief visit into a world of fantasy and fun; still others look to the clown as an ambassador of cheer. To children a clown is a living cartoon, an animated figure in the flesh.

Contrary to popular opinion, clowns are not strictly children's entertainers. Sure, children are attracted the most, but other people enjoy clowns too. Most parents, whether they admit it or not, love clowns as much as their children do.

Clowns are more than just crazy people who dress up in funny clothes and wear heavy makeup. They are performing artists. Circus clowns perform their crazy skits under the "Big Top"; others do magic, make balloon animals, and tell jokes at children's birthday parties, grand openings, malls, and school shows; rodeo clowns playfully flirt with wild bulls; religious clowns provide Christian entertainment in churches, on campuses, in hospitals, and in senior citizens' homes; and still others enjoy juggling, unicycling, and stilt walking at fairs, carnivals, parades, and picnics. Combining the talents of both actor and comedian, often in combination with circus skills, clowns portray exaggerated comic characters. Their purpose is to entertain, to bring smiles and laughter to audiences of all ages.

BEING A REAL CLOWN

To be successful, a clown must possess certain skills, just as any other entertainer does. Wearing a colorful costume or using clownish props does not make a person a clown any more than wearing a white jacket would make a doctor. At times children may ask, "Are you a real clown?" or more bluntly say, "You're not a clown, you're just a man dressed up."

Being a *real* clown, as in any profession or skill, involves training and knowledge. This book was written to provide both experienced and inexperienced clowns with the basics of the art of clowning. It goes a step further than giving instruction on the physical or mechanical aspects of the art; it teaches how to use traditional clown skills to amuse and entertain.

As the title of this book implies, *Creative Clowning* is designed to help clowns and aspiring clowns to look deeper than just performing tricks. A juggling clown, for instance, can be an expert juggler yet a poor clown because he lacks the ability or know-how to make people laugh. An effective clown can make the act come alive for the audience and induce spontaneous laughter. The audience must leave knowing they had a good time. If the clown has made them laugh and forget their daily lives for a few minutes, he has accomplished that goal.

In order to do this, you will need to know how to make ordinary things become funny. Three tennis balls in themselves are not funny or entertaining. Even if juggled, they have limited entertainment value. But if the clown combines them with clever dialogue and physical expression, he can make an audience roll in the aisles with laughter.

To make people forget themselves and laugh you can use a variety of methods beside juggling, such as magic, stilt walking, balancing, puppetry, mime, balloon sculpturing, and unicycling, all of which will be discussed in some detail later in this book.

There's more to making people laugh than just telling a funny joke. It's not so much *what* you say as *how* you say it. Have you ever heard a joke told by two different people? It's funny from one person but not with the other. They're telling the same joke and saying basically the same thing, but one gets roars of laughter while the other is met with stony-faced silence or perhaps nauseated groans.

The successful storyteller receives a good response because he lifts the listeners out of their present surroundings and places them in his own imaginary world, where they can experience in their minds the smells, tastes, and scenes he describes. They are following the story so intently that when the punch line hits, it's a total surprise and makes them burst out laughing.

If the same joke or story is told in a mundane way, it's boring. Listeners don't relate to it or may figure out the end before it's over. The difference between the two storytellers is basically attitude. One tells it with excitement and conviction, while the other just repeats something he heard, without vocal variations, emotion, or physical expression.

Combining dialogue with physical skills, such as juggling or magic, works by the same principle. Lead the audience into a imaginary world of your own creation, using vocal fluctuations, emotions, and physical movement. Avoid simply repeating jokes borrowed from someone else. As you read through the chapters on skills, keep this important concept in mind.

Clowns are silly, but acting silly and providing entertainment are different. People act silly and goof off solely for their own enjoyment; entertainers, on the other hand, do it for the enjoyment of others. This doesn't mean that the performer can't enjoy himself. Your speech and actions should appear spontaneous and be fun for both you and your audience.

A clown's purpose is to entertain others, and his actions and emphasis should be directed toward this goal. For instance, if the clown comes up to someone and begins to joke around, he should not try to embarrass or offend just to get a laugh. Spectators should never be the butt of any joke. The clown is the silly character—it is he, not the audience, who should end up looking like the fool or taking the short end of the stick.

Much of the joy in clowning is experienced by the performer himself. To evoke laughter in a child or smiles in a wheelchair-bound patient brings a sense of joy obtainable in few other ways. To have children giggle, laugh, and shout with excitement is immensely satisfying. In so doing, they are telling you that you're funny and appreciated. There have been occasions where, after a show, a child would come up to me, give me a hug, and say, "I love you." Sincere appreciation—what better reward could a clown receive?

THE ROOTS OF CLOWNING

The art of clowning as we see it today is the culmination of thousands of years of evolutionary development. Clowns share a common origin with comedians, magicians, actors, and other performing artists.

The first recorded reference to clowning dates from about 2270 BC. A nine year-old Egyptian Pharaoh is recorded as saying that they are "A divine spirit . . . to rejoice and delight the heart."

Clowning, in one form or another, is found in almost every culture and in every age. The art of clowning has existed wherever there have been people who enjoy "clowning around." Historical accounts trace the art from early Egyptian times through the rise of the Greek

City Boy: Look at that bunch of cows.
Farmer: Not bunch, herd.
City Boy: Heard what?
Farmer: Of cows.
City Boy: Sure, I've heard of cows.
Farmer: No, I mean a cow heard.
City Boy: Why should I care? I have no
    secrets from them.

Although we readily recognize the jester as an early ancestor of the modern clown, the vast majority of these mirthmakers worked on their own as street performers. Because they lived nomadic lives and often were skilled musicians and vocalists, they were referred to as traveling minstrels. They were also known for a wide variety of entertaining talents other than music and poetry—their acts included such things as juggling, acrobatics, storytelling, puppetry, magic, contortion, tightrope walking, fire eating, and working with trained animals.

Being street performers like their predecessors in earlier ages, they depended on donations from their audience to make a living. To be talented and skilled enough to be employed as a jester for one of the nobles was not only an honor, but was considered the pinnacle of success in the profession.

Life for the typical wandering minstrel was difficult at best. Many would hire their services to a mountebank and work as a "zany". Mountebanks were the equivalent of the traveling snake-oil salesmen who roamed America in the 1800s. They sold homemade elixirs and potions, and even extracted teeth. Depending on good salesmanship and the ability to attract an

and later Roman Empires. Kings and rulers often had their own personal fool or funnyman to keep them entertained.

The most recognized clowns in history are those of the Middle Ages and early Renaissance. We are all familiar with the court jester, often depicted juggling or strumming a lute. Employed by kings and nobles, these talented mirthmakers possessed a variety of skills. Jesters were a privileged class who often had freedoms granted to no one else. They were allowed to forego much of the formal behavior expected of others in the ruler's household. They could answer back to anyone in authority, and make jest of almost anyone or anything without fear of reprisal, although history does record severe punishments for some who had used this freedom too liberally.

During this time costumes began to take on the colorful and bizarre appearance we often associate with clowns. Comedians are masters of twisting ordinary things into the ridiculous, thus creating humor. Since the jesters were expected to be funny, they dressed to fit the part by wearing clothes with exaggerated or unusual designs. Often wearing bells, jagged collars, coats, and pointed caps colored with bright red, green, and yellow to complement their cheery, comical character.

Joseph Grimaldi (1779-1837) famous English clown.

audience to peddle his "medicines," the mountebank often employed a zany.

The zany would perform his juggling, magic, comedy and other skills to attract an audience. When a sufficently large audience was gathered, the mountebank took over the stage to peddle his wares.

The Theaters

After the beginning of the Renaissance, the clown transformed from a multi-talented street performer to that of an actor-comedian. With a resurgence in the arts, including the performing arts, clowns became common stage characters. Some achieving great popularity.

The Italian street theaters, which became popular in the 1500s, and remained popular for another two hundred years, played an important part in perpetuating this new image. In the commedia dell'arte, (comedy of professional actors), clowns played roles as clumsy, slow-witted servants or country bumpkins, yet retained the variety of skills that made them popular in earlier times.

One of the popular types of clown that appeared at this time was the Harlequin, a name which is still used to describe clowns. The Harlequin's distinctive costume of black and white patchwork coat, tights, and matching mask, made him easily identifiable.

In French theaters another form of clown emerged, the Pierrot. In contrast to the Harlequin, the Pierrot wore a white loose fitting costume. His most distinguishing trademark, and one that would be a standard for clowns in the future, was an all-white face. Powdered originally with flour and later with grease paint, the whiteface clown as we know him began to emerge.

Like their counterparts in Italy and other European countries, the theater funnyman or "zanni," as they were called, were accomplished actors as well as skilled technicians who often used their talents in tumbling and other forms of physical expression.

The word "clown" did not exist until the sixteenth century. The term was originally used in English theaters to describe a clumsy country oaf.

In the 1700s small traveling street theaters, which played primarily for the common folk, often used clowns or zanni to attract people to pay for the main show inside. These small troupes would compete with the large city theaters, who looked down on them.

To keep the acting profession at a more dignified position in society and to eliminate competition, laws were created to restrict street performances. The laws in England and France prohibited unauthorized performances but said nothing about silent acting. In order to continue their profession without harassment, performers in the street theaters turned to pantomime. This was to have a lasting effect on the development of clowning. Mime, or acting without words, is a basic tool of clowns today.

Perhaps the most famous clown of the theater was an Englishman by the name of Joseph Grimaldi. Born into a family of entertainers, Grimaldi began his performing career at the age of two on the stage of the famous Drury Lane Theater in London. From his debut in 1781 until his retirement in 1828 he was a regular performer in London theaters. His stage name "Joey" is used now as a term synonymous with "clown".

Dan Rice (1823-1900), American circus clown.

Circus World Museum, Baraboo, Wisconsin

Circus World Museum, Baraboo, Wisconsin

The Circus

The clowns we recognize today are a direct out-growth of the circus. Can you imagine a circus without clowns? Clowns fit into the circus like a hot dog in a bun. They go together naturally and have done so from the very start.

The first circus was started by a former British sergeant-major named Philip Astley. Outside London in 1768 Astley organized a show centered around the horsemanship and trick riding skills he had learned while in the cavalry.

One of Astley's early stunt riders was a man named Billie Button. Button's performances combined agility and skill with elements of awkward clumsiness, which delighted audiences and gave him the distinction of being the first circus clown. The popularity of Button and the other acts inspired Astley to enlarge his show with additional animals, tightrope walkers, acrobats, and, of course, clowns.

The word "circus," which means "circle," was first used when Charles Hughes, a former member of Astley's troupe, formed his own show, called the Royal Circus, in 1782.

It wasn't long until other circuses patterned after Astley's and Hughes' shows began to emerge through-out Europe. The clown being a primary character in all of them. By the 1820s small traveling circuses roamed across both the European and American con-tinents. Setting up their show inside roofless canvas tents, clowns, horsemen, acrobats and others performed for delighted audiences.

One of the greatest of the early showmen, who emerged in the 1830s, was P.T. Barnum. Starting out from Connecticut, he traveled around the country with a canvas-topped tent, exhibiting a comical midget named

Circus World Museum, Baraboo, Wisconsin

Tom Thumb. His show, which eventually included animals, clowns, acrobats, and human curiosities, be-came one of the leading circuses of the day. When combined with competitor James A. Bailey's circus in 1881, it became the largest attraction of its type in America and was billed as *Barnum and Bailey's Greatest Show on Earth*, boasting the world's largest collection of elephants and other animals.

The most renowned circus clown in America during the 19th century was a man by the name of Dan Rice. Calling himself "Yankee Dan" he sported a goatee, top hat, and red and white striped tights, which inspired cartoonists of the day to use him as a model for creating "Uncle Sam."

Begining his circus career in 1840, Yankee Dan toured successfully with several circuses until his retire-ment in 1882. His natural flair for creating humor made him immensely popular with his audiences. Often he would use trained pigs, dogs, and horses in his acts.

George L. Fox (1825-1877), offten called the American Grimaldi.

Still he is remembered best for his lighthearted quotes from Shakespearean plays, which won him the reputation as "the Shakespearean clown."

Inspired by Yankee Dan and his fellow performers, five brothers from Baraboo, Wisconsin named Rungeling opened up their own circus in 1884. Small traveling troupes of family performers were common in these days, especially in Europe. The Rungelings, calling themselves the *Ringling Bros. Circus,* went on the road with animal acts, a band, and (of course) clowns. The youngest brother John, becoming their first clown.

The one ring circus in which the performances were held gave way to the more spectacular three rings, which allowed three separate acts to be shown simultaneously. Tents grew larger, accommodating thousands of spectators.

By the 1890s the Ringling Bros. Circus was Barnum and Bailey's biggest rival. In 1907 after the deaths of both Barnum and Bailey, the Ringlings purchased their primary competitor's circus. This combined show, known as *Ringling Bros. and Barnum & Bailey Circus,* brought together the largest collection of animals and

Circus World Museum, Baraboo, Wisconsin

Circus World Museum, Baraboo, Wisconsin

Two of the most recognized clown faces in the world, Lou Jacobs (left) and Emmett Kelly (right).

variety performers ever seen; it was truly the greatest show on earth.

The early 1900s was the heyday of the circus, and Ringling Bros. and Barnum & Bailey continued to expand by purchasing other circuses. By the late 1920s it had 5000 employees and used 240 railroad cars for transportation.

The economic depression of the 1930s and later competition with television, movie theaters, and other forms of entertainment slowed the growth of the large circuses and choked out many of the smaller ones. By this time, clowns as we recognize them today had developed.

Modern Clowns

Until the mid-1800s most clowns wore very little makeup. They were of the category we would now call character clowns. The character clown is one who portrays a specific lifestyle or profession, exaggerating

the stereotyped personality associated with them. Many of the early comedians of the stage and screen, such as Buster Keaton, the Keystone cops, Laurel and Hardy, and The Three Stooges were considered character clowns. These performers developed their own distinct comic appearance and personality, many of which are copied today by modern character clowns and family entertainers.

The all-white face which started with the French Pierrot became typical of many circus clowns in the 1800s. The whiteface clown was that of a skilled comedian often exhibiting extraordinary talents in juggling or acrobatics. The bumbling half-wit character that is so often portrayed by clowns today did not become a trademark until the beginning of the 20th century.

This trend was inspired by the creation of a new type of clown known as the *auguste*. While performing in Germany in 1869, an American acrobat named Tom Belling, literally stumbled onto this new approach to clowning. Suspended from performing for a month because he had fallen during a routine acrobatic move, he remained back stage during the performances.

Having a natural sense of humor, Belling passed much of this time clowning around with fellow performers. On one occasion he took some old baggy clothes, turned them inside out, and put them on. To this he added a wig, which he wore backwards, tying the hair in back into a knot, which made it stick straight up out of the back of his head. While amusing his companions offstage, he accidentally ran out onto the circus arena during a performance, stumbled, and fell. The sight of this silly looking, awkward creature tripping onto his face evoked a thunderous roar of laughter from the audience. Joyfully they shouted "Auguste!" an old German slang word meaning "stupid" or "silly".

The audience enjoyed his brief appearance so much that it was added with embellishments to later performances. Unlike the typical whiteface clown, the auguste developed into the classical buffoon, who appeared to be clumsy and lacking in intelligence. His clothes became bright and colorful, and makeup matching his exaggerated personality, incorporating large eyes, mouth, and bulbous nose.

The auguste evolved into the boisterous, slow-witted, fumbling character we recognize today. The whiteface, on the other hand, became the smarter, more skillful clown, usually possessing talents in juggling, ropewalking, acrobatics and magic. Although in reality just as skilled, the auguste would appear to be unable to copy the whiteface's talents. The two types of clowns often teamed up, the whiteface taking the role of the more intelligent (or rather less unintelligent) straight man, and the auguste playing the role of the comic. It was the whiteface who set up the situations in which the auguste would get trapped in, thereby creating much of the humor.

Probably no other entertainer in history has brought more smiles to people in a live performance than Lou Jacobs of the Ringling Brothers Circus. Born in 1903, Jacobs has been entertaining audiences as an auguste for over 60 years. Recognized as a master clown, he has shaped the character of the modern august clown as well as influence the art of clowning as a whole.

The aftermath of the American Civil War gave rise to yet another breed of clown, the tramp or hobo. At the end of the war, a great many homeless and migratory workers began roaming across the American countryside, often relying on passing trains for transportation. These hobos were common sights to traveling circus performers.

In their performances, circus clowns often portrayed specific characters such as firemen, policemen, and dentists. The tramp characterization became one of the most popular, evolving into a standard clown character commonly seen today.

Many of the famous comedians of the early 1900s portrayed themselves as tramps. W.C. Fields began his career as a tramp juggler, changing his image as he moved into motion pictures. Charlie Chaplin, known as the "Little Tramp," was one of the best examples of the character clown. He was an expert at making people laugh at life's problems. Perhaps the best known circus tramp was Emmett Kelly. Kelly's character "Weary Willie" made audiences laugh and cry at the sight of a clown sweeping a spotlight around until it vanished. His success has set many of the standards emulated by today's tramp and hobo clowns.

Like the other clowns, the tramp's appearance evolved with time and more makeup was gradually added. With the increasing size of circus audiences, the faces painted on clowns became bigger for easier visibility. Spoken dialogue also became impractical, and clowns had to develop their routines around physical comedy and pantomime, using exaggerated movements and oversized props.

A hundred years ago most all clowns worked in the circus. Since the 1940s more and more clowns have found employment in a variety of other settings, ranging from birthday parties to business promotions and amusement parks. Retaining their circus heritage, clowns are easily identified by their unique makeup, colorful costumes, and comical often slapstick antics.

> Doris: If you put three ducks into a crate, what would you have?
> Daisy: A box of quackers.

CHAPTER 2

DEVELOPING A UNIQUE CLOWN CHARACTER

WHAT IS CLOWN CHARACTER?

You can make balloon animals, maybe do magic or juggle, but what makes you different from every other clown? Your unique personality and character—that's what. Your clown character, which is supported and enhanced by the makeup used and the clothes worn, is what separates you from the so-called "generic" clown.

What do Charlie Chaplin, Buster Keaton, Groucho Marx, Bill Cosby, and Pee Wee Herman all have in common? Nothing—except that each has a distinctive style. Each can be identified by his own unique comic personality.

If you put a spoonful of unflavored Jello gelatin into your mouth it will be bland and tasteless. But take a bite of cherry flavored gelatin and your taste buds perk up, your eyes twinkle, and your mouth waters. It's good—you may want more. What's the difference? The gelatin now has *flavor*. When flavor is added, the gelatin gains character and becomes an enjoyable dessert.

Clowns, like Jello, need flavor. Being a clown involves more than just putting on some makeup and a costume and acting silly. The personality or flavor that you add distinguishes you from all other clowns and makes you recognizable and remembered by audiences.

Your clown character is a person you create with personality traits, likes and dislikes, goals and desires,

strengths and weaknesses. Your clown character has a unique way of looking at the world. Your clown's appearance, way of moving, and actions and reactions are all influenced by your character's personality.

That personality should connect in some way with who you are. It might be an exaggeration of your own personality traits. I tend to be quiet, and by exaggerating that trait I created a silent character. It might be a personality driven by wish fulfillment. One clown I know said she had never felt very attractive, so she created a glamorous character. Your character might be an expression of your sense of humor. I love the Gracie Allen type of humor so my clown tends to give everything the same literal interpretation.

A phrase used by many clown instructors is "find the clown that is in you." That's how really successful clown characters are created. Your personality should enable you to portray one particular clown character better than anyone else. What makes developing a clown character difficult is that you must find it yourself. Nobody else can tell you what it should be.

Being in makeup and costume can free inhibitions. This may give a quiet person the freedom to be boisterous, but a quiet person can't force himself to be boisterous because somebody said he should. Your clown character has to be a personality you like and are comfortable with, because if you are successful you will be spending a lot of time with that character.

THE IMPORTANCE OF CHARACTER DEVELOPMENT

Bettmann Archive

Why is character development so important? First, because people are interested in character. Listen to conversations around you. You'll find that most of them are about people. Talk shows and fan magazines are popular because the public wants to know entertainers as people. If people were interested only in jokes, they would be content with reading joke books. People watch comedians because they are interested in the personality behind the jokes. Understanding the comedian enhances humor and gives it greater meaning.

To entertain people effectively, you must make them understand you and care about what is happening; you must get them emotionally involved. Very few people care if a magician makes a red handkerchief turn green, unless they care about the person trying to make it turn green.

The way to build rapport with an audience is by developing a character they can identify with. Gracie Allen's talent of interpreting everything literally gave her a unique comic personality. After telling her husband, George, that she was having troubles with one of the tires on their car, he asks her, "Is the tire flat?" Innocently she replies, "Only on the bottom." This was typical of her type of humor. In explaining why Gracie

Allen's humor worked so well, George Burns said, "Gracie's conversation on a radio broadcast often illustrates the way your mind might work underneath the surface of an intelligent, ordered conversation. Her logic is faultless, though usually mistaken. Gracie gets her laughs—we hope—because we often *think* the way Gracie *talks*, but we pride ourselves that we never talk the way Gracie thinks." By laughing at a clown, we laugh at ourselves. Watching a clown is like looking at ourselves in a funhouse mirror.

Because people are interested in characters, they begin to make assumptions about your character as soon as you appear. If you contradict those assumptions too strongly or too often, you make people aware that you are somebody who is dressed up and playing tricks. When your character's action and appearance are consistent with the personality your audience perceives, your character seems real. A strong, distinctive character heightens the fantasy.

Character development is not always easy, but once you know your character, the rest of your job will be easier. Choosing a new costume will be simpler because you know your character's tastes. You'll know how to react to a new situation because you'll know how your character perceives the world and reacts to

Buster Keaton in his youth, circa 1902 (left) and later in his career (right) with characteristic stone face expression, 1924.

it.

Humor depends on character. A fall can be either funny or tragic, depending upon who falls down. A pie in the face is not necessarily funny. What is funny is how a specific character reacts to it. The pie fight in Laurel and Hardy's *Battle of the Century* is considered the best ever filmed because of the richness of definite characters and the variety of their reactions.

Your clown's character is important because it is what makes your clown funny, interesting, and real.

GENERAL CHARACTER CATEGORIES

Clown characters have been divided into categories which correspond with the makeup designs.

Ideally you will decide on your clown's personality and then design a makeup to fit it. This is called developing a character from the inside out. If you are having trouble finding your character, you might pick a makeup style which appeals to you and experiment with the character type corresponding to it.

There has always been a hierarchy of comic characters. These characters tend to come in pairs. One is smarter, or at least thinks he is, instigates plots, and may be a trickster. The other is stupid, dooms plots to failure, and is the victim of practical jokes.

Let's take a closer look at the traditional clown characters.

The Whiteface Clown

Whiteface clowns top the current hierarchy. Their makeup consists of a white base and colored features.

Neat Whiteface. These are the clown aristocracy and act accordingly, looking down on other clowns and pulling tricks on them. They try to maintain their dignity at all times. In a music entree they may try to present a dignified violin or trumpet concert, but be continually interrupted by an auguste clown playing popular tunes on a tuba. In all acts they react in dismay to the auguste's stupidity.

The neat whiteface serves as straightman. In a talking act he sets up the punch line and establishes the timing. He may demonstrate a real skill, which is then burlesqued by an auguste.

When the whiteface doesn't possess a skill, he enlists the auguste's aid in faking it. He carries off his part flawlessly, but is revealed as an impostor through the auguste's stupidity. To impersonate a pianist, for example, the neat whiteface asks an auguste to hide and play phonograph records. During the first song the actions of the neat whiteface are in perfect synchronization with the music. Then the auguste gets the timing wrong, starting the music when the whiteface is not at the piano or getting distracted and not starting the music.

The makeup of the neat whiteface has simple, elegant features that are either red or black. In the past whiteface clowns wore white skullcaps, often with a tiny hat perched upon the head, but today most prefer to wear wigs.

The whiteface costume has traditionally been a one-piece jump suit or a two-piece loose fitting pajama type garment. The outfit is usually highlighted with a ruff around the neck and large pompons on the front. The neat whiteface costume is usually elegant, and color combinations are simple. At times he may even wear a tuxedo; it fits well, although it may have short sleeves and legs.

Bettmann Archive

Grotesque Whiteface. Another type of whiteface clown is called "grotesque" for reasons which are obvious when you see one. This clown uses the same colors in the same areas of the face as the neat whiteface, but applies greasepaint more boldly so the mouth and eyebrows become a large splash of color, and the nose often puffs into a large bulb. They may wear skullcaps, or more commonly, wigs. Their costumes are often a combination of bright colors, can be baggy, and may be an oversized or ill-fitting business suit once considered appropriate only for the auguste.

The grotesque whiteface is not as colorful in makeup or costume as the auguste, nor as zany. He is less intelligent and less skillful than the neat whiteface. The grotesque whiteface is an intermediate step between the characters of the neat whiteface and the auguste. He is not as dignified or wise as the neat whiteface, and may actually be silly or stupid. Although still the instigator of plots and a prankster, he might become the victim of his own tricks at the act's conclusion.

The Auguste Clown

The Auguste. The auguste is less educated, polished, and skilled than the whiteface. He misunderstands or

Neat whiteface clown (upper left). Grotesque whiteface Gary "Lupo" Willden (above). Bruce Johnson as Charlie the Tramp (lower right). Auguste clown Alberto Fratellini (upper right).

fouls up instructions. When doing an impersonation, he is exposed by his own stupidity. For example, after watching a whiteface manipulate three cigar boxes, the auguste may copy the routine and then with a box in each hand, spread his arms apart in a bow, revealing that the center box is securely attached to his belt.

It is the auguste who falls down, gets splashed with paint, drenched with water, and is the victim of pranks. But like a cartoon character is never really hurt.

The auguste's costume reflects this active role and the character portrayed. It is loose fitting for movement and easy to clean. A traditional auguste costume is an oversized plaid suit. Some performers desiring a youthful appearance wear a striped T-shirt, solid colored pants with contrasting cuffs, suspenders and sometimes a vest.

Instead of using white for the base color as the whiteface does, the auguste uses some other light color such as pink, orange, yellow, light brown, or even light blue. White is used around the eyes and mouth, and other features are generally red or black.

European Auguste. In Europe a slightly different auguste character is dominant, one that is a more natural "everyman" character. He may wander into the ring by mistake or be an audience member intruding on an act. He may be slightly inebriated and formally dressed, as if going home from a party. If not a partygoer, this character is dressed in ill-fitting clothes, including a jacket. Reflecting the everyman role their makeup is more natural.

The Tramp Clown

There is a great variation among tramps. Richard Snowberg divides them into three groups: (1) the hobo, who attempts to look nice and maintains his wardrobe; (2) the tramp, more pathetic and lowly, whose clothing is torn and tattered; (3) the bum, socially the lowest, with dirty clothes that are stained and rumpled. The bum is comparable to the skid row alcoholic and isn't often performed. Another classification system divides these clowns into happy hobos and sad tramps.

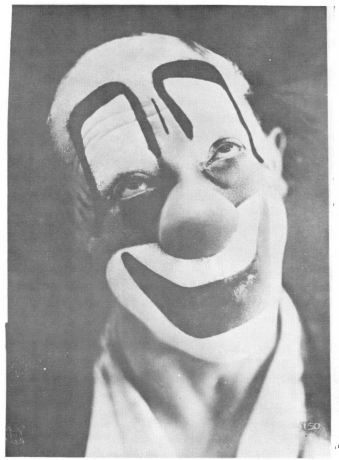

Bettmann Archive

The important thing to remember is that there are many options available. Some performers, considering Emmett Kelly the definitive tramp, attempt to copy him, but to be most successful you should create your own unique character instead of copying another. Here are some possibilities.

This first character corresponds to Snowberg's hobo. He is penniless, but pretends to a higher social position. He may carry an outdated edition of the *Wall Street Journal*. He explains his inability to pay by saying, "I seem to have misplaced my wallet" or "I'm having a temporary cash flow problem." He is eloquent, and a gentleman of exaggerated manners. He calls himself the Professor or assumes a title such as Lord. His clothes are shabby, but as neat as possible.

Another tramp variation is the character who knows he is penniless but doesn't care. He is happy-go-lucky, takes pleasure in simple things and is inventive about creating luxuries out of available materials. Red Skelton's "Freddy the Freeloader" is a good example of this clown type.

A third tramp is one who is unhappy about his status. He is sad, may move slowly and may be a little hostile. Things never turn out as hoped. He may be resigned to this, but continues to try anyway. Otto Griebling and Emmett Kelly are excellent examples of this character.

All tramps have their low social and economic status in common. Their makeup is distinguished by a white mouth and black greasepaint beard; they may also use white around their eyes. Their costumes vary, allowing room for character expression. The tramp's personality, lifestyle, and method of obtaining possessions can be shown through choice of costume and props.

Character and Specialty Clowns

In clown competitions, a fourth category is sometimes listed, the character or specialty clown. This is a catch all, and refers more to costume than character. It may include Chaplin imitators, special walk-around costumes, and characters playing a specific role such as chief, washer woman, or cowboy. Character is determined by personality. Just as in real life, the same person can have different roles, be a school teacher during the day, a security guard on weekends, as well as a father. A clown can have different roles and still be the same character.

How strict are these traditional categories? That depends on your goals. If you want to win clown competitions, including the skit categories, you must follow them strictly because judging criteria are based on them. If your goal is to do birthday parties, you have more leeway. A mother won't refuse to book you if you look like a whiteface but act more like an auguste. Solo performers are more likely to combine elements from the different categories since they serve as their own straightman and fall guy.

FINDING YOUR OWN CLOWN CHARACTER

Some people are lucky enough to discover right away a character that they are comfortable with and that works with an audience. Others struggle for a long time trying to find what is right for them.

Here's an exercise to help you identify your taste in characters.

- List your favorite comic strip characters, animated cartoon characters, comedians, and comedy figures from TV and the movies.

Character clowns David C. Montgomery (left) and Fred A. Stone (right).

Fred Garbo

and you are finished. There is nothing written in stone to make you keep the first character you try. Just as you change and evolve, so should your character. In 1942, for example, when their radio show was at the height of its popularity, Burns and Allen began losing their audience. George Burns discovered the problem. They were still doing the boyfriend-girlfriend insult jokes they had always done, but they were becoming too old for that type of humor. He changed their characters into a married couple and the show regained its high ratings.

As you work with your character, you will gradually learn more about how the character thinks and reacts to various situations. It took me years to understand the part juggling played in my character. My original concept of "Charlie" was that he wasn't

• Write a brief description of each character. Include the qualities that appeal to you and what makes them funny.
• List those things the descriptions have in common.
• Write a description of a composite character incorporating the things that your favorite characters have in common.

That composite character could be your clown character. You can't successfully portray a character or use a type of humor which you don't enjoy or find funny. Because you enjoy a type of character or humor doesn't guarantee that you will be capable of performing that way, but it suggests something to try.

The important thing is to try out a character in front of an audience. In the beginning, try different things. The audience will help you find your character. In discussing the creation of his character, Jack Benny said that he did a stingy joke one week, and people laughed. A couple of weeks later he did some more stingy jokes, people laughed, and before he knew it he had a stingy character.

If audiences don't respond positively to part of your original conception, change that part. Don't spend time justifying your original idea. Originally I thought my character, Charlie, was shy, but audiences didn't respond to that. Eventually Charlie became more outgoing and flirtatious.

Character development isn't something you do once

Red Skelton

Bettmann Archive

very smart and couldn't do anything right. When I added juggling to my act, I kept dropping balls on purpose and completed tricks awkwardly. As my juggling skills increased, I was hesitant about adding more difficult tricks to my act because I thought it was inconsistent with my character. One day I was performing several acts in a circus, all based around Charlie not doing things right. My last act was my juggling act. During it I heard a lady exclaim, "Hurray, he can really do something right!"

Then I realized what juggling did for my character, and I was able to establish a rapport with the audience. They didn't like to see Charlie fail all the time. People like to see the underdog win. Juggling was the one thing Charlie could do successfully and that ability allowed him to win in the end.

Now I start my act by juggling three balls to establish that my character can actually juggle. Then I juggle with two red balls and one yellow one. The yellow one is uncooperative, dropping repeatedly or going where I don't want it to go. Throughout the main part of my act, I continue to use comedy drops and visual gags, but the conclusion of my act is always a demonstration of real skill. Now my concept is: Charlie isn't very smart, and juggling is the only thing he can do right. The character's stupidity allows the audience to feel good about themselves because they're smarter, but that one quality rescues him from being inferior.

Character Biography

Within the general clown categories there is room for creativity. It is important to go beyond the general and create a specific character.

A tool frequently used in developing a character is to write a biography. Creating the biography helps you get to know the character and how he reacts to various situations.

Your biography doesn't have to be realistic. A fantasy character can have a fairy tale background set in a mystical kingdom or on another planet. If your character has magical powers, it's helpful to decide how those powers were acquired and what their limits are. Comedy characters usually have limits or obstacles that prevent their tricks from working as planned.

Your character's biography can be in the form of a story or answers to questions. In the beginning, you may have trouble creating a biography, but that's natural until you get to know your character. Make some choices. Each one will help you. If you later decide that a choice was wrong, the decision will bring

you that much closer to finding the right one. Answer as many of these questions as you can. Some may not seem directly applicable to performing but will help make your character's personality more real to your audience.

- Where was your character born?
- How old is he? When is your character's birthday? What sign was he born under?
- Who was your character's father? Mother?
- What is your character's educational background?
- Where did your character grow up?
- Does your character have any brothers or sisters? Are they older or younger?
- What is your character's occupation? Hobbies?
- What is your character's favorite book, sport, TV show (past or present), food, and color?
- What kind of music does your character listen to?
- What magazines does your character read? Why?
- What is your character's economic and social status?
- Where does your character go shopping?
- If you had to select one adjective that describes your character, what would it be? What adjective absolutely does not describe your character?
- What would your character consider a perfect day?
- What famous people does your character admire?
- What motto does your character live by?

W.C. Fields, circa 1925

- What are your character's goals in life? What are the obstacles to these goals?
- What are your character's strengths and weaknesses?

Abstract Biography

In addition to the biography, another helpful tool is to describe your character in abstract terms. This technique helps you get in touch with who your character is, what qualities he has. If I were describing my character as an animal, for example, I would choose a basset hound, because that dog looks sad, cuddly, gentle, and comfortable to be with. Answer these questions.

- If your character were an animal, which would it be?
- What kind of plant would your character be?
- What kind of bird would your character be?
- Which song best describes your character?
- Describe your character as a color.

If this abstract approach appeals to you, you can create additional questions.

Your biography may not be very complete now. The only way to develop it is to make some choices by performing your character and finding out what works. You have to spend time with your character to get to know him, but don't spend so much time creating your biography that you don't start performing. A character biography is a tool to help you as you develop your clowning ability, not an obstacle that must be overcome before you start. You'll come back to it many times through the years.

Using Your Biography for Character Expression

We make assumptions about people based on what they are wearing. If somebody is wearing tattered, paint-stained tennis shoes, faded blue jeans with grass stains on the knees, a Haverford college sweatshirt with frayed cuffs, a wedding ring, and a Coors baseball cap, what can you deduce about him?

The audience does the same thing with clowns. Your character's appearance and personality must be consistent to seem real. If you wear a highly exaggerated costume, the audience will expect a character just as exaggerated. If you dress predominantly in black, the audience will expect you to be an elegant or somber character.

Sometimes an article of clothing is the inspiration for a character. The performer finds a coat or hat he particularly likes, and discovers that it suggests a personality to him. He creates a character who would wear it, and makes the rest of the wardrobe compatible with it. Charlie Chaplin said that he knew his tramp's

Girl: I'd like a triple vanilla ice cream sunday with chocolate syrup, nuts, whipped cream, topped off with a slice of cucumber.
Waiter: Did I hear you right? Did you say top it off with a slice of cucumber?
Girl: Good heavens you're right, forget the cucumber—I'm on a diet.

personality as soon as he put on the costume he got from other Sennet comedians.

Since comedy depends on character, the sooner the audience feels they know your character, the more effective your act will be. Acts in the circus and variety shows are so short that a clown performing there must establish his character quickly. Clowns can take advantage of the tendency to make assumptions based on appearance and consciously use their appearance to reveal their characters' personality to the audience. This is called *character expression.* Your costume and props can be used for character expression.

This expression can be abstract: for example, dressing a character in blue because the qualities associated with that color are ones you want to project. Your abstract biography can be helpful here. Objects that share emotional qualities with your character may contain colors, patterns, or decorative elements that you can use for your character. I got the idea for wearing bags under my eyes from a toy basset hound. In the same way, to suggest stupidity, some court jesters wore hats whose shape was inspired by donkey ears.

You may also choose your costume and props the way your character would. If your character's favorite color is orange, choose props that are predominantly orange. This is one way your character biography can be helpful—by making your choices consistent and giving your act a unified image.

Try to picture how your character obtained his possessions. For my tramp character, I decided he wouldn't find a usable pair of shoes in one place. The right shoe may have come from a gutter and the left shoe from a field where a dog dropped it. My shoes are mismatched; the right one is brown and white, and the left is black.

Theatrical designers speak of "justification," making a choice in terms of the character. If you decide to work in pantomime, for example, you must have a reason for your character not speaking. In Walt Disney's *Snow White,* one of the dwarfs explains why Dopey can't speak—not because he's stupid, but because he never tried.

Justification can work in two ways. One is character development. You make a decision, and then rationalize your character's choice, which helps you to know your character better. The other way is character expression. You start by knowing how your character makes decisions, and make a choice accordingly. Both methods are valid and may be used at different times during your career.

Justification is a tool, not a rule. Use it when it is helpful. Sometimes you will see a prop or costume element which seems perfect without knowing why.

Morris Costumes

You can use it, based on instinct, as long as it fits the rest of what you do.

To be a funny, convincing clown, give your character a distinctive personality, get to know your character, and do everything as a result of that personality.

CLOWN CLOTHES

Putting Character Into Your Wardrobe

What's a clown without a descriptive clown outfit? . . . Naked that's what. Not physically naked, but bare in character. Clothes convey meaning. The clothes people wear and how they wear them are extensions of their personalities. The same is true in clowning. Each piece of clothing you wear tells others something about yourself. Some people are considered "nerds" just because of the way they look. Punk rockers are easy to identify by their distinctive clothes and hair styles. A proper wardrobe should be chosen with careful planning.

Once you have defined your clown character, you will have to design a costume to accompany it. The outfit you choose must support your clown personality. There are no hard and fast rules you must follow, but certain guidelines or standards are traditionally recognized and accepted.

In general, the more slapstick or silly your clown character, the more bizarre your makeup and wardrobe. The neat whiteface being the most intelligent and skillful of the clowns, wears a costume which is color coordinated and pleasing to look at. His facial features are small and more naturally proportioned. The auguste, and the grotesque whiteface to some extent, wear a variety of mismatched, odd sized clothes. Since these clowns portray more zany characters, their clothes should match their personalities. The more outrageous and comical the personality, the more outlandish the costume.

Contrary to popular belief, a good clown costume is not a mixture of mismatched clothes haphazardly thrown together. A good costume is a carefully selected arrangement of style, patterns, and colors. Unless you're a tramp clown, your outfit should not be composed of an assortment of old rejected Salvation Army wares. Most clowns will use bright cheery colors and designs which are not obtainable in second hand shops. The clothes must also smell fresh and be clean

Bobby walked into the house after completing his first day at school.

"What did you learn today?" asked his mother.

"Not enough," Bobby said. "I have to go back again tomarrow."

looking and pressed. Evan a tramp clown's costume should be clean and neat, although patches and tears may make it look old and worn.

Another factor is the type of print on the fabric. The usual prints are stripes, checks, and polka dots. These are fine, but you can be more selective and choose a pattern that may fit your character better.

Animals printed on the fabric of your costume suggest some affiliation with animals. If you use live or puppet animals, such a choice would make a good complement.

A juggling clown might wear prints of jugglers, balls (spots), clubs, and rings (circles). If you can find material with some design which fits your clown character, hire a tailor or seamstress to make you a customized clown outfit. Go to a few large fabric stores and look at what they have. They may even carry some patterns to make clown suits. Patterns not specifically designed for clowns can be modified slightly by a tailor to make a pleasingly unique clown outfit. Costume shops and several enterprising individuals sell custom made clown clothes. Periodicals such as *Laugh-Makers*, *The New Calliope*, and *Clowning Around* often carry ads from these people.

A custom made wardrobe is the most suitable. Costume stores sell only a few outfits. These are usually good but generalized, mass produced, and designed for the "average" clown, not for anyone specifically. They might work well with your clown character, but nothing is as eye catching as an original suit.

An outfit designed by you, using your own choice of colors and prints becomes your trademark. Such an outfit would fit your character and be unique.

Descriptive Costumes

Whiteface, auguste, and particularly character clowns often wear costumes which reflect a certain time period, national origin, profession, or lifestyle. Most all character clowns rely on their wardrobe as a character aid to identify their roles to the audience.

Many entertainers use different clown characters for different types of acts. Red Skelton, one of America's

Cathy "Sweetheart" Gibbons and Bob "Skoopy" Gibbons.

best known clowns, played the part of several different characters ranging from country bumpkin to a mischievous little child. Each character required a completely different wardrobe. His character Clem Kadiddlehopper wore an old plaid suit that was far too small, giving him a naive country boy appearance. The Mean Little Kid wore shorts, knee high socks, tie, and jacket, depicting a spoiled rich kid.

Members of any profession can generally be stereotyped. The marine drill sergeant, for example, brings to mind an unsmiling, rough, somewhat sadistic soldier who commands discipline. He is pictured as large, with a loud piercing voice and a closely shaved head.

There are also stereotypes for lifestyles, national origins, races, religions, and historical characters. We have preconceived ideas even for robots and space creatures. What physical and personality traits come to your mind with the following list: professional boxer, librarian, chemist, business tycoon, Arabian sheik, rock singer, Indian guru, romantic movie star, body builder, and hillbilly?

Any of these professions and lifestyles can be used by the clown. A policeman is recognized by his dark blue uniform. Add a billy club, a bobby's helmet, and perhaps large black bulbous shoes, and you have a silly Keystone cop character.

A chemist is considered intelligent and highly analytical, yet often absent minded and eccentric. He is recognized by his lab coat and white hair, styled like Albert Einstein's. His life is dedicated to making new scientific discoveries. The clown scientist can emphasize these traits and create a lot of funny material with his "new discoveries," like the no-stick lollipop which gets stuck on his tongue, shirt, tie, hands, pants, and the wall.

The key to designing an effective wardrobe is to make it reflect as closely as possible the personality of the character portrayed. Every piece of clothing conveys some meaning. Even the way the clothes are worn reveals something about the person. Take a night watchman for instance; what can you say about a watchman who wears his name tag a little crooked, has a shirt tail hanging out and a bottle of spirits in his back pocket? Compare him to a watchman with a spotless uniform, name tag in perfect alignment above his breast pocket, and hair neatly trimmed and combed. By appearance alone we can make some character judgments.

Adding certain accessories, even to a generic clown suit, will give it personality. Take the average man on the street; give him white socks, black shoes, and eyeglasses, hang a calculator on his belt, and stick six mechanical pencils in his shirt pocket and VOILA—you

have a "nerd". Those articles create a specific character out of an otherwise ordinary person.

Character Aids

Character aids are articles of clothing or accessory pieces of the costume which help define the personality portrayed by the performer. These include ties, suspenders, hats, handkerchiefs, boutonnieres, eyeglasses, beards, belts, unbrellas, canes, and the like. Let's look at some of the most important character aids.

Gloves. The most universal article of clothing for all types of clowns is a pair of gloves. Most clowns wear gloves as part of their wardrobe, white being preferred. The wearing of gloves is steeped in tradition and has become a standard practice. One of the major reasons gloves are so popular is because they cover the flesh colored skin of the hands, reinforcing the clown's cartoon like image.

Some clowns prefer not to wear gloves because they interfere with a particular activity, such as balloon sculpturing or juggling. Others have found that if the fingertips are cut off the gloves, they can wear them and still work effectively at these activities. Most tramp

clowns use fingerless gloves because it gives the gloves a well-worn look.

Hair. A clown's is one of the first things that catches the eye of a spectator. This first glance should tell the observer who the entertainer is and basically what type of personality he or she is potraying.

Although the audience will see the entire costume, their eyes will focus mostly on the clown's face. It is the face which conveys most of the clown's feelings and emotions and communicates to the audience.

The clown face is incomplete without an appropriate wig, skullcap, or hair style to go with it. The hair is, in fact, part of this all important clown face.

The style and color of hair (or lack of it) is one of the most important parts of your clown wardrobe. The effect of hair on our appearance can be dramatic. Even for nonclowns, dyeing or styling the hair differently can radically change a person's appearance.

Most tramp and other character clowns use their own hair and just style it for their acts. Whiteface clowns use their own hair, skullcaps, or wigs. Auguste clowns wear wigs or skullcaps.

The best hair colors to use are red, orange, yellow, and blond. These are bright cheery colors that match most clown costumes and are closest to natural hair

colors. Many clowns, however, choose to use blue, green, purple, and other less natural colors. Whichever color you use, it should match the rest of your outfit. A pink costume combined with green hair is distasteful; it is usually best to avoid color conflicts such as this.

Hats. One of the most important pieces of clothing in a clown wardrobe is the hat. Although not technically a part of the face, it is always right there next to it, and is therefore a part of the costume which is constantly observed by the audience.

Hats communicate more to the audience than most other pieces of clothing. The hat can be the single most important part of a costume for identifying the clown's lifestyle or character, especially for character clowns. For instance, a rustic cowboy type outfit with a ten-gallon hat brings to mind the Texas cowboy. The same outfit with a large Mexican sombrero would turn the character into a Mexican rancher or bandito. If a derby is worn, it would suggest a Doc Holiday type character. A carefully chosen hat can make a significant impact on your costume.

Shoes. Shoes are important for both identity and utility. Like all parts of a clown outfit, shoes must match and help define the clown. Equally important, they must be comfortable and durable, especially if a lot of walking or standing is to be done. Standing in front of a store for several hours or walking in a parade can be hard on your feet and ill-fitting shoes can become very painful.

A wide variety of shoes are available. Some manufactures make clown shoes in various shapes and sizes; most being very large and bulbous. They come in solid colors, two-tones, checks, and fancy designs.

The cheapest shoes are made to be worn around your street shoes. This type of shoe is adequate if you don't do much walking or performing, but will wear out quickly.

Specially made clown shoes designed to fit your feet can run up to $200 a pair or more. They are comfortable and durable. If your feet are going to get a lot of wear and tear, it's advisable to buy a pair of good quality clown shoes.

> One skeleton to the other: "If we had any guts, we'd get out of here."
>
> Mother monster to little son: "Please don't set in that chair! We're saving it for Rigor Mortis to set in."

Ed Wynn, 1923

An old pair of men's dress shoes can work well as clown shoes. By adding some bright colored acrylic paint, the shoe takes on new life. Two-tone colors work well.

White high top sneakers have been a favorite for many years. They are especially good for the more acrobatic or active clowns who need good footing. Jugglers, unicyclists, and others may prefer them when combining their skills with clowning.

Ordinary white sneakers can be brightened up, if desired, by painting them with acrylic paint. The paint is very durable, and the shoes can be washed in a washing machine to keep them clean

If ordinary sneakers are't zany enough for the character you portray, you can buy size 17 sneakers. Worn over your regular shoes these large sneakers make excellent (and inexpensive) oversized clown shoes.

Ties. Neckties are one of the most commonly used accessory articles of clown clothing. A tie can add a welcome splash of color and personality to your outfit.

In western culture the tie is worn with formal and semi-formal attire. It is worn by businessmen, diplomats, clergy, and the like, and is a symbol of proper dress.

People are judged by first appearances, so most people make an effort to look proper. Any deviation from the norm is unusual and can be funny. To wear a tie which is disproportionate or peculiar in color is

absurd and nonsensical. Such a tie shows the audience the clown's comical and naive nature. The clown thinks he is "dressed up" yet looks ridiculous. The more absurd the tie, the more ridiculous the character wearing it.

Pockets. One of the most important features of any clown outfit is the pockets. They can be used to help identify the clown or be simply a place to carry props and giveaways. Whether you use pockets as a character aid or not, you must have pockets—the bigger the better.

It's best to carry both props and giveaways out of sight by placing them in the pockets. In this way you can regulate the giving of gifts to make them last throughout the day. Also, pockets keep props handy yet out of reach of curious children.

Pockets can be any shape or in most any location. Some are sewn onto the outside of the suit and become part of the design of the costume. Others are sewn on the inside and are largely unnoticeable.

Fake pockets—openings which allows the clown to reach through the suit into bags or pockets underneath the costume—are also useful. An apron with large pockets worn underneath the costume can hold much more than ordinary pockets. Another advantage of the fake pocket is that it prevents mischievous hands from grabbing things.

Other Aids. Accessory pieces of clothing give clues to personality and odd habits, especially when used in excess. The clown who wears many different types of watches depicts a character who is obsessed with time. Whether he is late or always on time, he is always conscious of time. The same is true with an unusual number of anything such as flowers, buttons, handkerchiefs, horns and whistles, rubber balls, or pockets.

Makeup, too, can be used as a character aid. Freckles, for example, are associated with children, and the clown who wears them must also be childish or silly, lacking adult wisdom and knowledge.

Eyeglasses are one of the most popular aids used in the theater and normally suggest intelligence. Doctors, teachers, and scientists, are commonly depicted with eyeglasses. This is one reason why it is rare to see a whiteface or auguste wear glasses; it's out of char-

When your grandfather was born, they passed out cigars. When your father was born, they passed out cigarettes. When you were born, they just passed out.

acter. Most clowns who wear glasses do so because they can't see without them. If you need to wear glasses, make sure they match your makeup. Frames can be found in some unusual styles, particularly for womens' glasses. These may be used with good results.

Traits related to eyeglasses can be emphasized and exaggerated by the clown. The bookworm or scientist, although intelligent, can be extremely absent minded, forgetting where he put things—such as his hat when it's on his head. Clumsiness is also associated with eyeglasses; a clumsy person would rather sit and read than indulge in sports or other physical activities. When he does attempt anything requiring physical coordination, he makes a fool of himself.

Poor eyesight is another peculiarity that can be emphasized with eyeglasses. The cartoon character Mr. Magoo used this idea to the extreme. He was so near sighted that he kept making one mistake right after another, misidentifying people and objects, misreading signs and directions, getting himself in all sorts of trouble.

Ill-fitting and mismatched clothes depict a naive lack of intelligence which is characteristic of many clowns. Silly clothes tell the observer that this character has little cultural refinement or social grace. The clown, of course, is not aware anything is wrong with his clothes.

A degree of clumsiness can also be evident in the way clothes are worn. If they are not worn properly, it can mean the wearer is just plain uncoordinated. A straight tie with the skinny end dangling below the fat end would support this image. Other examples include a coat put on inside out, untied shoes, and a shirt buttoned wrong.

Otto Griebling

False buck teeth can be used in the mouth or painted on the lips. Buck teeth are associated with slow intelligence. The typical stereotype of a hillbilly with buck teeth is that of a mentally slow and culturally backward individual.

Beards and mustaches can be styled to depict several different personalities. A big bushy beard and messy long hair suggest a brash, ill-mannered character. On the other hand, a thin mustache conjures up visions of romance and daring. The Fu Manchu type mustache suggests an Asian background and lifestyle. A handlebar mustache depicts a 19th century character and corresponding cultural values.

Most whiteface and auguste clowns do not look good with beards. Yet some clowns manage to design a clown face complementary to mustaches and beards. Many tramp clowns use their own natural beards with good results.

Nose size and shape are another consideration. Large, round, bulbous noses are silly and funny looking; they make the wearer look ridiculous. Auguste clowns usually wear these types of noses; a pretty or neat whiteface clown will not use a fake nose. The shape of the nose can vary. Most noses are of the round bulbous type, but some clowns use putty so they can mold the nose to a desired shape for a specific clown character. The putty is then attached to the nose with spirit gum.

Body size and shape also suggest personality types. A person who is overweight is seen as jolly, like Santa Claus. Tall thin people are considered slow and uncoordinated, like a giraffe. Short people are thought of as spunky and active, like mice.

A person's natural build is difficult to change, but certain physical traits can be created artificially. Large plastic hoops, much like thin hula hoops, sewn into the waist of a clown suit make a clown appear overweight. It doesn't fool anybody but sure looks amusing, and the person wearing it can act the part of a jolly fat clown.

The print on the material of the clown suit can also help. Horizontal stripes visually broaden things; a person will look wider and fatter wearing horizontal striped clothes. The opposite is also true; vertical stripes make a person look taller and thiner.

When designing your wardrobe, stop and consider each article. Ask yourself these questions: What type of character would wear this? What personality traits do people associate with it? Are these traits consistent with my clown character? Will it match the rest of my costume? Don't stick on or wear something just because it looks cute. Make sure it fits your personality and style or don't wear it at all. Following these principles will make your appearance one that is truly professional.

Ed: There is a new book out called *How to Be Happy Without Money*.
Fred: How much does it cost?
Ed: Nineteen dollars.

CHAPTER 3

THE CLOWN FACE

CLOWN MAKEUP

What is a clown without makeup? Distinctive makeup separates clowns from most other comedians and family entertainers. Every clown face in the world is different (or should be) and serves as a distinctive means for identifying the clown.

This chapter will explore how to create a clown face. We will go step-by-step through the process of properly applying makeup so that you can have that "professional" look. Too often novice clowns don't pay enough attention to their makeup; they put a dab of eye shadow here, some lipstick there and presto, they call themselves clowns. But a poor makeup job easily identifies a novice as an impostor—a person dressed up as a clown, not a REAL clown. With proper instruction and a little practice, even a beginner can look like a professional.

Although makeup alone doesn't make the whole clown, and a clown's performing ability shouldn't be judged solely by what he or she wears, makeup is a highly visible part of the clown costume. Through it the audience gets a feeling for who the clown is, what he or she is like, and what to expect. If you want to be accepted as a real clown, you're going to have to look like a real clown.

Portions of this chapter have been reprinted from a series of articles written by Tony Blanco for *Magic Manuscript*.

DESIGNING YOUR OWN CLOWN FACE

Designing a professional looking clown face and applying makeup correctly, are basic skills that all serious clowns must learn.

The first step towards creating your own clown face will be to decide which of the three clown types you want to be: whiteface, auguste, or character. Keep in mind that the clown face you choose must be consistent with the character you portray. Is your character wacky and clumsy like a tramp or an auguste, or smart and skillful like a whiteface? If you choose whiteface, do you want it to be a skilled neat whiteface or a clumsy grotesque whiteface?

A great deal of the clown's personality is displayed through the facial features. The large exaggerated nose, mouth, and eyes of the auguste and the grotesque whiteface clowns depicts a more zany character. In general the less bizarre the facial features the more intelligent and graceful the clown becomes. Your first step in designing a clown face is deciding which type of clown you want to be.

Every clown face should be unique—just as your own natural face is. A clown face is a type of trademark, and nobody should copy the face of another clown. Many of the same features or markings can be used, of course, but each face should be original.

Start by looking at pictures of other clowns; skim through the pages of this book. Visit a local magic shop or costume store and look through the books with clown pictures. How do these clowns wear their makeup? What type of markings do they use? Examine the different ways that have been used to outline the mouth and eyes. These pictures will give you the background information you need to create your own face.

After deciding on the general type of face you want and before you even touch any makeup, sit down in front of a mirror and examine your face. Is your face long or short? Round or thin? Do you have a long nose? A dimple on your chin? Is your chin round or square?

Examine all your natural lines and wrinkles. Make faces—smile, frown, look surprised, laugh. What lines or folds in your face are most distinguishable? These folds will be used as guidelines for designing your clown face.

> City Boy: Is it hard to milk a cow?
> Farm Boy: Naw, any jerk can do it.

One of the biggest mistakes that new clowns make is to wear makeup as a mask. For best results, makeup should not hide but should enhance your natural features.

Take a pencil and paper. Sketch a picture of your head. Put in all the prominent lines that are naturally in your face. Using these lines as a guide, design a clown face. Outline the mouth and eyes, add any additional markings you desire. Make several different drawings until you have one or two which suit you the most. This will be your blueprint.

With your sketch to guide you, take a black lining pencil and outline the features on your face. (Men should be cleanly shaven before applying any makeup.) Look at yourself in the mirror; how do you look? When you add white and other colors, will they help bring out your expressions or mask them?

These black lines can be removed with baby oil, baby shampoo, or skin cleanser. Apply one of these cleansers to your face, let it soak in a few seconds, and rub it off with a disposable paper towel. Don't try to remove makeup with ordinary soap or you will have a mess on your hands (and face!).

Take the black liner again and try another face. Does it look better then the first? Keep trying new

Tramp clown Donald "Dee Gee" Gonsalves

designs until you have one you're be happy with. Now wash your face completely and dry it off.

GENERAL PROCEDURES

The following procedures apply to any type of clown face you choose to use. Each of the three types of faces will be described in detail later.

In preparing to do anything, it helps to have have the right tools. The same thing applies when you're putting on makeup. Before you start, here are a few things that you will need. (1) A tin of clown white—the greasepaint which you will smooth evenly over your face. The best brands to use are Stein's, Bob Kelley's, and Mehron because of their smooth and well balanced formulas. There are many other brands—some good,

The Fratellini Brothers. Top to bottom: Paul (character), Franesco (whiteface), and Alberto (auguste).

others not so good—but these are the brands the professionals use and trust.

The other tools are: (2) a shaving type brush/or soft one-inch wide paintbrush; (3) a 100% white cotton sock with baby powder in it (pure baby powder of just talc and fragrance); (4) paper towels; (5) a plastic shower cap; (6) mirror; (7) Q-Tips; (8) a few (two or three) very thin art brushes (00 or 01 gauge); (9) baby oil or baby shampoo; (10) paint creme liners, Bob Kelley's or Stein's tube red.

Applying makeup can be a messy procedure. If at all possible, delay putting on your clown outfit until after your makeup is in place. Pieces of clothing which have to be pulled over the head may smear your makeup.

If you must wear some part of your costume, be sure to use an apron. You will get the greasepaint on your hands, paper towels, and the table. No matter how careful you try to be, some will find its way onto your shirt or pants.

Put on all the other parts of your wardrobe associated with your face and head, such as wig, fake nose, and hat, after your makeup is complete.

Apply the makeup with as much care as you possibly can. A good job will take time, perhaps 40 minutes or more. Don't be in such a hurry that you make your features unsymmetrical or uneven. The smile on the right side of your face should be the same size as the smile on the left side. Any outlining around one eye should be equal in size and shape to that around the other, unless of course your design is intentionally uneven.

Take care to keep outlining as sharp and even as possible. Messy outlining gives an amateurish look. Other problems to avoid are sagging, smearing, greasiness, caking, and skin showing through.

When you begin to apply makeup, put on the lightest color first. Progressively add the darker colors as you go. White or a flesh tone is used as the base color which all other colors and markings surround. The base color will cover most of your face and any exposed skin.

After each application of a color, you will need to "set" it by powdering the fresh makeup lightly with baby powder. There are several different methods of applying powder to the face. If you use the cotton sock, filled with the powder, shake or hit the sock several times before applying it to your face. This will force the powder through the cloth to the outside where it can be lightly patted onto the face. A powder puff may be used instead of the sock if you wish. Use plenty of powder. If the sock or puff doesn't have enough powder, you run the risk of transferring colors and making a mess of your face.

To avoid the problem of messing the makeup while powdering, some clowns prefer to throw the powder or jiggle the sock above the face, letting the powder fall without touching the makeup. Once a thin coat of powder is on the face, the sock or puff can be patted on the face to get an even coat.

After powdering, look in the mirror. If you see any damp or wet spots, put on more powder. Then take a shaving brush or a soft one-inch paintbrush and brush off all excess powder. Brush from the lightest colors to the darkest so that if some areas are still wet, you won't smear the makeup. Repeat the powdering and brushing process as often as necessary to eliminate all wet spots and get an even coating.

The next step is to remove any excess powder remaining. This is done by splashing water on the face or by taking a wet washcloth and patting with it lightly—do not rub your face! Without the water treatment, makeup tends to turn gray and colors fade because of the extra powder that was not removed. Use a soft towel to soak the excess water off your face. Powder applied in this way will give you a professional dry look and prevent the makeup from coming off when touched.

Powdering serves three important purposes. First, it sets the greasepaint keeping it from sagging, and smearing. Without powder, makeup tends to sag, especially when the weather is hot. On a warm summer day, the makeup may begin to look more like a Halloween mask than a clown face. Second, powder eliminates the greasy wet look of the makeup. Third, it makes the makeup dry, so it can be touched without smearing or coming off.

A clown's appearance is sharply improved with a fresh dry look that powder gives. On a long hot day the powdered makeup will last several hours; a light powdering in the middle of the day is enough to freshen it until the end of the day. Applying powder is essential to good clown makeup and commonly one of the major differences between "lipstick clowns" and professional looking clowns.

After applying your base color and powdering, check your face. If everything is OK, proceed on. Outlining features and small designs go on last. These are most commonly black and red. Once these are on, powder as you did before. Don't worry about putting white powder over the colored makeup, it will be absorbed and will take on the color of the makeup. Remove any excess powder.

Now that you know the general procedure, I'll describe in detail how to apply makeup to create each of the three clown types.

THE THREE TYPES OF CLOWN MAKEUP

The Whiteface Clown

Figure 3-1(a) shows your author freshly shaven, with a clean face and with shower cap in place. To begin, place your fingers into the clown white and remove a small dab (less is best); rub your hands together to warm up the greasepaint to your body temperature. Spread it evenly on your face (Figure 3-1(b)). Cover your eyelids and eyebrows (rubbing the makeup in), apply it under your eyes and on your lips.

Now pat or slap your face lightly all over to even out the white mask, (Figure 3-1(c)). This technique is very important: patting the makeup with your hand, which still has makeup on it, evens out the base so flesh tones won't show through in blotches on your face. Using a Q-Tip, remove the makeup from areas where you will place designs or features (Figure 3-1(d)). To make a shape for your nose, use a towel or a tissue (Figure 3-1(e)). Once this has been done, clean the greasepaint off your hands with a towel. While your makeup is on your face in its wet state, you can mix colors to blend in with the white (Figure 3-1(f)).

After you have the look you want, the baby powder comes next (Figure 3-1(g)). Powder your face by either shaking the sock above your face (eyes closed) or by patting your face with the sock as you turn the sock around. Use your shaving brush to gently remove excess powder (Figure 3-1(h)).

To apply colors, use your art brushes. Dip a brush lightly into some baby oil to get it wet, then into the color. Begin painting the clown's designs and features (Figures 3-1(i), (j), and (k)). In Figure 3-1(j), you will notice the design that is being painted in under the eye. The white greasepaint was not removed with a Q-Tip beforehand. Why not? Well, in doing under-the-eye work, it's easier just to paint over the white because you're outlining a small natural feature. Outline designs need not be removed because you are *outlining* not *creating* a feature. The design by the eyes has been finely outlined in black. Please note that two hands are used in painting these features; one hand to paint and one hand to steady the movement of the other.

Once again, powder your face and remove the powder (Figures 3-1(l) and (m)). To give the appearance of rosy cheeks, a commercial women's blush has

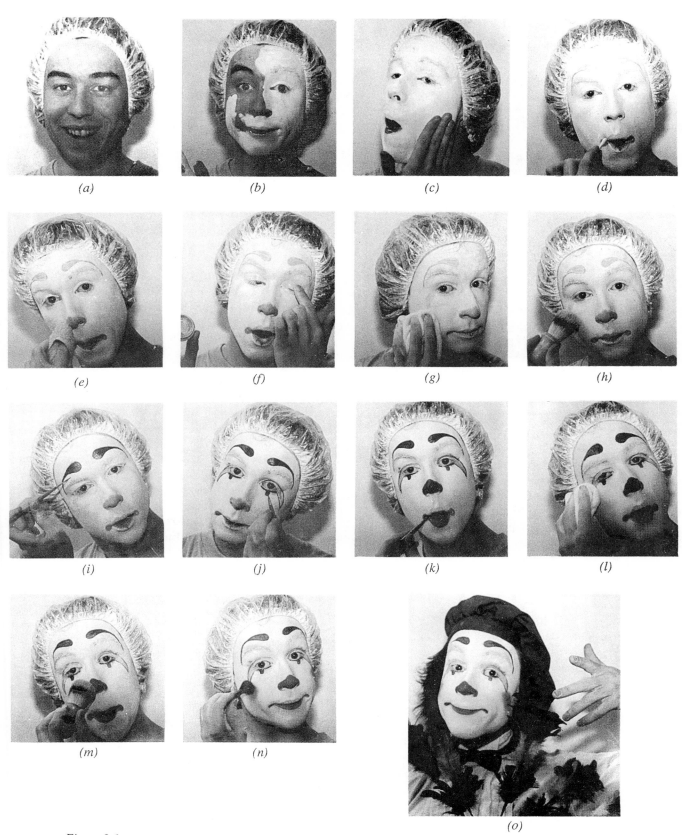

(a) (b) (c) (d)

(e) (f) (g) (h)

(i) (j) (k) (l)

(m) (n)

(o)

Figure 3-1

been used on top of the dry clown white (Figure 3-1(n)). That's it; the finished product is a whiteface clown design (Figure 3-1(o)).

This makeup design was created for you to learn by. Try the design step by step, but do create your own face. This is what will make you different from every other clown. Experiment, look at books, visit the circus until you feel you've designed something special.

The Auguste Clown

Each clown type has its own particular characteristics. The auguste clown is the most slapstick of the bunch, the one who gets into the most trouble and does the silliest things. Consequently the auguste has the most bizarre and exaggerated facial features. Some whiteface clowns, such as the grotesque whiteface, approach the auguste in character and have similar features. The whiteface, however, always has the characteristic white base color.

The main difference between the look of the whiteface and the look of the auguste is that the auguste has fleshy tones in the makeup and uses two different color bases. One base is white, the other is either pink or a deep flesh tone, such as suntan.

Our model, Bunnie Collins-Blanco, is shown with a clean face and her hair pulled back (Figure 3-2(a)). She uses a sweatband which helps to anchor her wig.

Bunnie's skin is normal (part dry, part oily), so she will wash her face thoroughly 45 minutes to an hour before she begins the makeup application. This gives her skin time to replenish its natural oils. If she does not wait, the replenishing skin oils will make the greasepaint bubble as they push the greasepaint out of the pores. Needless to say, this "bubbling" does not become her, or any clown.

It's always best to learn the application of the whiteface first. Practicing the whiteface makes applying the auguste easier—but not easy.

Look at Figures 3-2(b) and 3-2(c). The auguste makeup is applied from lightest colors to darkest. White, being the lightest, goes on first. Draw designs first with a paper and pencil, so you have an idea of what you want. Remember though—sometimes a design may look perfect on paper but awful on your face, so as you are learning, don't be afraid to change. The only way to learn how to apply clown makeup is by constant practice, trial, analysis, and more practice.

For the auguste, white is usually applied only in the areas of the eyes and mouth. Shapes vary according to taste and the size and shape of your face. The object is to identify features that move and enhance them with the makeup to exaggerate your expressions.

Once the white is applied in the areas you desire, use a cotton swab (such as a Q-Tip) to remove the white greasepaint from the larger areas where you will apply other colors (Figure 3-2(d)). Bunnie uses black to outline, and black on her lower lip (red also could be used on the lip). The outline has so fine a line that it isn't necessary to remove the white, but for the color to hold better on her lip, it helps to remove the white greasepaint there.

After the white is removed where needed, comes the most important step in the proper application of clown makeup—powdering down. If the white is not powdered down now, the outline colors may run and blotch into the white—yuck!

Some makeup artists use a powder sock but Bunnie prefers a puff. Powder is applied liberally over the greasepaint. The powder absorbs the oils, leaving the greasepaint dry and touchable, though it may streak, smear, and get all over the "touche's" fingers. After the powder sets or dries the greasepaint (about 45 seconds), brush off the excess powder with a soft brush.

Figures 3-2(g) and 3-2(h) show the second base being applied, in Bunnie's case pink base. Depending upon whom you learn makeup from, you may or may not decide to apply this base to your neck, ears, and the back of your neck. After checking to make sure the pink is not streaked and is on evenly, Bunnie proceeds to the next darker color: red.

Since Bunnie wears a red wig and nose, she keeps the red area small and uses it only to accent the white mouth (Figures 3-2(i) and 3-2(j)). Too much red is overpowering. For this fine linework, a brush makes the application much smoother, leaving a sharp edge between colors.

Black is applied last, Figure 3-2(k), starting from the top of the face and working down—eyebrows, eye accents, and mouth.

Figure 3-2(l) shows the last powder down. Don't forget to powder your neck, ears, and the back of your neck if you choose to do them.

Figure 3-2(m) shows Bunnie brushing off the powder. She learned to use two different shaving brushes: one for the white areas and one for colors. Sometimes colors are picked up on the brush and ruin the white area, giving an unprofessional look.

In Figure 3-2(n) all excess powder has been removed. The powder should not dull the makeup much. (Again: PRACTICE!) Figure 3-2(n) also shows one method of holding on a false nose: white elastic.

Finally Figure 3-2(o) shows our complete clown: wig, hat, and smile!

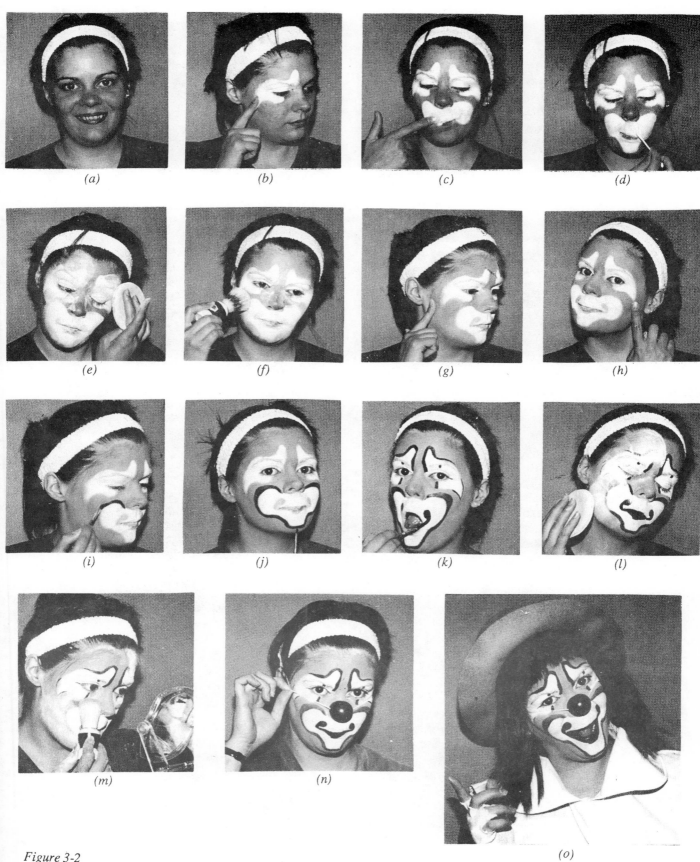

Figure 3-2

(a)

(b)

(c)

(d)

(e)

(f)

(g)

(h)

(i)

(j)

(k)

(l)

(m)

(n)

(o)

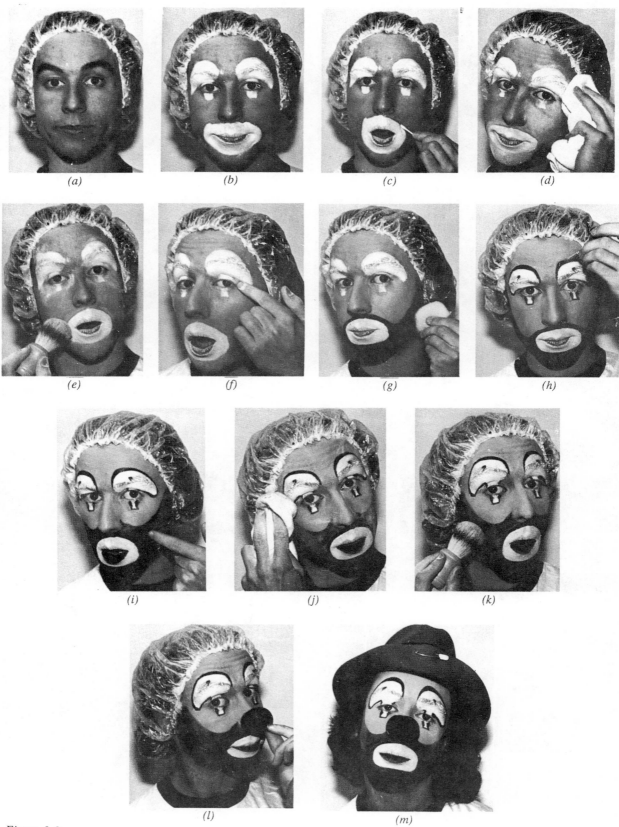

Figure 3-3

The Hobo Clown

The character clown is made up in a wide variety of styles, and can be as simple as Charlie Chaplin or nearly as bizarre as the auguste. By far the most popular type of character clown is the hobo or tramp clown.

Unlike other clowns, the hobo does not have have a happy face. He is sad and down on his luck. He appears dirty and unkempt. His clothes are old and worn out, usually black or gray, lacking the sparkle that other clowns have.

Begin with a clean, freshly shaven face (Figure 3-3(a)). In this case stubble won't hurt because you'll be blacking in this part of your face. In Figure 3-3(b), notice that the white makeup has been applied for shape around the eyes and the mouth. Choose a shape or style that works for you. Pat these areas down so that they are even in whiteness.

Figure 3-3(c) shows how to use Q-Tips to further shape out the mouth and the eyes. You can also use the Q-Tip to remove unwanted makeup. Wait until the white is dry before adding the base color. Figures 3-3(d) and 3-3(e) show how to powder these areas and how to remove the powder with a brush. In powdering your face, either shake the sock so the powder mists out on your face or pat your face with the sock, turning it as you pat.

Figure 3-3(f) shows the application of the base color. (I chose a pink base around the white areas of the eyes and mouth.) Smooth out this color and pat it in place for even texture. Figure 3-3(g) shows the main part of the makeup; some clowns blend this with white to create a greying effect instead of a bold black beard. Either way, use a piece of polyfoam or cut sponge to make the beard appear stubbled. Use one of the art brushes to make the beard join under the nose.

Outlining is important for all the clown faces we have discussed. It makes your clown face stand out well at a distance, a crucial consideration in large auditoriums such as Madison Square Garden. Figure 3-3(h) shows the outlining of the white areas on this hobo face. Figure 3-3(i) shows a choice that you might consider—the blending of a red area above the beard to add greater color to the hobo. Also paint in your bottom lip with the red greasepaint at this time. As mentioned before, some choose to blend white with the black before powdering to make a shade of gray.

Once again powder all the colors down (Figure 3-3(j)), than remove the excess powder with a shaving brush or a wide soft paintbrush, (Figure 3-3(k)). I can't stress this point enough! If you don't powder your makeup, your clown, whether whiteface, auguste, or hobo, will look bad. When you meet with children, the makeup will come off on them, and you won't be liked by the parents.

A word about noses. Choosing a clown nose is a personal choice. Emmett Kelly would make a fresh nose for his clown from nose putty; others use rubber clip-on noses. Some clowns perform very fast and thus secure their noses with elastic string around either their head or ears. In Figure 3-3(l) I use a magic sponge ball split open in the back and glued on with spirit gum.

This makeup design is my version of a hobo I created for you to learn by. Work out the steps and then create a face that you can live with. Always refer to circus books and movies; see the circus when it comes to town, but remember to create something that's yours. Don't rehash what's been done!

REMOVING MAKEUP

It was fun wearing the makeup, but how do you remove it? Simple. Sandpaper and Comet! . . . No, only kidding . . . please don't do this! The proper way is to use either baby oil or baby shampoo, depending on your skin type. Use baby oil if you have normal or dry skin, and baby shampoo if you have

oily skin. Baby oil will make dry skin moist; baby shampoo will soak up excess skin oil nicely. Both do the job of cleansing the skin and conditioning it.

Apply your choice of clenser by smoothing it in the palms of your hands and rubbing it into the makeup. You will get a grey mess on your face, which will wipe right off in a towel. Use disposable paper towels or a cloth towel. If you choose a cloth towel, make sure you use one devoted totally to removing your makeup.

The grease will wash out, but the makeup may stain the towel. (Don't use mom's good towels.)

Occasionally the red makeup may leave a stain on your skin. Don't panic! Just apply the baby oil or shampoo again and let it soak in for a few minutes, then wipe it off your face. If some red still remains, it will fade away completely overnight. Don't scrub and scrub to remove the red, or you will remove your skin and leave it red from irritation—not makeup.

CLASSIC CLOWN GAGS

Throughout the years many clown gags have come and gone, but some we see over and over again, and have become classics. Some people may ask "Why perform an old gag or tell an old joke?" The answer to that question is simple—because it's funny. Just because a gag is old doesn't mean it's not funny, and if it is funny, who cares how old it is. Sure, many people may have witnessed the gag at one time or another, but each clown has his own personality and method of delivery which gives old gags a new appearance. Not only that, but new generations are continuously coming along who have never seen these classics. For these reasons old gags and jokes can be repeated over and over again with just as much amusement as when they first appeared.

There are many clown gags and skits which use a similar punch line or blowoff, "Let me have it" is one of these. This phrase could refer to a bucket of water, a rubber hammer, or a cream pie waiting to be pushed into an unsuspecting face. Here is one version known as "The Telephone."

The Telephone

Two clowns enter, Dumbbell and Jingles. Jingles is holding a bicycle inner tube which has been cut to make a long hose.

Dumbbell: Hey, Jingles, what have you got there?

Jingles: It's a telephone.

Dumbbell: A telephone! You got to be kidding?

Jingles: No I'm not. Would you like to see how it works?

Dumbbell: Sure, let me have it.

Jingles: Just a minute, since I have a phone let's use it. Here, you grab this end and stand over there and I'll take this end and stand over here. (The tube is tightly stretched between the two.) Now when I say 'Ring-ring' you answer the phone and say 'Let me have it.'

Dumbbell: OK, I'm ready.

Jingles: Ring-ring.

Dumbbell: Hey, your phone's ringing.

Jingles: I know that, stupid! You're supposed to answer it and say 'Let me have it.'

Dumbbell: Oh yeh, let's try it again.

Jingles: Ring-ring.

Dumbbell: Hello—Avon calling.

Jingles: No no, you knucklehead! You're suppose to say 'Let me have it.'

Dumbbell: OK, got ya.

Jingles: Ring-ring.

Dumbbell: Ahh . . . what was it I was suppose to say?

Jingles: (Screaming) LET ME HAVE IT!

Dumbbell: OK (Releasing the tube, it flings back hitting the other clown and knocks him off his feet.)

CHAPTER 4

THE SILENT ART OF MIME

Mime, or pantomime as some call it, is the art of silent expression, portraying an action, thought, or concept through movement and emotion, without the use of words. Through mine the clown creates an illusion, making the invisible visible.

All of us use mine, in a sense, every day when we communicate with others. We express feelings and thoughts by the way we move our hands, or arms, or by our posture. Nodding of the head up and down, for example, is universally recognized as meaning "yes" or signifying acceptance or approval.

When done skillfully, physical movements can be used to express almost any thought or action. By using mime, performing artists are able to represent scenes from life, usually in an exaggerated or ridiculous manner, as entertainment. Clowns, too, rely heavily on mime to create much of the physical comedy characteristic of their art. For this reason all clowns should gain experience in expressing themselves through pantomime. Many clowns, in fact, perform entirely in mime, never speaking a word during their shows.

In mime you must look at things as if they were invisible to everyone, and with your movements be able to make them visible to all who are watching you. A simple exercise to try while you're holding this book is to turn your head from left to right as you glance down the page, then turn to the next page. In doing this, imagine that you're reading this book as a speed reader. Now put the book down, yet pretend that you're still holding a book and mime the movement of reading. In a performance you would be creating an illusion, but what would really help the scene is your reaction to what you're reading. Read, then express happiness, then show sadness. By doing this your audience can *feel* the story in the book.

BODY LANGUAGE

Mime, as in any art form, depends on a sense of understanding and knowledge of people and the world. To mime (or mimic) someone, you must interpret a person's personality with body language.

Understanding body language is something one must develop an eye for. Notice people as you walk down the street. Look closely at how they walk and carry themselves. Notice the youthful and carefree walk of a child, compared to the harsh, forceful strides of a businessman who is trying to beat the clock. In a restaurant, look at how some people eat. Study the contrasting styles of a person in a rush scarfing down his food and a little old lady peacefully having a cup of tea. Observations like these are important to you so that you can call upon them for your skits when

Tony Blanco

you need them. Always keep your eyes open; learn to look more closely at life. It's a pretty funny world out there if you know how to look at it.

The following is a short list of "people types." Stand in front of the mirror and place yourself in the attitude or use the body language that you think belongs to each of these people. Give thought to placement of hands, the way you tilt your head, and how you stand.

> Three-year-old girl
> Sixteen-year-old boy
> Happy housewife
> Busy father
> Tough truck driver
> Nerd
> Policeman
> Burglar

Even if you never use most of these characters, you should have a sense of how you might perform them. In performance the three-year-old girl might hop around and act very innocent and a little silly. The teenager might be glued to a Walkman radio or always be combing his hair, and (of course) chewing gum. Practice techniques for conveying attitudes.

WRITING SKITS

Let's set up a skit using pantomime. If a skit was titled "The Big Date," you might show a teenager who wants to borrow his busy dad's car. An understanding of both father and son is needed. In your skit the son, listening to a loud radio, might approach his dad, who is busy preparing income tax returns.

Showing the contrast between the characters establishes who each one is. The teenager mimes to his father about a big date, showing all the details—miming out getting dressed up, the shape of the girl, and driving the car. Dad mimes that the car has a flat tire and that he's too busy to fix it. The son mimes that he will fix the flat if he can borrow the car. Dad agrees. They shake hands and get to work . . . Blackout.

This skit (or piece) had a beginning, a middle and an end (resolution, or blowoff). In putting together a skit these elements are important for the audience or they will never know what happened. When opening a skit, establish who your character is, where he may be, what he has to do, and when it has to be done (if the scene calls for a specific time). Remember this rule: do what a news reporter does, tell who, what, where, when, and how.

I have a confession to make. I don't like mimes. I have said it, very mean, if every mime on the face of the earth would disappear, the world would not be a worse place. They had to drag me kicking and screaming to see Avner the Eccentric, a one man mime show, but when the show was over, they had to drag me kicking and screaming out of the theatre. I wanted more...I laughed for 2 solid hours. The show only lasted an hour and a half. The last 30 minutes I remembered and laughed all over again.

You know the most critical element in comedy? Ask me, what's the most critical element in comedy? Timing. And the timing, the pacing, the bits that fly off the wall and out of nowhere are so good, you are never aware there is just one silent man with some silent props entertaining you.

—Joel Siegel ABC-TV

PERFORMING SKITS

When performing mime, you are creating an illusion. Each scene, skit, or bit must be as clean as if you were actually performing the action and you must always be conscious of *space* and *size*. Space referring to where you are in your skit and where things are around you in your mime world. When you're miming that you're in a kitchen, for example, remember where each pot and pan is, where the spoons are, and even where the cupboard is. Nothing is as bad as a mime who opens doors (and doesn't close them) and then walks right through them.

Avner Eisenberg as Avner the Eccentric

Size refers to the shape and weight of the objects in your mime world. If you're going to show a ball to the audience, what kind of ball is it? How much does it weight? Is it round? Is it hard or soft? These are the type of questions that you have to ask yourself before you perform a skit or scene. Because if you're not sure what you're doing, then your audience will never know.

Theater Games

Let's begin with some simple theater games which will give you a better sense of both space and size. Don't forget that a great imagination also helps. These games can be practiced by yourself or used when working with a group of people. If you're working by yourself, use a mirror to check your movements, but don't live in front of the mirror—move around.

What It Isn't. To open up the imagination, try this game which I've named "What it isn't." Choose an object, any object (wallet, notebook, box, handbag, pocket calculator) and use your imagination to show the audience *what it isn't.* If the object is a wallet, you might mime that it is a portable radio, a camera, a sandwich, a steering wheel, or anything other than a wallet.

As an exercise, this game will help you develop a very strong sense of how to improvise. Improvisation is the art of performing a skit or scene on the spot, without any rehearsing. Most of the world's greatest clowns (Charlie Chaplin, Buster Keaton, Laurel and

At the county fair, a pilot offered to fly anyone in his old, open-cockpit plane for $5. One farmer and his wife, who had never been up in a plane, wanted to take a ride but the price was to high.

"Come on," said the pilot. "If you promise to be a good passenger and don't do any back seat driving I'll take you up for nothing."

The farmer and his wife readily agreed and went for a ride with the pilot.

While up in the air the pilot gave the couple a thrilling ten minute ride with some pretty facy tricks.

After landing, the pilot said to the farmer, "You did very well for your first flight. I didn't hear a word out of you."

"That's right," said the farmer. "It was pretty hard. I almost said something back there when my wife fell out."

Hardy, Abbott and Costello, Red Skelton) have this sense of "impromptu timing." In training yourself to be a professional clown, strive to gain this timing because there will be situations where you might not have a magic trick with you and you are asked to perform. Improvised entertainment can be funny (even funnier than a rehearsed bit) because it's live and exciting, not knowing what your brain will create next.

People, Places, and Things. This game extends your new found ability to improvise in front of your audience. Ask the audience to give you the following situations. A person (famous or common), a place (anywhere within this solar system), and a thing (problem, job, or goal). Take these suggestions and put them together in an improvised skit. Whether it turns out to be comical or tragic is up to you. If you do this in a group, you'll be amazed to see how three or four people will improvise together. To keep the skits interesting, limit these games to under three minutes.

Passing the Object. As a group effort, passing objects (mime objects) also helps to build up your skills as a mime. One person begins by passing an object (a book, a hat, loose jello) to the next person without telling anyone what it is. By the way the first person handles this invisible object, the rest of the group must figure out what they are about to hold. When the object returns to the leader, the rest of the group must tell what they held. Only then does the leader reveal what was passed out in the beginning.

The Mask. This is an exercise in expression development. Pretend that you have a mask; each time you place it in front of your face, create a different facial expression: happy, sad, mad, goofy, spaced-out, and so forth. In a group, pass this mask around and have each person display a different expression.

Classic Skits

In the world of mime some skits or vignettes are classics, which all performers of mime should experience. The following are a few of these "classics," with a brief description of how you might perform each skit. These descriptions are given only to help you understand the scene; improvise and add your own personal touches.

The Wall. The mime enters and begins to create an invisible wall in front of himself. This is done by placing the hands with open palms in front of the body (arms slightly bent) and fingers spread open to

Walking

Tug-of-War

show the solidness of the wall. Open the fingers, stop, relax the hand, and move that hand away from the space which is the wall. To get a better idea of how to do this, place your hands on a real wall, then relax the fingers.

In performing this you will want to have the hands move in a even motion (don't put your hand through the wall you've just created). By moving the hands faster and more frantically you will give a solid feeling to this invisible wall.

The Box. As with the wall, you will want to show the solid interior of the box. Working with your hands and arms, feel and push out the sides of the box to give it shape. Don't forget to indicate the presence of a top. In performance this box could become a telephone booth that you get trapped in. With a closed fist bang on the wall of the box.

Tightrope Walker. The last two skits dealt with objects, now you must create the character of a brave tightrope walker (or maybe one who is not so brave). In performing this skit, start by climbing up an imagi-

Tightrope Walker

Leaning on Fence

Sitting

Body Lean

Rope Pull

nary ladder to the platform of the tightrope. Place your foot on the rope to get the feel of it, juat as someone might stick their foot in a pool to see if the water is cold. Pantomime the pole that the tightrope walker uses to keep his balance. Remember to place your feet in a toe-to-heel position and to walk in this fashion when on the tightrope. Try to create different things to do once you've made your first mime walk across the tight-rope—mime juggle, balance on one foot, do a head-stand.

Tug-of-War. This skit can be done solo or with a group, but as a solo the skit demands more work. You will have to show how you are pulling the rope and then how you are being pulled by someone else (who of course is not there if you are doing this solo). A great exercise to really sense the pulling of the rope is to get a real rope and actually have a tug-of-war with some friends. Observe the actions of pulling and the reactions of being pulled. After this exercise, try to recreate the same actions and reactions without the rope.

Preparation

In all that has been discussed on the subject of mime, observation is the most important of all. Notice and then notice again how situations occur in the real world so that when you perform a skit or a piece in mime, it will appear clear to the audience. Watching the way people move will help your performance of "character types." To be a great mime requires a constant awareness of how people act. Look at each detail of how people act so that when and if you ever need to imitate something it will be waiting in your brain to use.

For clowns, mime is a tool used to entertain and generate laughter. The following chapter on physical comedy will go into more detail on the use of mime in creating comedy.

Ed: Once I lived for a whole week on a can of sardines.
Fred: Wow! How did you keep from falling off?

CHAPTER 5

PHYSICAL COMEDY

BUILDUP AND SURPRISE

Imagine the following scene. A man with somewhat less intelligence than average, perhaps a Rodney Dangerfield look-alike, is strolling through a Neiman-Marcus department store when he spots the girl of his dreams. It's love at first sight.

She doesn't appear to notice him. He must get her attention and strike up a conversation with this beautiful lady. He straightens his tie, pushes his hair back, making sure every strand is in its proper place; shoes are buffed vigorously against the backs of his trousers. Knowing the importance of first impressions, he wants to knock her off her feet with his charming looks and personality.

Lifting his head confidently, he walks slowly toward her. As he steps near, she turns and looks at him. Their eyes meet, she smiles.

He is overjoyed and quickens his pace. As he approaches he opens his mouth to utter his carefully planned introduction. "Excuse me miss, I—" Unexpectedly he steps on a discarded banana peel. His leg slides out of control, propelling the foot up into the air making him look like Big Bird doing the cancan. His arms swing wildly, eyes roll around in his head and he squeals "YAACH!"

Falling onto his face, he lies on the floor looking like a idiot. The woman turns quietly and walks away, pretending that she never noticed him.

In a movie or on TV an event like this would have brought a round of laughter from the audience. What made this scene funny? For that matter, what makes anything funny?

One of the major elements of humor is the occurrence of something unexpected. It could be verbal, like the punch line to a joke, or physical, like the man who tries to impress the woman with his charm but ends up foolishly spread on the floor.

Any deviation from the expected sequence of events has the potential to be funny. A clown notices that his shoe is untied. He bends down to tie it. As he does so, he accidentally bangs his head against the top of a table. Straightening up, his eyes roll and he drops into a heap onto the floor.

Hitting one's head and falling on the ground is not part of the normal process of tying a shoelace. The clown hitting his head was unexpected and took the audience by surprise. This is the basis of all humor. If the audience had expected the clown to bang his head, the incident would have lost its element of surprise and would not have been funny.

If the audience expects a certain thing to happen, and it does, there is no surprise and the event is not funny. The funniest jokes require spontaneity; there should be little or no warning something unusual is about to happen.

Surprise alone, however, will not guarantee a laugh. The unexpected event or punch line must be related to something that is going on at the time. If the man who slipped on the banana, for example, was just walking through the store when he stepped on the peel and fell, much of the humor in the event would be lost. But because he was trying to impress the woman with his charm, the fall had more significance. The addition of unexpected arm swinging, facial expression, and body contortions while falling compounded the humor of the incident.

The same is true with jokes. A good story or buildup is what makes the punch line (or blowoff, in the case of a skit) funny. Take the guest at a hotel as an example. This guest is a Jack Benny type. During his entire stay the bellhops avoid him because he never tips for their services in spite of using them frequently. Yet they put up with him, as good hotel employees should. While checking out of his room, he spots a bellhop and says, "I'm leaving now. Would you call me a cab?" The bell hop looks at him one last time and says "OK, you're a cab!"

The punch line "You're a cab" by itself is not funny. But it becomes funny when used in the context of this story. The more effective the lead, the funnier the punch line or blowoff.

PHYSICAL EXPRESSION

Humor can be separated into two broad categories, verbal and nonverbal. Verbal comedy is relayed by speech through jokes and stories. Nonverbal or physical comedy is expressed by body movement and facial expression.

Clowns rely heavily on physical comedy to express themselves and create laughter. Clowning and physical comedy are in fact inseparable, you can't have one without the other. Many clowns use no verbal dialogue at all, but depend totally on pantomime.

To convey emotions, thought, personality, and actions through physical movement alone requires an acute awareness of body language. Clowns are not the

bumbling fools they seem to be; they are skilled performing artists. An inexperienced or untrained clown is readily detectable because he lacks the skill to express himself effectively. Conscious awareness of body movements and practice will help a clown master the skills of acting like a fool without being one.

Some of the great comedians of the past such as Charlie Chaplin, Red Skelton, and Laurel and Hardy, relied heavily on physical comedy. The slapstick humor of the Keystone Cops and the Three Stooges was drenched with physical nonsense.

We are all familiar with the pie in the face or getting a foot stuck in a bucket. Although old situations, we can watch them again and again with as much amusement as when we saw them for the first time. In verbal comedy a joke gets "old" after a while and loses its humor; it no longer comes as a surprise. It's different with physical actions, however. Because each actor reacts differently, the same situation takes on a newness that makes it funny time and time again.

VISUALIZING YOUR STORY

Visualize the following pantomime, with all accompanying facial expressions and body movements. Picture it in the funniest way you can. No words are spoken; all emotions and actions are conveyed through body language alone.

The scene opens in the living room of a couple celebrating their wedding anniversary. The wife opens a present from her husband. To her surprise she finds a brand new frying pan. Maybe not the best anniversary present in the world, but she thanks him and excitedly hands him a present from her.

The husband opens the box and finds the ugliest tie he has ever seen. He winces at the sight of it, but quickly forces a smile of pleasure. She beams with pride as she tells him she made it herself. Not wanting to hurt her feelings, he pretends to act as if he loves the gift.

Noticing his lack of genuine joy, she gives him a stern look of disapproval. Defensively he insists that the tie is beautiful and that he's happy with it. Motioning for him to try it on, she leaves momentarily to go into the kitchen.

The husband reluctantly puts the disgusting thing around his neck. To see how ridiculous it looks, he heads toward the bedroom, where there is a mirror. The door into the bedroom is stuck, and he has to push it hard to open.

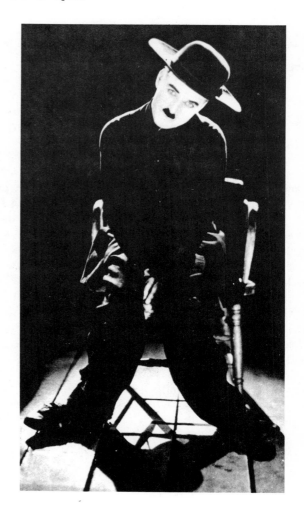

On closing the door one of his fingers becomes stuck between the door and the doorframe. He winces in pain and tries to pull his finger free, but it won't budge. He pulls harder, but it still won't move.

Lifting one foot and bracing it against the door, he tries to pull the finger free, unaware that pushing on the door with his foot just tightens the door's grip on his helpless finger. Seeing his mistake, he chuckles to himself for being so silly.

Grabbing the edge of the door, he pulls with all his strength. His trapped hand is joyfully freed. Happy to escape the door's viselike grip, he turns and begins to walk away. As he starts to move, he is yanked back.

Shocked, he sees that a finger on his other hand is now trapped by the door. He pulls on it, but it won't come loose. Using both hands, he frees his finger, but only at the expense of trapping the first finger again.

He tries again to pry the door open, only this time he leans his body against the door for added leverage. Both hands slip safely away from the door. Free at last, he happily starts to walk away, only to be yanked back with the door clinching tightly to his trousers.

He pulls his leg, but the trousers remain stuck. Yanking the leg brings no results. Frantically he kicks and pulls, but no luck. Anger is building up inside him. Grabbing the door with both hands, he pulls and tugs with all his strenght.

The leg slips loose. Immediately he looks at both legs and arms to verify that he is indeed free. Chuckling as if to have the last laugh, he begins to walk away. Then his eyes widen and his tongue sticks out as he is yanked back to the door by his tie.

He pulls, but it won't come loose. He pulls harder but still remains trapped. Spotting a pair of scissors on a nearby table, he reaches for them, but they are too far away. As he stretches he slips and falls. The tie, locked tightly in the door, acts as a noose and begins to choke him.

His eyes roll in circles, his checks puff out with comical choking expressions. Scrambling back to his feet, he rubs his neck and swallows deeply, twisting his head from side to side to relieve the pain.

He tries again but this time he grabs the edge of the table and pulls the scissors within reach. Picking them up he cuts the tie in two. Free at last!

At this moment his wife walks into the room, pushing the stuck door wide open. Half of the husband's new tie drops freely to the floor.

She looks at him and points to the scissors in his hand and to his tie, which is now totally destroyed. He tries to explain, but she doesn't believe him. She becomes furious that he ruined the tie she had worked so hard to make. Gripping the new frying pan, she slams it against the top of her husband's head. He screams and runs away, with his wife in hot pursuit.

As you read this pantomime, could you see the shock in the husband's face when he opened his present and found that ugly tie? Could you visualize his frustration as he repeatedly got stuck in the door? Did you see the anger in his wife's face as she saw the mangled tie, and the frightened look in the husband's eyes as he tried to explain to his wife what happened?

If you can visualize these things in a funny way, you can recreate them physically as you act out a skit or a routine.

One of the first steps in creating physical humor is to define what expressions, feelings, and actions you want to convey. Do you want to express anger, frustration, desperation, or determination? Or do you want to show actions such as driving a car, asking for directions, and painting a sign?

To express yourself and convey thoughts and actions to others without words, you need to practice ways of communicating with your body. In this way your will have a storehouse of information which you can use to express yourself in a clownish manner.

SPEAKING WITH THE BODY

Communication without words is body language. We wave our hands "good-by," nod our heads "yes," hold our stomach if it's upset, rub our eyes if we're sleepy. Physical comedy uses body language to communicate humor.

Facial expressions can be a great tool in communicating with the audience. A face with little expression has the same effect on an audience as a speaker talking in a monotone. All great speakers put a lot of expression into their speaking voices, and to be effective at physical comedy you must use a variety of facial expressions.

The face physically expresses emotions, feelings, and thoughts. It is the single most important means of nonverbal communication. Because of the great importance of facial expressions, every clown should spend time practicing as many different faces as can be imagined.

Ed: Knock knock.
Fred: Who's there?
Ed: Adolph.
Fred: Adolph who?
Ed: Adolph ball hit me in the head. That's why I talk like this.

Go to a mirror and practice each of the following emotions. Look at yourself from someone else's perspective. Would they be able to readily identify these emotions expressed by you?

happiness	surprise
laughter	remorse
anger	confusion
sadness	excitement
fear	pain
pleasure	revenge

All the feelings listed above can be expressed by the face alone, but body movement can enhance or assist in conveying the proper mood. Review the list again, adding movement from the entire body

Personality and character traits can also be displayed with a proper combination of facial and body movement. Go back to the mirror and practice the following personality traits.

stubborn	stylish
clumsy	sneaky
determined	talker
conceited	snobbish
shy	nervous
confident	boisterous

Use your imagination and past experience to act out these traits. Make every movement project a feeling or thought. Let's use a pie fight as an example. Imagine that someone has just smashed a chocolate cream pie onto the top of your head. What is your reaction? How does it feel? Can you feel the cream drip down the side of your face and neck? Is it hot or cold? What does it smell like? Is it sticky or smooth? These are the kinds of things you must consider when acting out a part.

Practice expressing thoughts, feelings, and activities in front of somebody and ask them to try to identify your actions or feelings. Use the following list to get started. This practice will also help develop your mime skills.

hot	cold
surprise	hammering
eating	taking pictures
sewing	digging a hole
hunger	roller skating
sleepiness	swimming
windiness	driving a car
running	fighting
searching for something	drunkenness
getting a new idea	smelling an odor

CLOWN MOVEMENT

Clowns and comedians, unlike other actors, don't always display normal actions. Clown movements are performed with obvious exaggeration. Much of the humor and the joy of watching a clown is derived from these bigger than life actions. A clown must learn to express his emotions, thoughts, actions, reactions, and personality with the entire body.

A clown's expressions and movements are a caricature of normal movements much like that of a cartoon. The clown is in fact a living cartoon character. His actions should be like those of Bugs Bunny, Fred Flintstone, or Scooby-Doo.

You will notice that clowns, like cartoon characters, exert a tremendous amount of energy which seems to accomplish very little. In a chase scene, for instance, a cartoon character who begins to run away from something will jump up in the air and pedal his legs before actually taking off. The clown too, may jump and begin moving his legs before starting on a run.

The chase scenes in cartoons are filled with wasted motion. Turning a corner isn't just a simple turn but may involve hopping on one foot as the turn is made. Participants take the most ridiculous routes, run in circles, and bump into each other. The clown chase scene is done the same way. It's silly sure, but that's what clowns are for.

All actions can be exaggerated or made clownish in same way. Take something as simple as walking. Rather than simply starting to walk, lift one knee high before stepping out. Remember Jackie Gleason's walk? He would raise his elbows up and lifting one leg, bent at the knee, across the other before straighening it out to take a large sidestep. This movement added a lot more color than a simple step.

Excitement can be expressed by jumping around clapping your hands, hugging yourself, and showing others what made you feel happy.

Anger can be displayed by flexing the muscles in the face into a tightly contorted frown. Raise your fist and shake it, stomp your feet, show your teeth, jump up and down. Express yourself fully.

If you're tired and worn out, walk very slowly, feet dragging, arms limp, mouth open, tongue hanging out, and shoulders slumping. You may stumble as you walk, stopping periodically to rest and wipe your brow.

To deliver a punch, pull your arm all the way back, maybe even winding it up, and then swing it in a wide arc so as to be seen easily by the entire audience.

Eating can take various forms. Smack your lips and lick them with your tongue. Open your mouth wide to take a big bite. Make chewing obvious, perhaps even sticking your tongue against the inside of your mouth to make it appear to be stuffed with food. Pick up a few crumbs that happen to fall and pop them into your mouth—savor the flavor.

These are only a few examples of exaggerating ordinary actions. Go back to the lists of emotions, thoughts, personaliy trates and actions. Practice each one again, using slow, exaggerated movements. Remember to act as if you were a cartoon character.

When practicing facial expressions in front of a mirror, take some time and make some silly faces. Move your eyeballs and eyebrows, puff out your cheeks, and twist your lips. Find several combinations that you like. If you have the ability to do something unique or unusual, such as wiggling your ears or nose, add that. I have the ability to flex certain muscles in my face which makes my nose wiggle. This simple skill adds another gimmick I can use for creating laughter.

Funny faces can be used whenever other humor doesn't produce a strong enough reaction. Moderately humorous jokes and gags take on new life and become effective simply with the addition of a goofy looking expression. Use funny faces freely, but don't overuse them. Too many of the same faces lose their appeal, so use several different faces for variety.

ACTION AND REACTION IN PHYSICAL COMEDY

Reactions are a vital element in physical comedy. If there is an action that affects the performer, there must also be a reaction.

Stepping on a banana peel is an action. Sliding, swinging arms wildly, kicking the legs up, and eventually falling down is the reaction. Stepping on the banana peel wasn't funny but the reaction was.

Slapstick Comedy

One of the major types of physical comedy is slapstick humor. Originally a slapstick was a device made from two flat sticks and a hinge or wedge, which would make a loud sound when struck against a performer's backside. Slapstick is a term used now to describe comedy using physical discomfort and pain, such as slaps, blows, and falls. Like a cartoon, the actors never really gets hurt and the audience knows this.

Just being hit or falling is not funny. It's the reaction to the hit or fall that makes slapstick effective.

I learned the principle of action-reaction early in my juggling career. When I began working up my first short juggling routine, I was a real novice. I thought slapstick humor was an easy way to get laughs.

I would toss a ball into the air and "accidentally" let it hit me on the head. "Ouch," I'd say, and wait for the audience to laugh. This however only produced a few snickers and a lot of silence.

Later I repeated the same routine but added a more expressive "OUCH!" This reaction produced a much better audience response. I found that the more exaggeration I added, both verbal and physical, the more the audience enjoyed it and the better the routine became.

Dropping a bowling ball on your toe can be hilarious if you follow it by screaming, showing great pain, and contorting your facial muscles as you lift the injured foot and hop around with it in your hands.

Remember, all reactions must be larger than real life. If you're struck by an object or another performer, the reaction is to fall, jump, or move in the direction of the force. The reaction to a kick in the seat of the pants would be to arch the hips out forward. The head, arms, and legs lag behind, accompanied by appropriate facial and verbal expressions.

A punch in the kisser is an action. A reaction might include a stunned or dazed look on the face, eyes rolling around in their sockets, and spitting out a mouthful of teeth.

If a large hammer comes down on your head, bend your knees and come down slightly with the force of the hammer, at the same time, raise your shoulders to exaggerate the movement. Add facial expression, stick out your tongue, and act as if you're seeing stars by rolling your head around in a circle.

Non-Slapstick Comedy

The action-reaction principle works with non-slapstick humor as well. While standing in front of an audience, the clown bends over to pick up a fallen prop. As he does so, he hears a loud "RRRIP!" A surprised and worried look crosses his face as he realizes that his trousers have just given way. His face shows fear and embarrassment. Grabbing the hat off his head, he hides the rip on his posterior. Smiling nervously, he backs cautiously backs toward the exit.

Ripping of the clown's pants was the action; how he handled the situation was the reaction. The number of possible reactions is limited only by the performer's imagination. What and how each clown reacts is highly variable and subject to personal preference and the character portrayed.

One often used reaction is the "double take" or "second take," one of those second glances that confirms the unexpected or sometimes even the expected. Imagine a man, who has stopped during a walk in the woods. Casually he begins to pick berries and eat them. A furry bear paw appears, holding out a handful of berries. The man takes some and pops them in his mouth; he may even say, "Thank you." Suddenly realizing where the berries came from, he looks quickly (the double take), lets out a yelp, and runs for the hills—a classic comedy scene.

The greatest comedians have the talent of getting the most laughter out of any situation by the way they handle their reactions. Although carefully rehearsed, each reaction looks spontaneous.

I have seen many acts that had a lot of funny material but lacked well executed reactions. Even though the performers may have received laughs, their presentations would have been much better if they had added exaggerated vocal tone and body movement. Carefully planned actions and reactions add variety and give the act a more professional appearance.

Practice your reactions to each of the following situations. Use full expression and get the most out of them.

Put your toes into icy cold water.
Sit on a burning cigarette.
Drink a very strong beverage.
Drop a juggling club on your toe.
Eat a chewy piece of candy.
Step on a very sticky piece of gum.
Get a finger caught in a dresser drawer.

Even ordinary actions can be made funny if the reaction dramatically exaggerated. It's not what you do that's important, but how you do it.

TIMING

Timing in comedy is very important! A punch line delivered at the wrong time could be disastrous, even if only a few seconds too late or too early.

The punch line should accommodate the laughter from the audience. Let the laughter die down before continuing. If you have several possible lines in a joke or an effect and they're too close together, you may have half of the audience asking the person next to them, "What did he say?" Give them the pleasure of laughing as long as they can before continuing. Cutting the laughter short is almost like telling the audience to be quiet so they can hear the jokes. Because of audience response and reaction, the entertainer must learn to pace himself. Observe and note your audience's reaction time. Learn from them while giving them what they need, when they need it. Most important, always leave them wanting more!

The great comedian and clown, Red Skelton is a master at this. His tramp clown character, Freddie the Freeloader, would get excited about something and walk quickly across the stage. About midway, he would give a little kick and jump in the air, while the sound effects man in the back would jingle a cowbell. The audience

but he was more intelligent than his companion. The Three Stooges were all idiots, but Moe was the most intelligent and Curly the least. Larry was in between, playing the buffoon when interacting with Moe but assuming the intelligent role when interacting with Curly.

Clowns who work as a team should pair up in similar fashion. The whiteface clown traditionally plays the role of the smart clown. Although he may look like a fool, he is more intelligent than the other types of clowns. The whiteface will team up with either an auguste or a tramp (or other appropriate character clown). The auguste and tramp play the role of the buffoon.

In the past a whiteface was always teamed with an auguste, but now it is common to see two whiteface or two auguste clowns teamed together. In such cases the makeup and wardrobe of the clowns must allow the audience to distinguish which one is the buffoon and which is not. The one wearing the most bizarre makeup and clothes will always play the fool.

The concept of action and reaction plays an important role in comedy partnerships. The whiteface or straight man sets up the situation, which the dumber partner reacts to. Although comedy teams use some jokes and gags, they work primarily through situation comedy. A particular event or situation becomes funny as a result of the interaction between the performers.

would grow accustomed to hearing the bell, and after several times the bell would sound either too early or too late. This routine, combined with second takes, brought the house down with laughter. The audience would watch in anticipation to see what would happen the next time he jumped.

Running gags are my favorite part of physical comedy. The audience is usually set up in advance to be thrown off course. One oldie, but still a goodie, is when a clown or magician continually wipes his brow with a handkerchief. After each time, he throws the handkerchief on the floor and each time it bounces back, compliments of a rubber ball sewn into it. The third time, the hanky with the ball is replaced by an identical hanky with a clay ball. The result is a thud as it hits the floor where it remains lifeless. The performer follows this with an unexpected double take.

COMEDY PARTNERSHIPS

The most successful comedy teams have been those which combine a straight man with a buffoon. Laurel and Hardy, Abbot and Costello, the Smothers Brothers, Hope and Crosby, Martin and Lewis—in each team one was more intelligent than the other. The straight man didn't always know the right answer or act intelligently,

Getting a shave or a haircut from a barber isn't particularly a funny situation, but if the person cutting the hair is a clumsy idiot pretending to be a barber, you have the potential for many laughs.

An auguste may play the part of the inexperienced barber. The whiteface could play the part of the real barber, who left the shop in the care of his friend as he went out on a quick errand. A whiteface would also play the role of the unsuspecting customer who comes in for a haircut.

The customer may be in a hurry, and he doesn't listen when the auguste tries to explain that he is just tending the shop until the real barber returns. The whiteface demands a haircut then and there, setting up a situation for the auguste to get laughs. The novice barber would then proceed to make a mess out of everything and destroy the whiteface's hair.

BREAK A LEG!

In the last two chapters we have covered many of the basics of physical expression as used by clowns. Combining physical movement with comedy has become

a trademark of the art of clowning and is one of the characteristics that separates clowns from other comedians.

Many skillful entertainers, using only mime, make their audience laugh with amusing movement and body language. Most clowns combine both physical comedy and verbal humor in a synchronized display of tomfoolerly. All clowns should learn to develop their skills of physical expression. Practice the exercises discussed in these chapters and always be aware of how you visually express your clown character. As they say in the theater for good luck, "Go out there and break a leg!"

Ed: OUCH! Oh my ear, my ear!
Fred: What's the matter?
Ed: I just bit myself.
Fred: That's impossible. How can sombody bite themself on the ear?
Ed: I was standing on a chair.

CHAPTER 6

WORKING WITH YOUR AUDIENCE

CONTROLLING THE AUDIENCE

Are your shows filled with fun and excitement? At the end, do the people in the audience feel they've been truly entertained? Was your show memorable, or just another clown act?

A really good performer is one who has developed a special magic that can touch each member of the audience. It doesn't matter if it's a clown act, a magic act, a skit, a play, or even an opera. The actors or performers grab the audience's attention and sweep them into a world of make-believe.

In a skit or play with two or more actors, the dialogue and the action cause the spectators to experience the performer's emotions. When the hero is in trouble and racing against time to save his life or that of another person, the audience feels the tension and excitement. As observers, we actually feel as if we were physically involved. We perspire, grow nervous, and cry in anguish, only to breath a sigh of relief when the crisis has passed.

Next time you watch a good show, especially a dramatic and emotion-filled one, try to sense the feelings you have as you watch it. You'll notice that you actually feel sad when the main characters are distressed, happy when they are happy. You ride through an emotionally packed experience, feeling everything the actors feel. That's a sign of a good performance.

A clown, magician, stand-up comic, or any other per-former should be able to grab the attention of an audience and lead them to feel any emotion desired. For clowns, the performance will be slanted heavily toward humor and fantasy.

When your act consists of a skit involving two or more performers, it is relatively easy to project feelings of love, jealousy, revenge, embarrassment, anger, and other emotions through dialogue and action. When you work with a partner, whether it's a real one or a wooden dummy, you are actually performing a play.

For the single performer, the method of conveying emotion is slightly different. Instead of talking to another actor, a puppet, or an assistant, you must talk to the audience. The skilled clown can evoke responses from the audience through a careful choice of actions and words. This is done by talking to the audience and asking for a particular response or by performing universally recognized physical movements.

When on a stage, the performer may travel from one end of the stage to the other, but most of the time he will gravitate directly to the center. Without speaking, he can indicate to the audience when to applaud by stepping toward the front and center of the stage and waiting. This move is usually enough to signal an audience response, but spreading the arms slightly reinforces the first sign and tells the audience, "I am through with this particular bit—please respond."

Other nonverbal signs are used to control the au-dience. A wave of the hand when entering the stage signals a happy "Hello." A wave while stepping back will tell the audience that it was fun but the act is over and now you are leaving. A hand held up to the ear or a palm lifted upward is a signal for the audience to respond louder or with more vigor.

Use these and other types of body language to communicate with your audience. Treat the audience like a group of friends.

One of the primary ways of communicating with an audience and getting them to respond is simply by talking to them. Tell them to do something; have the entire audience participate; choose helpers to come up on stage to work with you. One of the best ways to liven up a show and make it memorable for the audience is to have them help you. In this way they feel like a part of the show. Ask an audience full of children if there is anyone who would like to help, and kids will go wild with excitement.

COMMUNICATING WITH THE AUDIENCE

Have you ever been in a conversation with a person who does all the talking? You feel lucky if you can squeeze in a word or two, and even then the other person doesn't seem to listen. Trying to communicate with such people can be discouraging because you are essentially left out of the conversation.

Audiences can feel this way too. The performing arts are a form of communication. The clown or performer expresses thoughts, emotions, and humor to the audience. The audience responds with applause, laughter, groans, or even boos, which express their feelings about your performance. Even with the absence of any of these responses, the audience is expressing what they think of you. If nobody laughs at your jokes, they're telling you something.

This form of two-way communication continues throughout the show. When you enter the stage, you may get welcoming applause.

Every time you do or say something funny, the audience laughs. A particularly good gag or display of physical or vocal skill will bring a round of applause. The audience is showing immediate approval and satisfaction. The opposite is also true—a sorry joke will bring groans if the audience is enjoying themselves and boos or stony silence if they are not.

The applause and laughter also tell the performer *how much* the audience enjoyed or is enjoying the show. The louder, longer, and more frequent the response, the greater their enjoyment.

You can increase an audience's enjoyment by allowing them to participate in the show. This will increase their communication with you and get them more involved.

AUDIENCE PARTICIPATION

Participation—this is a key word for keeping the attention and interest of an audience. It makes the audience feel special and creates a more personal relationship with the performer. The performer becomes a real person who will be remembered, not an object

like a TV that can be turned off.

All good shows involve some type of audience participation. Use the audience as often as you can. If you've ever been in an audience of kids that is given a chance to yell or move, you know what effect it has. Games, sporting events, songs—anything is more enjoyable when we get to participate and the same is true for shows.

How do you engage an audience? Where do you start? A good place to start is with a warm-up before the show actually begins.

Warm-Ups

A short comic routine involving the entire audience helps to set up the performer as the one in charge during the show. You also warm-up the audience and let them get to know you.

Using a participation routine to start off your show has several advantages. For one, it gives stragglers a few minutes to come in and sit down without missing any of your "prepared" material. It can also act as a means of attracting people into your show. It also announces to everyone already there that the show is beginning and to pay attention. The warm-up is a good way to spark everyone's interest and prepare them for the good time they are about to have. It says, "This guy is fun and we're going to enjoy this show."

Casual Greeting. A very simple method that at first may not seem like a participation technique is the casual greeting. Instead of entering on the stage, as is usually done, come up to it by walking through the audience.

Starting from the back, advance toward the stage, shaking hands and waving to everyone. Playing some warm-up music as you appear will help announce your presence and signal the start of the show.

By walking through the audience like this, you stir up some excitement and generate curiosity.

The Hello Echo. An old favorite is the echo technique. As you come out on stage say "Hello." Bring your hand up to your ear to signal for the audience to respond. They will give back a half hearted "Hello." Look disappointed and signal for them to speak louder as you repeat your "Hello" with a little more force.

They will come back with a more synchronized and louder response. Shake your head and signal again for them to yell louder as you holler "HELLO!" They are warmed up now and will give you all they've got.

This activity has perked them all up and they're now ready for the show. You can use this method any time during the show when a solicited response lacks enthusiasm.

Applause Contest. Using applause to warm-up the audience is a technique that is commonly used. It's fun and easy to do, and establishes you as the leader.

A popular form of warm-up is an applause contest. This is great for outdoor shows where the audience can come and go freely, such as you find at many fairs. The thunderous applause you generate will be heard by others in the vicinity. They will wonder who is getting this fantastic ovation and are likely to join your audience.

Split the audience into two halves (or three halves?). Call one side "Group One" and the other side "Group A" (nobody likes to be second). Have one side applaud as hard and as loud as they can, then have the other side do the same. Go back and forth a few times encouraging them to do it louder each time.

You can finish with a short gag, like having both sides give it all they've got at the same time. When the noise dies down bow humbly and say, "Thank you, thank you, I'm glad you enjoyed my show. Good-bye . . . Oh you mean I haven't done it yet? . . ." Then start into your regular act.

Without the warm-up many people may still be talking to each other or otherwise be distracted. Audience participation forces them to give you their attention so that when you begin with your regular routines they're ready to follow you into your world of fantasy.

An active warm-up like this is one of the best ways to get an audience prepared for your show. You have introduced yourself, and by the time the warm-up is over, they will know you a little better. Jokes and other comic patter will help make the warm-up even more enjoyable.

Goofy Applause. Add some creativity to the applause. Here is an idea you can use as part of your warm-up and as a running gag throughout the show.

This bit can be added after your entering applause or after your first trick or stunt (you may have to encourage them to applaud if not given spontaneously). After receiving applause, say something such as "Thank you for that marvelous round of applause. I appreciate it but you know, there was something missing. In order to give a *round* of applause as it should be given you need to clap while your hands move in a circle like this."

Show the audience how a real round of applause works and have them do it. Kids especially enjoy this type of activity because it's silly and gives them a chance to expend some of their energy.

You can continue by saying, "That's how you give a real round of applause. There are other ways to applaud besides that, let me show you another . . ."

You then can demonstrate one of any number of imaginative forms of clapping, such as the lip applause. Instead of clapping with your hands you clap with your lips. Have them pucker up and vibrate the lips quickly with a finger while humming. It's amazing what a crowd of vibrating lips can sound like. The audience will choke with laughter at this. Throughout the show, you can teach them other ways to applaud.

This is a good way to add variety and fun to any type of show, and an excellent way to get audience participation. Here are some examples of other kinds of applause.

Belly Buster: Stand and clap hands while bending over at the waist.

Knee Slapper: Slap knees with both hands.

Horse Applause: This includes three separate claps done several times in succession. First clap both hands together, then quickly slap the right knee with the right hand, followed by the left knee with the left hand. Repeated several times makes the sound of a galloping horse.

Bottle Applause: Open mouth and slightly pucker lips while slapping the cheek. This sounds like a bottle being emptied. It can also be done in stereo by slapping both sides of the face.

Jump for Joy: Jump up, clap, and fall back into the seat.

Tarzan Applause: Beat on your chest.

Chicken Applause: Bring hands up to armpits and flap elbows like wings.

Balloon Applause: Make a fist and put your thumb to your mouth as if to blow up a balloon. Blow, and one by one open up the fingers like an expanding balloon. When they are all out, wiggle them. Both hands can be inflated then placed on the nose or ears while sticking out the tongue. Yes it's crazy, but it's fun.

Duck Cheer: Shout, "Quack, Quack."

Skunk Cheer: Say "Pee-you" while holding the nose. This goes well after a sick joke.

Combine the tricks or gags you do with a related applause. For example, after juggling a rubber chicken or doing magic with eggs, end with the chicken applause. After a balloon trick or gag, use the balloon applause.

I don't like spinach and I'm glad I don't like it, because if I did like it I'd eat it—and I hate the stuff.

_____

Why don't you learn to play the guitar and stop picking on me?

Participation Techniques

Using applause is an easy and effective way to get the audience to participate with you and become more involved in the show. Directing them to say or do things or asking for spontaneous responses will open up the channel of communication.

The following are some ideas that have been used successfully by performers to generate audience participation. These are just a few ideas to help jump start your imagination into creating your own techniques.

Cheering Section. Choose a cheering section—one, two, or five people, or the entire audience. Sometimes it's fun to select a single bystander and have him or her respond. Choose likely-looking candidates, teenage girls make good guinea pigs—oops, I mean volunteers for this bit.

Tell them that in order to keep enthusiasm up, they must respond in a certain way every time you give the clue. You might stamp your foot and wave a hand, or stick your thumbs in your ears, smile and wiggle your fingers. Anything will do as long as the clue can be recognized.

Tell them to respond by clapping frantically and scream "Oh good golly, that was great!" Have them try it out a couple of times for practice. I guarantee that for the rest of the show, your cheering section will be paying close attention.

You can signal them any time you want during the show to get a response. Added at the right time it can be hilarious. If you tell a joke that doesn't go over well, give your cheering section the clue and turn a poor joke into a belly buster. While the rest of the audience is moaning, a loud voice will be shouting, "Ha ha ha that was really funny!"

Experiment with various sayings such as "You're great, do it again," "That was fabulous," "You're the funniest guy I've ever seen!"

You may choose two or more participants and have each one give a cheer to a different signal.

Magic Words. Get the audience to help perform magic by having them shout out a magic word. The word can be almost anything. It can relate to the theme of your show or the trick you're performing.

If you're talking about bicycle safety, the word might be "axle grease." At a picnic it could be "barbecue." At a birthday party it could be "ice cream." If your trick involves animals or food say, "Beetle cookies." Use a nonsense word such as "Pagillaschwagal."

When the audience yells "Pagillaschwagal," proceed to perform the trick, but the trick doesn't work. For example, if you're trying to pull a rabbit out of a hat, pull out a bullfrog instead.

Explain that the audience didn't say the word correctly and that it must be said exactly as you say it or it won't work properly. When they all say the word a second time, reach into the hat yell and pull out a mousetrap clamped onto your finger. Have them repeat the word one last time to finish the trick correctly.

Another reason that a trick doesn't work properly is because the audience didn't say the magic word loud enough. Have them yell louder each time. Can you imagine a full audience yelling, "Silly willy wiggly bumpers" or some such ridiculous thing? It's fun.

In the Audience. Go down into the audience. Mingling will make you a real person rather just a figure on stage. By going into the crowd, you bring the action directly to them.

Your reason for coming off stage could be to talk or ask questions, perform a trick, or run wildly through the audience, as in a chase sequence.

In one creative act I witnessed, the performer jumped off the stage, sat in an empty chair, pretending to be a spectator, and yelled up to the stage. He then jumped back on stage and replied to the comment from the "audience." It was a crack-up!

Magic Movements. You can tell your audience that in order to perform a certain magic trick, you will need their help. The trick will work only if everyone rolls down their socks and croaks like a frog. This can be very funny. Try the trick, and if it doesn't work say, "Who didn't roll down their socks?"

A drunk is sitting at a bar next to a man and his wife. Suddenly the drunk lets out a tremendous belch.

"How dare you" the man angerly says. "What do you mean, belching before my wife."

"Pardon me," says the drunk, "I had no idea it was the lady's turn.

The clown can have the audience do any number of crazy stunts. Flapping elbows and squawking like roosters, and closing eyes while patting heads and rubbing their stomachs are just two of the many possibilities.

Show Amazement. Whenever you perform a difficult juggling or magic trick, tell the audience to show amazement by saying "Woo!" Have everyone try it.

When they all say "Woo," the performer frowns and glances at someone in the audience and says, "It's Woo, not Boo!"

Have them practice it again on your signal. Then do a difficult looking trick using this signaled response.

Balloon Fun. Here is a good activity for those who work with balloons. Tell the audience that you will turn an "ordinary" piece of rubber into a rabbit (dog, elephant, or whatever) using magic. In order to do it, though, you will need the help of everyone in the audience. As you say the magic word, the audience must repeat it to generate the force needed to complete the transformation.

The word (or phrase) can be a long multisyllable nonsense word of your own, such as "super-drooper-fifi-snozzel-figgle-che-hoggy-fat." As each segment of the word is said in turn, the audience repeats it until the whole word has been said. This not only gets the audience to participate but also gives you time to create the rabbit. You can vary the speed at which you say the word so that on the last syllable the balloon has finished its transformation.

The Worm. When using some unusual creature in your act, such as a worm, tell them all to impersonate that creature. What does a worm do? Not much. After waiting a couple of seconds ask, "Well what's the matter? Haven't any of you seen a worm before? Let's hear some worm noises."

Still little response. "I see you haven't had too much experience with worms . . . let me help you. When I say the name of my pet worm 'Ralph' you make a worm sound . . . If you don't know what that is, they go like this: 'Yum—Yum—Yum.' Worms aren't too smart and can't say too much."

Have them practice. "When I say 'Ralph' What do you say?"

They answer "Yum—Yum—Yum."

"Good. Let's try it again, but this time I will use the key word in a sentence . . . I stuck my hand into the greasy slime and pulled out a fat hairy worm named Ralph."

The audience responds with "Yum—Yum—Yum."

USING SELECTED PARTICIPANTS

In addition to using the entire audience, you can select volunteers to help you on stage. Although not taking part personally, the rest of the audience will still feel involved.

For those who know the helpers, the jokes and stunts become funnier and more interesting. These things are happening to their friend Harvey, not to some actor or unknown person.

The volunteers are even more delighted. They become co-stars, so to speak, with a visible and active part in the program. This makes them feel special, giving them an ego boost and something they can tell their friends about later. A gag or stunt is funnier if someone you know is involved. It makes the show more personal and consequently more successful.

Choosing Volunteers

How do you choose your stage assistants? Should you start by asking for volunteers? If you do, be prepared for uncontrollable chaos; kids wildly waving their arms, jumping, and screaming "Choose me!"

Most children relish the thought of going up on stage with the performer. To maintain control and avoid a mad stampede, use the military method of getting "volunteers"—choose them without asking. By not asking for volunteers you avoid the frenzied response

and you can choose whoever you want without hurting anyone's feelings.

When you're about to choose a helper, don't say, "I'm now going to pick a helper." Instead pick out the person you want and announce that you would like this particular boy or girl to come up on stage to help you.

When asking this volunteer to come up, be as specific as possible. Don't just say, "I'd like the little boy with the red hair to come up and help me on this next trick" or you'll be surrounded by little red-headed boys. Describe several things about the youngster so that there is no mistake. "I would like the blonde-haired girl with pony tails and the red dress in the second row to come up and help me." Everyone will know who you mean this time.

When you choose a helper in this fashion, nobody is disappointed for not being chosen. Most of all, you remain in control.

What type of assistant should you choose? When you choose your own helper without asking for volunteers, you have complete control in selecting exactly who you want. You can choose the sex, age, physical build, and (to a lesser degree) personality.

Some kids are easily entertained and will laugh and giggle at almost anything silly. Others may be funny in their own way because they are open and vocal or just because of the way they act. But then you have kids who are shy or easily frightened.

Avoid, if at all possible, asking any child to come up who appears to be shy or who looks as if he or she may burst into tears while on stage. If you choose a child who doesn't want to come up to help you, don't force him or her, just choose another. A crying child doesn't help any performer, especially if he's trying to be funny. Unfortunately, you can't always tell how the child will respond until he or she is up on the stage

On Stage

Talking with your new assistant and asking questions will give you an indication of what you can do. If the child is shy, you may want to be cautious so he doesn't burst into tears. On the other hand, a child who is soaking up the attention with glee can be kidded to a much greater degree.

The first thing you must do when you get a volunteer in front of the audience is to get to know him. This serves several purposes. (1) It helps the volunteer become familiar with you and lets him know you're his friend. (2) It erases his fears of being on stage. (3) It introduces him to the audience so they can get to know him. (4) It gives you an idea of the type of helper you have and how cooperative he'll be.

Many kids become nervous when standing in front of an audience. The introductory chat with the performer helps to ease these fears. Bending down to his level and putting your hand on his shoulder helps reassure him.

What questions should you ask? Here are a few common examples. Add any "bit of funny" you can to loosen him up and keep the audience entertained.

What's your name?
How old are you?
Do you have any brothers or sisters?
What grade are you in at school?
Have you ever been on stage before?
Have you ever helped a magician (juggler, balloonologist, etc.) before?
Are you married?
What do you do for a living?

If there is more than one child on stage, mixing up their names is funny, especially when a boy's and a girl's name are crossed.

Asking other seemingly innocent questions can give you unexpected responses that only a child could dream up or dare say. When asking your helpers what they would like to be when they're older, you get your typical responses such as doctor, fireman, and police-man. You will also hear a few unusual answers. When I asked one four-year-old what he would like to be when he grew up, he answered without hesitation, "A dog."

Once they tell you what they would like to be, question them further as to why they have chosen this particular profession. One young man explained why he wanted to be a lawyer: "Cause my mom says I talk so much all the time I might as well get paid for it."

Asking your helpers to tell you what their parents do for a living can be interesting. After asking one boy this question he said "My dad's a school teacher."
"Does he like it?"
"Yah, he likes it fine, all except for one thing."
"What's that?"
"The kids."
You can ask many other questions that will lead into a short interesting conversation. Here are a few you might like to try.

What do you like to do most?
Who's the boss around your house?
What's the funniest thing you've ever seen around your home?
Have you ever been in love?
What would you do if you were president of the United States?
How did your daddy and mommy meet?
Do you have any secrets?
What type of animal would you like to be?
What do you like to do the most?

Follow up these questions with why, where, or how. The reasons behind many of the answers can add a lot to the conversation and often shows the child's innocent reasoning skills. Some kids will naturally give you a good response and you can ask them more questions and work more silly stuff with them, ad-libbing where appropriate. When I sense that I have a child who doesn't respond well on stage, I take it easy with him and stick strictly with the planned routine.

Billy: Boy, was I in hot water last night!
Johnny: How come?
Billy: I took a bath.

———————

Doctor: The best time to bathe is just before retiring.
Billy: You mean I don't have to take another bath until I'm almost 65 years old?

How To Use Volunteers

Now that you have a volunteer to help you, what do you do? Your helper can assist you in a variety of ways, ranging from detailed involvement to a passively holding a prop.

What your helper does on stage doesn't have to be elaborate or even necessary for you to complete a particular routine. Having your helper hold a sign while you do your clowning gives you the opportunity to use volunteers without designing special routines for that purpose.

Some of the funniest bits of humor can come from volunteers. Their actions and responses are spontaneous and totally unexpected. Some kids suited perfectly to these situations and love to play along with you, adding to the success of your routine.

Have volunteers come up and try to do magic, juggle, or make balloon animals, mimicking your movements. These kids will get a kick out of it and, if handled in a humorous way by you, can be very amusing. An assistant may just stand still as you or you and a partner juggle around him. Adding a live body between two jugglers who are passing presumably razor-sharp axes greatly increases the audience's enjoyment.

Contests can be fun. If you are a balloonologist, have a contest to see who can blow up a balloon the biggest. You can rig the contest beforehand. Invite two or more kids on stage and give them each a balloon. Have one pre-blown and stretched so that it will inflate easily. (Pencil and apple balloons are naturally difficult to inflate if you have not had much experience with them.) Give the prepared balloon to the smallest contestant and give the unstretched balloons to the others and have them go at it. The contestant with the prestretched balloon will easily blow up his, but the others may not even be able to start theirs. This can be very funny when combined with a few well placed jokes.

Try a talent contest. Choose four or five volunteers from the audience and give each one a card. Each card will have a different activity written on it: "sing," "dance," "hum," "whistle." Then as you hold each card up to the audience, the contestant does what it says on the card. After they have all participated place your hands above each child in turn. The one who receives the most applause is the winner. You can finish by giving out prizes to all, with some special recognition for the child who won. This contest not only gives you an opportunity to use volunteers on stage, but gets the entire audience involved in choosing the winner.

You can do a variation of this contest by using musical instruments such as a harmonica, a whistle, bongo drums, and a kazoo. The music each contestant produces can be very funny.

A technique you can use for contests or any other type of volunteer help is the *whispered command*. The performer tells the volunteer to do or say something in order to get a specific response. In this way the clown leads the helper into a prearranged routine. The audience does not hear the commands, and what your helper does appears totally spontaneous. Your volunteer gets a laugh and you end up looking like a master comedian with the ability to turn any situation into a humorous experience.

Let me give you an simple example of a bit you can do using whispered commands. Have a small boy or girl come up on stage. Since he is much shorter then you are, you will naturally bend over to talk to him. As you do, whisper to him to get down on his knees. When he does this, look at him and then at the audience with a puzzled look. Get down on your knees and try to continue. As you do so, quietly instruct him to sit down flat on the floor. After he is sitting, again look at him questioningly and then at the audience.

Sit down on the floor beside him and say, "We can't go much further," and proceed with your show.

Here is another example that can be used in a magic show. Give your helper a miniature magic wand about three inches long and tell him to wave it over an object to make it vanish. After he waves the wand and nothing happens, whisper to him to tell you that the wand isn't working because it's not big enough.

Give him another wand which is about six inches long and tell him to try that. He waves the wand without results. Secretly instruct him again to tell you that the wand isn't big enough. When he makes this comment, hand him a very large wand (three feet or so) and say, "Is this big enough?"

"Tommy, can you read and write?" The woman asked.

"I can write," he replied, "but I can't read too well."

"Well then, let me see how you write your name."

The boy writes something down on a piece of paper.

"What is this?" she asked as she tried to read the scribbling.

"I don't know," Tommy answered. "I told you I can't read."

Giving a gift to helpers is a practice some children's entertainers swear by. It's the clown's way of saying "thank you," and adds a little extra reward for their assistance. This gift can be a piece of candy or a small toy. A photo of yourself will also do nicely and this is what most clowns choose.

BE SENSITIVE

When you interact with groups of people there is always the possibility of offending someone. As an entertainer you need to be aware of this. Your job is to entertain and make people happy. It is important, whenever you interact with a spectator, to avoid ridiculing or embarrassing anyone. You should never try to get a laugh at the expense of others. Use your skills to make the audience laugh at you. If anyone is to be the butt of a joke, it should be the performer, never the volunteer or the audience.

It may seem funny to have a coiled snake jump out of a can and scare an unsuspecting volunteer, but is that good showmanship? I think not.

The clown is supposed to play the part of the fool or buffoon. The clown should always end up as the victim of any gag. The coiled-snake trick can still be used, but instead of playing it on the volunteer, the clown should be the one who opens up the can and be startled by the snake.

Out of sight of the helper on stage, the clown can show the audience the coiled snake and pretend to play the trick on the volunteer. But the trick doesn't work when the volunteer is given the container. The clown can't understand what went wrong. Taking the can, he opens it up, only to be surprised by the leaping snake.

If you want to use jokes and gags on selected members of the audience, tell them beforehand or plant

an assistant to play the part. Prearranged remarks and responses can make the gag turn out much better than an actual volunteer.

A clown has no bias; he treats everyone alike regardless of age, sex, ethnic or religious background. Avoid any joke that may cause embarrassment or ridicule to any part of society.

Clowns are family entertainers, and as such their language and actions should be clean and unoffensive. I am always offended when I hear other performers resort to vulgarity or off-color humor, especially when observers of all ages are present. I do not think it funny or appropriate. Many people in the audience may laugh, but others are insulted. There are plenty of unoffensive topics to joke about without relying on these tactics.

Simply because someone people laugh at offensive jokes doesn't mean they please the entire audience. Although you may not please everyone in every audience, you can avoid jokes that are clearly offensive to some. Any show you give is better when no one is ridiculed or offended.

HOW TO HANDLE TROUBLEMAKERS

What do you do about the heckler or the kid who knows it all? You will often have a heckler who shouts, "I know how you did that" or "I seen where it went."

Some kids, and grown-ups too for that matter, get their kicks (for whatever reason) out of yelling wisecracks and disrupting the show. This can be embarrassing and distracting for everyone, performer and audience alike.

One of the major reasons people act this way is to get attention. Unless you can get control of the situation, they will continue to disrupt you as they strive for that recognition. One of the best ways to quiet a heckler is to have him help you with one of your routines. He can come up on stage or stay in the audience, just as long as he is able to satisfy his need for attention.

If you invite trouble makers to assist you, usually they will be more than willing to help and will cooperate once they become a part of the show. In this way they receive the attention they wanted, and will return to the audience and remain quiet. They are now a part of the show and as co-stars do not want to ruin it.

Asking the heckler a few standard opening questions and having him hold a sign or some other prop as you continue with your planned routine may be all that is needed to satisfy his thirst for attention.

Invite him up when you plan to use a volunteer from the audience, or even create a special routine beforehand for just such occasions. Like any other volunteer, you need not ridicule him or play a trick on him to get even. He will be more cooperative on stage and back in the audience if you try to become his friend.

Most hecklers will make their presence known early in the show. Some may settle down a bit as the show progresses and can be ignored. Others may continue to badger you and make a nuisance of themselves. It is best to take care of them as soon as possible, or they will make the show a chore for you. If you can get a troublemaker to settle down, you will be more comfortable for the rest of the performance.

Troublemakers are everywhere and every performer has to deal with them at one time or another. Fortunately they are few in number, but even a few can be too many. You won't have hecklers in every audience, in fact most audiences will be trouble free. But be prepared for the few times you will. If handled wisely, at the end you will have had a successful show and you will have made a new friend.

> Fred: I'm hungry but I don't have enough money to buy anything decent.
> Ed: I know a restaurant where we can eat dirt cheap.
> Fred: Who wants to eat dirt?

CHAPTER 7

EFFECTIVE USE OF PROPS

HOW TO USE CLOWN PROPS

What is a clown prop? It is any object used by a clown for comedy. It can be a common object such as a diaper pin used as a clown's tie tack, or it can be a specially built object such as a book about Moby Dick which squirts water.

Props in themselves are rarely funny. What makes a prop effective is how it is used. There is nothing inherently funny about forks and dinner rolls, but when Charlie Chaplin in the film *The Gold Rush* performed a little dance while seated at a table, using dinner rolls and two forks, the results were hilarious.

Three brightly colored balls have little entertainment value until a juggler begins to work with them. A puppet is merely a doll until somebody brings it to life.

The way a prop is used can make all the difference between a good prop and a fantastically funny prop.

Even with props which are considered funny, the way they are handled influences the audience's reception. I once built a series of walk-arounds for a circus, including an oversized hot dog fitted into an Invisible Dog Leash. The first clown I gave it to simply carried the leash, and the gag received moderate response. The next clown who used it acted as if he were walking a real dog. He would stop and twirl the leash to make the dog turn a somersault or he would flirt with a girl, but the dog would continue to yank him along. He treated the hot dog as a co-star and the gag became a big success.

To get the most from the props you use, think of them not as lifeless objects but as co-stars or assistants who are helping you get a laugh. Put life into your props by working with them rather than just showing them and hoping that will be enough to get a laugh.

Gene "Cousin Otto" Lee has a gigantic Kodak Instamatic camera that he uses in parades. The sight of him with this enormous prop brings smiles to those who see him. But he goes a step further by working with the prop, adding physical and verbal humor as he pretends to take pictures of the spectators. He explains to the people that he is the "official parade photographer" and needs a picture for the parade yearbook. Getting two children together, he takes a snapshot. "Since this is an Instamatic," he tells them, "the picture will be ready in an instant." Pulling out a photograph, he looks at it, smiles and tells them, "It came out do a brief solo or partner gag. Walk-around props can be used for picnics, parades, and atmosphere entertainment, as at a shopping center or an amusement park. Although visibility is important in these settings, verbal humor can be added to the routine. Because of the short amount of time the performer has, the gags must be short and sweet. Consequently the props must lend themselves to brief comic bits. A rubber chicken, for example, is placed in an invisible dog harness, which is scurried along by the clown as if he were out walking his pet.

Hidden walk-around props are popular with clowns. A sign on a box may say "Danger—Baby Rattler." The content of the box is hidden from view until the audience reads the sign. When they look into the box, instead of a snake as they expected, it is simply a baby's toy rattle. When I do the Baby Rattler, I use a basket and toy flute. These snake charmer trappings increase the surprise when a toy rattle floats out of the basket. (A thread running through the end of the flute lifts the rattle.)

Some hidden gags use a literary reference and are more effective if the box looks like a book. One of these is *The History of Aviation, Vol. 1*, which opens to reveal a large fly.

Gene "Cousin Otto" Lee

great." When he shows it to the audience he reveals a picture of two monkeys. This little bit of tomfoolery is much more enjoyable than just seeing a clown carrying a large prop. Develop such routines; don't just *show* a prop, but *use* it and magnify its humorous potential.

TYPES OF PROPS

Though it would be impossible to discuss all the different types of props here, I would like to describe breifly some general categories of props commonly used by clowns.

Walk-Around Props

A walk-around in the circus is an act where all the clowns move around the track, stopping occasionally to

John "Krako" Guthrie

Although created as walk-arounds, these props don't have to be used that way. Having one on a table near you when face painting or distributing balloons allows you to include an entertaining gag without slowing down the line.

Clowns work at various distances from their audiences. The hidden object should be large and should be placed against a contrasting background so it can be identified from a distance, and yet should be detailed enough to be interesting when viewed close up.

Visual Puns

A visual pun is visually representing an alternate meaning for words or for similar sounding words. Most hidden walk-arounds are based on visual puns, but they don't have to be hidden. A large letter "J" which has been painted blue and put into a birdcage, can be labeled as a "Blue Jay." Signs or name plates are used to identify the pun.

Frankie Saluto with giant light bulb.

Jumbo Props

Oversized props are an important tool for clowns. They are used in circuses and on stage because normal sized props can't be seen and identified from a distance. Jumbo props are not necessarily funny, but can be used in a variety of funny ways.

One way is to inappropriately use a large tool for a small job. Emmett Kelly used a sledge hammer to crack a peanut. It did crack the shell, but also destroyed the kernels inside.

Another approach is to have a funny reason for using a big object. At a birthday party, announce that you are an official ice cream taste tester, obtain permission to try just one spoonful, and then pull out a giant spoon.

Jumbo props can become funnier by contrasting them with small characters or objects. Sometimes a large container is used for a small object, as when a bass fiddle case is used to carry a tiny violin, or a small container is used for a jumbo object, as when the clown reaches through a slit in the back of a small change purse to pull out a large wand hidden in his sleeve.

Sometimes a progression is used. For example, a tall clown enters wearing a small hat. Each succeeding clown is shorter and wears a larger hat. The last clown is a midget or a child wearing a hat that comes down to his knees.

Jumbo props are also effective when adults portray children because the contrast makes them appear smaller.

Squirting Props

Props—like a slice of watermelon, that squirt a stream of water when bitten are popular.

Adult enema syringes, ear syringes, catsup bottles, and hot water bottles can all be used for squeeze bulbs. Hudson (garden) sprayers and Coleman stove gas tanks can be used to produce a continuous pressurized stream. Aquarium air line tubing makes an excellent hose which, fits like a nozzle when combined with a medicine dropper.

Although some kids love to be squirted not everyone likes to get wet. In most situations aim the water so it falls in front of the audience. In gags where you start squirting someone, hold your aim steady so your victim can escape. When squirting water from stage, shoot it in a long high arch and sweep quickly from side to side. This insures that the water will be at some angle visible to everyone, and nobody will get hit by more than a few drops.

Cabinets

Many clown acts rely on a cabinet representing a machine. Frequently the interior is painted black, and a black drape creates a hiding place near the back. Horns, bells, flashing lights, smoke, and discharges from CO_2 fire extinguishers are used frequently to make the machine appear to be working. The title or purpose of the machine is prominently lettered on it. For ease of transportation, cabinets can be temporarily held together with loose pin hinges or can be designed to fold up.

An example of a cabinet act is the steam cabinet. A fat clown enters, and after being "steamed," a shrunken clown leaves the cabinet. An identically dressed midget or child hiding behind the drapes switches places with the fat clown.

Break-Aways

A break-away is a prop designed to come apart or collapse as if broken. There are two types. One is a fragile version, such as a balsa wood chair, which is intended to actually break, These are seldom used by clowns because a new one must be made for each performance. The other type is designed to be easily reassembled, it is either hinged with a release or joined together in loosely fit pieces. Break-away costumes are loosely basted with thread or joined with Velcro.

Many clowns use a prop that breaks when handed to a volunteer. This is more effective if you use a duplicate non-breaking prop earlier in your act, which increases the surprise of the break-away, and prevents the perception that the prop's only purpose is to embarrass the volunteer.

You can get longer laughs if you reverse that presentation. If a fan works when you fan somebody else, but breaks whenever you try to fan yourself, laughs will build with each repetition. Conclude by letting a child successfully fan you off, and try it yourself for a final failure and laugh.

Break-aways are smashed over characters in TV and movie fights, but rarely in clown acts. They can be combined with slapstick. A clown can carry something that breaks when he trips and falls. A break-away may form the blowoff, such as a fight between two clowns over a chair, climaxing when the victor sits down triumphantly in the chair and it collapses.

The break-away can also be effective if the clown does not know that something has been broken, such as when a clown moves a pedestal table without

Tony Blanco

realizing the base has fallen off. When he attempts to set it down in a new location, it crashes to the floor.

Manipulative Props

Many props require special skills or training in order to operate effectively. Skills such as magic, juggling, and music use specalized props to create their effects and humor. I will not discuss these props any further here, as they will be covered in detail in later chapters.

COMIC INVENTIVENESS

One way to use props to make people laugh is through *comic inventiveness*—finding an unusual solution to a problem or using an object in an unusual way. Tying a string between a clock pendulum and a cradle to rock a baby is comic inventiveness. So is using an all day sucker as a fan.

Comic inventiveness is the result of a character seeing the world from a fresh or unusual perspective. The result follows some logic and the character is

Fred Stelling seen here holding a paper butterfly attached to a whipcord in the pantomime "The Elusive Butterfly."

serious about what he is doing. When Gracie Allen put salt in the pepper shaker and pepper in the salt shaker, it was because people always pick up the wrong one and she wanted them to be right even when they were wrong. Comic characters don't do funny things, they do things for a funny reason.

Comic inventiveness can be a result of playfulness. A clown looking for an audience volunteer may pretend that a juggling club is a telescope, and then use the club as a microphone to interview the volunteer. Most volunteers go along with the game and speak into the club.

Mistaken Identity

Related to comic inventiveness is *mistaken identity*, using a prop in an unusual way because you think it's something else. If you use a microphone and place it on a table, then juggle clubs and place them on the same table, get a volunteer up on stage, pick up a club, speak into it, and act as if you can't figure out why the "microphone" isn't working—that's mistaken identity.

Use the approach that is consistent with your character. They all require the ability to look at things in an alternate way, an ability that can be learned and practiced.

Creativity Exercise

This creativity exercise will help develop that ability. Choose a common object and make a list of fifty unusual uses for it. To get the most benefit, don't settle for obvious answers. For example, if you choose a drinking glass as your object, listing "holding toothpicks" and "holding sugar packets" is not going to stretch your creativity. Look for ideas like "repairing a broken high-heeled shoe." Don't be concerned about making all your answers funny. The purpose here is to exercise your creativity, not create usable material. Of the many answers you come up with, some will be funny. The more times you do this exercise, the more potentially usable ideas you'll create.

Here's a realistic group exercise. Stand in a circle, take a common object and pass it around. When each person receives it, he or she must use it as if it were another object. For example, if you use a balloon, one person may use it as a crystal ball and tell a fortune. Another might use it as a pillow and go to sleep. Going around the group out of sequence will make everyone keep thinking all the time.

In doing this group exercise you'll find that something somebody else does will give you another idea. This is an example of brainstorming. Two people working together will come up with more and better ideas than if they combined the ideas they two would have created working separately. If possible, brainstorm with somebody else when working with a new prop.

When brainstorming, express all your ideas, don't censor them. A bad idea might be the genesis of a terrific one. Piggyback your ideas, creating a variation of one that somebody else expressed. Generate as many ideas as you can. The more you have, the more probable it is that some will be good.

Brainstorming is an effective way to find new uses for a prop or to create comic lines to use with it.

CREATING JOKES

You can increase a prop's effectiveness by pairing it with verbal comedy. Clowns use puns extensively and base jokes on alternate meanings of words. You can learn to create this type of humor. I'll use my hot dog, Frank, to illustrate.

The first step is to list everything you can think of that is associated with your prop. For Frank there are two points of departure, animal and food. The animal list is as follows:

purebred
papers
leash
tag
license
police dog
guard dog
chase—cats, cars, sticks
bark
tricks—roll over, play dead, sit up
obedience training
heel
pooper scooper
bite
bark is worse than bite
a dog's life
doghouse
bone
dig
can't teach old dog new tricks
puppy

The food list that I came up with is as follows:

catsup
mustard
relish
buns
sausage
napkin
steamed
cheese
all beef
vendor
ballpark frank
sauerkraut
chili
corn dog
wiener
pork and beans
potato chips

The second step is to go through the lists and look for things with more than one meaning. If you have more than one point of departure, look for similar things on both lists. Read the lists out loud and play around with sound. Create as many lines and variations as

you can. My concept is that Frank is a real pet dog, so I am particularly interested in talking about him as an animal using food terms. This type of comic line is a sentence that uses more than one meaning, often changing meaning in the middle. Here are some possibilities.

Relish means "chopped pickles and spices," and "to enjoy, do with zest." I could say, "Frank does his act with relish."

"Purebred" and "all beef," and "papers" and "napkins" could be paired from both lists and result in "He's a purebred—all beef. Do you want to see his papers?" Pull out a napkin.

"Sausage" sounds like "saw such" so I could ask, "Did you ever sausage a dog?"

The third step is to go through your lines and edit out any that are in bad taste, off-color, or not funny.

Putting the lines into a logical, smooth flowing order is the next step. For Frank, I might end up with something like this: "I'd like you to meet my dog, Frank. Did you ever *sausage* a dog? Yes, he's funny looking, but he does have nice *buns*. He's a purebred— *all beef.* Do you want to see his papers? (Pull out napkin.) He was in a movie when he was a puppy. You may have see it—Young *Frank N Stein.* When he got older he wanted to be a police dog, but he couldn't cut the *mustard.* He got in trouble for chasing

Harold "Buster" Black

Steve Kissell

catsup bottles. Boy, did I get *steamed*, so I took him to an obedience school. He wasn't their best *pup-l* but he did manage to learn a few tricks. Would you like to see his act? He does it with *relish*. (By manipulating the leash you can make him sit up, play dead, and roll over.) Thank you and good night!"

The last step is to do the routine in front of an audience to see how they respond. A line is a joke only if it makes people laugh. Change the wording to see what gets the best response. Add new lines as you discover them. If a heckler calls out a funny line, add it to your act at the next show. Take out all the lines that consistently don't get laughs. A five minute act full of laughs is funnier than a ten minute act with the same number of laughs. Remember, the audience is always the final judge.

CREATIVE USE OF STANDARD PROPS

Standard props and accompanying routines are used by many clowns and other entertainers. They are mass produced, which makes them affordable and easy to obtain. Some of them are very funny, with proven audience appeal. Others are terrible, but still get passed from clown to clown. Unfortunately some of these routines have been used so often that most people in the audiences have seen them performed before. To be most entertaining, your act should fresh and new.

When using a standard prop, keep two things in mind. First, you don't have to do any routine that comes with it or that you've seen used by others. Second, the appearance of the prop when you use it does not have to be the same as when you bought it.

One creative approach is to reverse the standard presentation. For instance, the Magic Coloring Book is gimmicked so that when you're flipping through it you can show the pages blank, with line drawings, or fully colored. The standard routine is to show the line drawings, magically color them in, attempt to remove the color but remove the lines as well, and finally restore the lines.

Let's consider reversing that. Suppose you start with the pages colored, and something happens to remove the color, possibly a sneeze. Your routine could be to proudly display the beautiful job of coloring you did, and start to sneeze. You prevent the sneeze by holding your finger under your nose. You show your book to the other half of your audience, and start to sneeze again. You stop it with your finger, but this time when you remove your finger you sneeze without warning. Colored confetti that you've been hiding in your hand flutters to the floor. Flipping through the book, you discover that your sneeze blew off the colors. You sneeze again, blowing off the black lines. With this premise, it wouldn't make sense to magically restore the book so you set it aside. Continue to use the premise and have everything you try to do in your act destroyed by a sneeze. The act could end with a gigantic sneeze which blows your pants away, revealing the funny shorts you're wearing. The result is a creative way to use a standard prop which allows you to build more and more humor.

Another approach is to ask what else could the prop become? How can its appearance be changed? This time let's look at the Break-Away Wand, a magic wand made of plastic segments with a cord running through them. Keeping tension on the cord holds the segments firmly end to end so they look like one solid piece. Releasing the tension allows the segments to separate and fall disjointedly. The Break-Away Wand is a well made prop and a funny idea which can be made fresh and more entertaining with a little creativity.

A wand is long and round. What else is long and round?

Ed: Knock knock.
Fred: Who's there?
Ed: Awkch.
Fred: Awkch who?
Ed: Gesundheit.

Kinko "The Human Pretzel" and his midget car.

A pencil. Screwing a piece of wood onto one of the wand's tips and sanding it would give you the pencil point. The wand could then be painted yellow. This would be added to your Magic Coloring Book routine. While trying to draw the lines back in, a sneeze could break the pencil.

What else could the wand be? The stem of a feather flower, which is destroyed by a hay fever sufferer's sneeze. It could also be the handle of a papier-mache lollipop. As part of a safety message you could demonstrate the hazards of running with something in your hands and trip, breaking the lollipop. The wand could also be a giant match which snaps when you try to light it, an exaggeration of real life. It could be an orchestra leader's baton which shatters when a singer hits a high note. What ideas can you think of?

With any prop ask yourself, "What else can I do with it?" One standard gag is to show a large book titled *Paradise Lost*, and opening it reveals a pair of

---

"I'm so depressed; I had to shoot my dog."
"Was he mad?"
"Well, he wasn't exactly pleased."

"You look like Helen Green."
"I look worse in pink."

Wise man says:
Anyone who goes to a psychiatrist ought to have his head examined.

---

large dice and the caption "Pair a Dice Found." If you make the dice removabie you can use them in your next routine, such as a Sliding Die Box, or another of the many dice tricks listed in magic catalogs.

USING A THEME

To make your act unique and unified, choose a theme that fits your props. Marvyn Roy is famous as Mr. Electric because of his magic act which he does entirely with light bulbs. To see how this is done let's look at lollipops as a theme.

The first step is to decide which qualities of your prop can be exploited. A lollipop is a flat circle with a long thin handle. Lollipops come in different colors and sizes.

The second step is to decide how to use these qualities. How could they be used for juggling? The lollipops should be made of wood for strength and should be of all-day-sucker, or a larger all-week-sucker size for visibility and ease of handling. Because the handle has its center of gravity near one end, they could be used as juggling clubs or for balancing. Two handsticks could be used to toss and catch one of the lollipops in what is called a devilstick routine.

A standard routine using an object with a long thin handle is the Giveaway, or Straw Flower. The stem of a flower is inserted into a straw. You offer the flower to somebody who naturally grabs hold of the straw. Then you pull up on the flower, leaving him holding only the straw. You can do the same thing using a lollipop with the added advantage that you can afford to give him the lollipop after the laugh, preventing disappointment.

Another possibility would be to give a papier-mache lollipop a handle made from a doorspring. Gimmick it like a Wilting Flower so the lollipop will duck out of the way when you try to lick it.

Your theme doesn't have to center around a particular prop, but can be a setting or topic. If you use a western theme you could wear a cowboy costume and use related props. Reading as a theme is fun. You could pull all your props out of boxes which look like books and each routine would be about a type of book, such as pulling a Chick Pan out of a cookbook and magically baking a cupcake.

BUILDING AUDIENCE INVOLVEMENT

You increase the entertainment value of your act when the audience becomes actively involved. Don't hide behind your props; use them to interact with your audience. One way is to have a prop do something when you're looking in another direction.

A Wilting Flower is a flower made of feathers on a doorspring stem. Fishing line is connected to the spring in such a way that pulling on it makes the spring bend in the middle. Releasing it allows the flower to straighten back up. Smell the flower, look away, and make it wilt. Somebody will tell you it has wilted. As you turn your head to look at it, allow the stem to straighten so it's normal when you see it. Look at the person who told you, and make it wilt again. More people will tell you to look at the flower. Repeat this bit of business several times to build audience reaction. At some point have it wilted when you look at it, but look away before you realize what you saw. By the time you look back, it is normal again. Eventually the flower remains wilted and the ending depends on how your specific character would react to a wilted flower.

Your props can be conversation pieces. When I was using my Blue Jay at a small amusement park, one of the guests said, "That's a nice blue jay, but he looks a little pale." I asked him if he thought it might be sick. (I perform in pantomime but carry paper and pencil in my pocket to ask questions or make short comments.) Soon I had a small group discussing my Blue Jay. The general consensus was that he wasn't sick, just lonely, and that he would perk up if he had a friend like a Spare-O.

Pay attention to your audience and respond to their reactions. Another day at the same park I was using a different gag. A guest with a season pass asked, "Where's your Blue Jay?" He thought it was great when I responded, "He took the day off to visit his friend, the Spelling B."

Every line you create on the spur of the moment won't be funny, but that's OK. Your audience won't remember the bad lines, and might not remember the good ones. If the joke was funny, they'll remember laughing. The important thing is that you are interacting and they are involved. It takes practice to come up with lines quickly. When you're with friends, use them as an audience while you practice.

What if a good response comes to you after the performance? It's never too late to create a good line. Write it down before you forget so you can use it if the opportunity arises again.

You can ask the questions and let your audience create the lines. I replaced my Blue Jay with a badminton birdie, also called a shuttlecock. I started asking people, "What should I name him, or is he a she?" I got responses like, "He's a he, because if he was a she, he would be a shuttlehen," and "Call him Rudolph because he's got a red nose." All the responses weren't creative, but almost everyone had some type of answer, and got involved. I wrote the good responses down, and if I get the chance I'll use them myself.

Don't let your props become a barrier between you and your audience, but use them in such a way as to bridge the gap between you.

CLASSIC CLOWN GAGS

The Mugger

Two clowns are used in this short skit—one a whiteface or auguste and the other a tramp. The tramp plays the part of the mugger and the other clown assumes the role of the parent of a baby who is sleeping in a baby carriage.

The parent clown being very quiet, is gently rocking the baby to sleep when a mugger creeps up and points a gun at him and says, "Stick 'em up!"

Clown: Shhhh—quiet please.

Mugger: Did you hear me I said stick 'em up!

Clown: Shhh not so loud—the baby's asleep.

Mugger: What are you some kind of a wise guy? Shut up or I'll let you have it.

Clown: Would you be quiet, you'll wake up the baby.

Mugger: This gun won't wake up anybody. It's got a silencer and won't make a sound.

Clown: You mean it doesn't make any noise?

Mugger: That's right and nobody can hear it, not even your baby.

Clown: Well, why didn't you say so. Go ahead and shoot!

The Letter

The clown peeks out to the audience, looks around to make sure no one is around. In his hand is a letter. He giggles and explains to the audience that this is a letter from his girl friend and that he didn't want any of his clown friends to know about it because the letters get mushy. He opens the envelope, looks inside, and SQUIRT! A stream of water hits him in the face.

This gag works by concealing a small rubber bulb and tube which shoots water. It is the same as those sold at novelty shops for squirting flowers. The bulb is filled with water and held in the hand which holds the envelope. The short piece of tubing goes into the envelope through a small hole in the bottom of it. The envelope is opened, the clown looks inside, and get a squirt.

The Third Arm

The clown walks about with his hands, in gloves, hanging down at his side. When he approaches some youngster a third hand suddenly slips out from the clown's waist to shake hands or do some other clown buffoonery.

A glove is stuffed and sewn onto the end of the clown's right coat sleeve. The sleeve is also stuffed to give the appearance of having an arm inside. The coat is put onto the left arm but only hung over the right shoulder concealing the arm.

Props may also be manipulated by the third hand. The clown may do magic tricks, juggle or work a small hand puppet who may be too shy to come out from under the clown's protective coat.

Juggler's Delight

During a juggling act the clown juggles three wooden blocks. A couple of the blocks are accidentally dropped to demonstrate to the audience that they are truly solid blocks. As he juggles the blocks, he sticks one of them in his mouth with one hand and removes it with the other, (this is an easy trick any juggler can learn to do with a few minutes practice).

After putting the block into his mouth a couple of times he stops juggling, licks his lips and begins eating it. "Mmm—good."

How does he do it? The clown uses a raw potato cut in to a cube the same size as the two wooden blocks. (Color can be added to the cube by using food coloring.)

CHAPTER 8

HOW TO PERFORM MIRACLES

ENTERTAINING WITH MAGIC

A miracle can be described as any phenomenon that is contrary to the laws of nature or rational thought. While no magician ever performs a real miracle, he creates the impression that something impossible has occurred through his magic tricks.

Performing tricks of magic has stimulated and entertained audiences for thousands of years. Children especially enjoy watching a magician perform seemingly impossible stunts. Among the variety artists (i.e. jugglers, rope walkers, ventriloquists, etc.) magicians are perhaps the most popular. In my own experience in performing at birthday parties, whenever a group of kids learn that they are going to see a special performance, they ask in wide eyed excitement, "Are you going to do magic?"

Even if you prefer to specialize in some other skill of clowning, learning a few magic tricks is well worth the time and effort. Many simple tricks can be learned in a matter of minutes. Short, easy tricks are good time fillers and attention getters. They are ideal for walk-arounds or children's parties where the performer is close to the audience. The amount of equipment you use can be very small, perhaps only a single coin or small ball, or you can work many tricks and use large props that require a full sized stage.

The subject of magic is so extensive that I can cover only the basics in this book. Enough information will be supplied to you so that you can gain a good basic understanding of the principles behind magic and seek out further information on your own. There are literally hundreds of books written on magic and how to do magic tricks. Many of these are readily available in libraries, bookstores, and magic shops. These books can give specific examples of how to perform certain tricks. Most of them also provide sample routines giving the reader an understanding of how to present the tricks.

Before you can understand and perform clown magic, you should have an understanding of the basic principles of serious magic. After gaining this knowledge, you can deviate into the world of clown magic. Clown magic isn't just a haphazard fumbling through a series of tricks; it's a well orchestrated routine, often requiring all the skills of an experienced magician.

CAUSE AND EFFECT

One of the first principles a magician needs to understand is that of cause and effect. The *effect* is the magic the magician has created: the disappearing of a coin, the finding of a hidden card, or transforming a red scarf into a blue one. Every time a trick is performed it must be *caused* by something the magician does, such as a wave of the hand, a tap of the foot, a magic word or phrase, the sprinkling of magic powder, or an invisible force radiating out from the fingertips. The cause is the magical gesture which seemingly produces the effect. Magic doesn't just happen, it must be caused to happen.

There are at least 12 distinctive effects a magician can cause to happen; these are not tricks but the elements of magic that make a trick appear like a miracle. Pulling a rabbit out of an empty hat is a trick; the effect is the creation of something from nothing. Here are the effects:

1) Vanish. Causing something to disappear.
2) Production. Creating something from nothing.
3) Transformation. Changing an object into some thing else.
4) Transposition. Causing something to go from one place to another.
5) Restoration. Destroying something, then restoring it as it was originally.
6) Identification. Identifying something which other wise should not be known.
7) Psychic phenomena. Effects involving E.S.P., X-ray vision, mind reading and communicating with spirits.
8) Penetration. Passing one solid object into or through another.
9) Levitation. Overcoming the forces of gravity and making something float in the air.
10) Attraction. Causing something to attract or stick to something else.
11) Animation. Bringing an inanimate object to life.
12) Escapes. Removing handcuffs, escaping from strait jackets or from a locked cell, etc.

Anyone designing a magic act should be familiar with these categories. A magic show should consist of a variety of effects, not just one or two. An act which consists almost entirely of vanishing tricks, for example, would become boring. A mixture of effects will help keep interest alive. If you use two effects from the same category, make sure they're separated by at least one other effect.

MAGICIAN'S GUIDELINES

To make your magic successful, you must practice. Remember you're going to try to fool your audience. You can bet they will be trying to figure out how you do your tricks and will watch very closely every move you make. If your timing is slightly off or if you're a little careless and they see something in your supposedly empty hand, they will let you know. This could be embarrassing. Avoid poor magic by practicing beforehand. Use a mirror; think about people sitting at an angle to you. Can they see anything you don't want them to see?

Here are some basic rules or guidelines that most all magicians try to live by.

Keep it secret. Magic is supposed to be mysterious and unexplainable, so don't give away the secret of any trick. If everyone knew how the tricks were done, magic would lose its appeal.

Do it only once. A good magician never performs the same trick twice for the same audience. Unless you use a different method to do the trick, the audience will be prepared for it the second time and your element of surprise will be gone.

Know your angles. Be constantly aware of the angles of vision of the audience. What may be hidden from someone directly in front of you may be visible to someone sitting off to the side.

Be an actor. Good magicians are good actors. Your movements should appear totally natural and innocent. Convince the audience that you really did pick up the coin or that you're reaching into your pocket to get some pixie dust, and not depositing a sponge ball which is suppose to vanish.

Practice. Practice each trick until it looks perfect, then practice it some more before showing it to an audience. Use a mirror to see if you can detect anything unnatural or if anything is showing. Kids can be unmerciful if they spot a flaw.

Be original. Never copy another performer's routine word for word. Sure you can use the same tricks and same ideas, but change the act by adding your own patter and style.

BASIC METHODS

Gimmicks, sleights, subtleties, and misdirection are the methods used by magicians to produce the effects of magic described previously. Each magic trick is performed by using one or more of these methods.

Gimmicks

Gimmicks are objects specially designed to assist the magician in accomplishing a trick. Some tricks using gimmicks are very easy to use and require little practice.

Others can be complicated and expensive. A box with a trap door, a thumb tip, linking rings, multiplying sponge balls, a scarf with a hidden pocket are all gimmicks.

All props that rely on illusions or that have hidden compartments or doors are gimmicks. They are manufactured to look like ordinary objects, yet each has some "secret". Magic shops carry hundreds of prepared props for the magician. Articles such as trick coins, glasses, cards, books, boxes, paper, balls, and keys appear to be ordinary, but have a secret that allow the magician to perform magic with them.

Sleights

A sleight is a movement which causes a trick to work without being detected by an audience. In many cases sleights require much more skill or physical dexterity than gimmicks. Sleights depend on the magician's ability to disguise the magic while maintaining normal, natural movements.

Some sleights are very simple and natural; others can be very difficult and require a good deal of practice. Many card tricks make use of the sleight. The ability to deal off the bottom of the deck but make it look as if a card is being removed from the top is an example. Making a fake transfer of a coin from one hand to the other is a common sleight that has many variations.

Subtleties

A subtlety uses principles of physics, biology, mathematics, psychology to accomplish the trick. These principles are worked in such a way that they are unsuspected by the audience. Number games and tricks fit into this group.

A simple example of a subtlety is to write on a piece of paper "Why the Dime?" stick it in an envelope, and hand it to a volunteer without telling anyone what you wrote. Now display three coins on a table: a penny, a dime, and a quarter. Ask your volunteer to choose any two of them. If he chooses the penny and quarter ask "Why did you choose to leave the dime?" Have him open the envelope and read what you wrote on the piece of paper, and the trick is over.

If your volunteer chooses the dime and one of the other coins instead, you instruct him to place one of these two coins in your hand. If he places the dime in your hand, ask, "Why did you choose to give me the dime?" If he keeps the dime and gives you the other coin, ask, "Why did you choose to keep the dime?" In either case you are making it look as if he has chosen the dime. When the envelope is opened and his choice is confirmed, everyone is amazed at your physic abilities. A subtle trick, but works every time.

Misdirection

Sleights and gimmicks fool the eye; subtleties and misdirection fool the mind. Misdirection is an important element that should be incorporated into most all magic tricks. Simply stated misdirection is directing the attention of the audience to one thing while secretly doing the "magic" somewhere else. The audience's attention is focused in the wrong direction, or they are made to believe in something that is not so. This doesn't mean that you tell the audience to look at your right hand and then do something sneaky with your left. Such primitive forms of misdirection rarely work. The audience must look at your right hand without your even telling them to do so. In this way it seems as though the audience is in complete control of what they are looking at. It gives a strong psychological impression that they see everything you do, when in reality you make them see what you want them to see.

Misdirection is also used to create the belief that something which is not there, really is, such as pretending to put a coin in the hand. The hand then holds an imaginary coin as if it were real, creating the impression that a coin really is there.

In essence, the art of misdirection is good acting. The magician creates the impression that a box is empty by easily picking it up, or that he is holding a pair of dice by the way he clenches his fist.

To act out the movements of misdirection you must practice the movement using real objects. This practice is very important, sure you may have made this movement thousands of times in your life, but you have never analyzed exactly how you do it. In general, a person who pretends to pick up an object and hold it, looks fake. Subtle movements or positions will give you away if you're not careful. You almost need to believe that the object is in your hand in order to make other people believe it.

People are always watching to see the magician slip something out of his sleeve or pocket. Misdirection can be used at critical times to draw the audience's attention away from the hand as it does a sleight or reaches into a pocket.

All eyes are drawn to the miraculous appearance of some object. While you produce a scarf in one hand, the other hand works the sleight. This move takes only a second and everyone's eyes will be on the scarf at that time. This psychological phenomena works every time; the audience will focus on the action or the spot where the magic appears to be taking place.

Misdirection and sleights go hand in hand. To execute a good sleight, you must also use misdirection. Don't let the audience know that anything out of the ordinary is happening. The sleight is the physical manipulation of an object, while misdirection leads the mind to believe that something else is happening.

Gimmicks, sleights, subtleties, and misdirection can all be used separately to perform magic. Most tricks, however, use a combination of these methods. Many will require the use of two or more to be successful. The classic multiplying ball trick uses both sleight of hand and gimmicks. A specially designed shell is the gimmick, but sleight-of-hand skill is needed to manipulate the shell and balls between the fingers.

Learning Magic

Many good books on magic are available and can provide more specific information on individual tricks. Read several of these and learn the tricks they describe. Even if you don't want to be a clown magician, a few selected magic tricks can add variety and excitement to any show.

You'll find an overwhelming amount of material on card tricks as you search through magic books. Cards

are very versatile and adapt easily to many of the magician's methods. Almost all books on magic contain their share of these tricks. Many books have been written entirely on the subject, giving the impression that card tricks must be very popular. This is far from the truth. Card magic has its merits and is entertaining for adults, but many children don't like them. To a young child magic with ordinary playing cards are abstract and unimpressive. However, using cards specially designed for children has been successful. These cards are usually much larger then ordinary playing cards and may have pictures of animals on them rather than spades and clubs, which kids often don't understand. If you want to do card tricks for children use one of these special decks.

CLOWN MAGIC

The magic that clowns perform is different from that which magicians do. The magician entertains his audience by amazing them with his magical powers. Magician comedians often use comic "patter" (verbal

accompaniment) with the serious magic in their act. The magician performs with flawless precision and timing. He is a master craftsmen of the mystical arts and his skills are unquestionable. The clown magician, however, is primarily a clown, and clowns by their very nature are supposed to be clumsy, foolish halfwits. A clown who possesses magical powers and fools the audience is out of character; the clown is the one who should be fooled.

I have seen many clowns in full costume perform with ropes, rings, and doves, much as a magician would on stage. I personally found them unappealing because they were performing serious stuff and the audience was expecting comedy magic. On the other hand, I have seen clowns perform full stage illusions which were accompanied with clown music and done with a comic flair. Seeing them perform the "serious" stuff in a comic manner was delightful and refreshing.

One of the best examples of clown magic that I have seen is the "electric deck." It is a small packet of cards that are attached either by staples or strung together. The clown displays the deck as a serious magician would and attempts to perform some difficult feats of shuffling. After a brief time the cards are accidentally dropped and the packet is exposed as being tied together. The clown looks competent at first, but then appears very foolish; the audience laughs at his attempt to be something he's not.

The magic performed by clowns should seem accidental and not a result of magical powers. Two basic types of magic which clowns can do, bungling magic and fake magic, are discussed below.

Bungling Magic

Everyone knows that clowns can't do anything right. A clown's attempt at doing anything serious invariably winds up bungled. When trying to perform magic, something unexpected happens to spoil the outcome, although the clown wins a hearty laugh from the audience. The humor is highlighted by the fact that the clown is trying to show off.

The clown may try to make a coin disappear. He says the magic word and opens his hand, but nothing happens. He tries it again with a new magic word. Upon opening his hand he finds to his surprise that the coin has turned into a small sponge ball. Much embarrassed, he tries to turn it back into a coin by saying an appropriate magical phrase. Opening his hand he finds that the ball rather than turning into a coin, has vanished. The original trick has now been accomplished but supposedly without the clown's control.

The clown performs some clever magic tricks, but he presents them in such a way as to make it appear that he is not in control. In this way the clown magician can perform most all the same tricks as a regular magician and retain his clown image.

Bungling magic can be accomplished in several ways. The tricks may not work right because of the clown's lack of knowledge; he forgets the magic word, says the wrong thing, or taps the wand rather than wave it in the air.

A clown also may bungle tricks through his lack of concentration. When mixing things together, he accidentally drops or spills something that will later spoil the trick he's trying to perform. While attempting to pour some milk into a mug he looks at the audience and smiles, paying no attention that the milk is actually poured into his hat. He says the magic word and presto—the milk has vanished from his mug, which he shows to the audience. With a smile of satisfaction

Daisy: I just had my appendix removed.
Doris: Have a scar?
Daisy: No thanks, I don't smoke.

he pops the hat onto his head. A look of surprise crosses his face as he realizes his mistake. Then lifting up his arm he pours the milk out of his sleeve and into the mug. This type of trick requires some degree of skill with magic, but all the audience notices is the clown's lack of control.

A third way the clown can mess things up is to use a magic device such as a wand or a hat which won't cooperate. The device may appear to have a mind of its own and do whatever it wants. The magician's top hat, for instance, may be mischievous and play tricks on the clown. When he reaches into it to pull out a rabbit, he pulls out a hand full of soggy spaghetti noodles instead.

The clown may attempt to make a cake by magic, placing eggs, flour, and water into the hat. After saying the magic word, he finds the cake did not appear, and his hat is empty. Frustrated he places the "empty" hat on his head only to have the gooey cake mess come out and slide down his face.

A fourth way to bungle magic is to use a helper from the audience. The magic clown can make the helper appear to be doing the magic unknowingly. As an example, the clown may show two soft sponge balls to the audience and tell his helper to hold one of them while he does some magic with the other. The clown attempts to make the ball transform into two balls but he just can't make the ball obey. Thinking that his ball is defective he decides to trade balls with his helper. The helper opens his hand, and to everyone's surprise two sponge balls pop out. The clown looks at him with a curious frown and asks "how did you do that?" The helper didn't realize it but the clown had secretly slipped him two balls at the start.

Fake Magic

The second major type of clown magic is the fake. The clown acts clever and tries to do magic tricks, knowing full well he can't really do any. With this type of magic, he tries to deceive his audience yet never manages to work the tricks well enough to fool anyone.

The clown may attempt to pull things out of an empty box which is on top of a table. Concealed under the table is another clown handing things up to him through a trap door in the table and a hole in the box.

The magician clown pulls one or two objects out of the supposedly empty box to the surprise of the audience. On a later attempt the assistant clown holds on too long to the object being passed up through the opening and the audience sees his hand come up out of the box. The assistant may also sneeze, rock the table, or even peek out to see the audience, revealing the secret.

In another situation, the clown magician may try to make a cookie disappear. Holding a handkerchief in front of his face, he hides the cookie and begins to eat it. At the same time he could be saying a magical phrase mixed with a few munching and chewing sounds. Pulling away the handkerchief, he expresses delight at having made the cookie "mysteriously" disappear.

The clown doesn't need to have much real skill in magic to pull off these gags, he is trying to pull one over on the audience.

Silly-Magic

These next tricks I call silly-magic because that's just what they are, silly. No skills in sleight of hand or special props are necessary. These tricks are so simple that most everyone can master them with little practice. The tricks work best with younger kids but can be worked into routines for all ages.

Finger Pull-Off. Hold your up left hand, palm toward you and fingers slightly spread. With the right hand grab the index finger of the left hand as shown in the figure below. The left index finger bends forward to hide its upper half. The right hand moves away as if holding the top half of your left index finger. "Voila" the finger is gone! Put it back on to restore the finger to its original position.

This trick won't fool anybody, but that's why it's called silly-magic. It's not supposed to deceive anyone, the clown tries to act clever and acts as if he had shown a good magic trick.

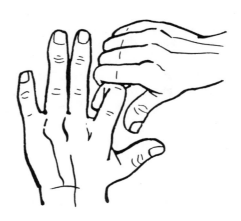

Linking Fingers. This is another bit of silly-magic. Bring both hands up with the thumbs touching the index fingers, making two "O" shapes. Show the audience that you have made two separate rings with your fingers. Lift your hands over and behind your head so no one can see them and say a magic word. Out of sight, link the two loops together.

Now bring your arms around in front to show the audience that you have magically linked the two rings. Unlink them in the same manner.

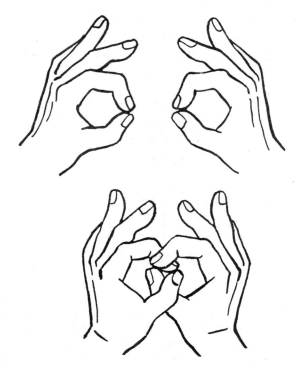

Anti-Gravity. The clown magician claims to have power over the force of gravity. To prove his claims he tries to make things float in the air. Wiggling the fingers of the right hand, to limber them up, the inner magical force is generated.

Once the force is built up, the clown points the fingers at an object and claims he can raise it up against the force of gravity. Pointing his fingers at his own foot, he makes it rise up and down as if done by the magic force. The same thing can be done to the other foot and the left hand. Even the head can be moved by this "mysterious" power.

These tricks are goofy but fun. When combined with a good buildup or story they can be very effective. A magical clown need not impress children with amazing abilities of dexterity and illusion; he needs only to make them laugh while impressing them with his magical abilities, or rather, lack of ability.

A few choice magic words during the show adds flavor. Use phrases like "tuna fish ice cream"; "hocus pocus, your camera is out of focus"; "hocus pocus, chicken bones will choke us"; "frog sandwiches"; "Prestobismol"; and other crazy sayings. They'll love it.

Story Development

Not too long ago I saw a magic act performed by an amateur magician which illustrated an important principle. This magician had a lot of magic tricks and props (some rather expensive) and a portable stage. His tricks were clean and well executed, but his show lacked magic. Oh sure he performed a lot of magic tricks, but there was no real magic—the magic of entertainment.

This performer assumed, like many beginners, that magic shows consist of a bunch of tricks. He even used volunteers from the audience but that didn't help. The show lacked a story or theme and consequently it was bland and faceless. It was interesting to some degree seeing him perform one trick after another, but he did and said noting to spark interest and hold the audience's attention. When the act was over, I didn't feel entertained.

This experience demonstrated to me that magic tricks lose much of their real magic if they are not accompanied by jokes or stories or some other clever patter. Tricks can become lifeless by themselves. For older audiences or in dramatic magic presentations, other techniques besides the stories and jokes are used to attract and retain the audience's attention. Children demand more action or verbal accompaniment, particularly in the form of jokes and gags to be entertained.

To be effective each trick must have its own accompanying patter or story. Since most magic acts are composed of several different tricks or routines, a central theme or story line is needed to relate one trick to the next. Each trick should flow into the next. This can be accomplished merely by saying after the Egg Bag Trick for example, "Speaking of chickens, let me tell you what happened to me the other day in my barnyard," or something to that effect.

Your entire show may revolve around a single topic such as bicycle safety, health, Christmas, Halloween, eating yellow lizards, or whatever. It can also be composed of individual tricks and stories which are linked together with carefully chosen patter.

Ed: How can one person make so many
    mistakes in a single day?
Fred: I get up early.

The following short clown act provides a good example of using patter and a centralized theme with magic. The magic skills needed are minimal, relying on silly stuff that anyone can do.

My Magic Pencil

For this routine an ordinary pencil is used. The clown must wear long sleeves without tight elastic so that the pencil can slide in and out easily.

"I have here a very unusual pencil. This is no ordinary pencil but a special magic pencil. It looks ordinary, and in fact is indistinguishable from the type you use at school. But this pencil possesses magical power—yes, magical power. To prove it to you, I will take a piece of paper and with this pencil I will be able to write down things about one of you that I could not possibly know. Let me have a volunteer. You, young lady, have you ever seen me before? Say no."

"No," she says.

He continues. "Good. Would you give me a hand with this magic trick?"

"Yes," she replies.

"This girl does not know me and I do not know her. I could not possibly know anything about her, including her name. But with the power of this magic pencil I will be able to write down on this paper things about her such as her name and age. Let me show you . . . I will write your name."

He writes a name on the slip of paper. "Your name, according to this magic pencil, is—Paul Harvey."

"No," she says.

"No? . . . It's not?" He looks curiously at the name on the paper. "Hmm . . . that is a strange name for a little girl. Let me try again."

He writes another name on the paper. "OK, I've got it now. Your name is Bertha Ann Bellyhose—No? . . .What about Sarah Jane Figwiggle?"

"No."

"Judith Finkelstine?"

"No."

"Well, what the heck is your name?"

"Susan," she says, or whatever her name is.

"Susan! . . .What kind of a name is that? . . . Oh well, let me try something else. I will write your age."

> Doris: Did you hear about the cross-eyed teacher?
> Daisy: No, what about her?
> Doris: She had no control over her pupils.

He writes something on the paper. "According to my magic pencil your age is . . . " He looks at the paper, acts surprised, looks at the girl, then back at the paper and back at the girl again. Making a funny, inquisitive face, he asks, "Are you 28 years old?"

"No."

"Hmm . . . maybe I've got the figures backwards. How about 82? No, that can't be right . . . Maybe this isn't my magic pencil after all." He thanks the helper and sends her back to her seat.

With a doubtful expression, he examines each side of the pencil. "Let me try something else. I'll put it in this hand, like this." (See illustration below.) "Bringing it behind my back, I'll do some magic."

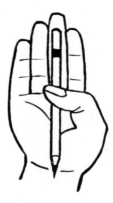

He brings his hands around in front of him, palms down. The right hand is cramped to make it look as if the pencil is in that hand. "Which hand is it in?"

The kids will all choose the correct hand. The clown turns both hands over and looks surprised. "Hmm . . . it was supposed to disappear. I must have done something wrong . . . oh I know, I didn't say the magic word. Let me try it again, this time using the magic word."

He keeps the pencil in the same hand and puts both hands behind his back. While his hands are out of sight, he slips the pencil up the sleeve of the other arm. He says the magic words, "Liver pudding . . . what did you expect me to say, abracadabra or something ridiculous like that?" Bringing his hands out in front and raised so that the pencil doesn't fall out, he holds the backs of his hand to the audience at about chin level. The hand which originally held the pencil is bent slightly, still pretending to hold it. "Which hand is it in now?"

Everyone will think it's in the crimped hand. "Nope," he says and shows them the empty hand. The kids will say it's in the other hand, but that is shown to be empty too.

"Ha ha, it's gone. See, I knew it was my magic pencil." Some of the kids might think it was stuck behind the clown's back, but to prove that he didn't, he turns around. "See, it's not behind my back either." As his back is turned he palms a coin out of his pocket.

"I will now make the pencil reappear." Holding the empty hand out in front, palms down, fingers crimped slightly, he says the magic words, "Liver pudding on a stick, the pencil will now reappear quick." He turns his hand palm side up, but it's empty. Nothing happened; no pencil. He tries it a second time. Still nothing happens. He looks puzzled.

"Hmm . . . what's wrong? . . . Oh, I see," he says. Reaching over with the other hand, which secretly holds the coin, he grabs something from behind a child's ear. "How silly of me. Those magic words always make the pencil appear from behind somebody's ear."

Mauri "Binkie" Norris

Pulling his hand away he says, "Here it is." But instead of the pencil he's holding a coin.

"Hey . . . this isn't my pencil! . . . That's all right, I needed the money anyway." He sticks the coin into his pocket. Reaching over, he gently grabs the child's ear and looks in. "Got any more in there?"

Slowly a giant sneeze begins to build up in the clown's nose with exaggerated accompanying facial expressions. "Ah . . . ah . . . ah . . . AAAH!" Turning toward the kids he makes as if he is going to give them an unwanted shower. The sneeze builds to its final climax as the kids squirm, "AAAAAAH!! . . ." ending in a comical and almost inaudible "hew."

With a smile on his face he says, "Scared ya, didn't I?"

Wiggling his nose to relive a tickle he continues, "Let's see where could that pencil have gone to?" The pencil is secretly allowed to slide out of the sleeve and into the clown's hand. Suddenly he begins to build up another big sneeze. "Ah . . . AAAH . . . CHOOOO!!"

Just before sneezing he clasps his hands to his nose, concealing the pencil. As he sneezes he opens both hands wide and gives the pencil a little flick so it flies out as if it were the cause of the clown's ticklish nose. "Why there's my magic pencil. That's the problem with making things disappear—you never know where they'll wind up."

This routine can be broken down into its basic elements by eliminating the dialogue. What we have left are four elementary magic tricks. The first was a psychic demonstration, trying to guess the girl's name and age. The second was vanishing the pencil, followed by the appearance of a coin, and finally the reappearance of the pencil.

Each of these tricks could have been done seriously without patter, but they would have made a terrible magic show. With clever dialogue, tied together by a central theme, these simple tricks became a successfully funny clown act.

The theme on which the dialogue was built was the clown trying to prove that he really had a magic pencil, but none of his tricks did what he wanted them to do. Children enjoy it when an adult (a clown or a magician) makes an error, such as forgetting a name, mispronouncing a word ("Ladies and Germs"), or when a magic trick appears to goes wrong. Telling the audience that you're going to do one thing and then doing something else, often to your displeasure and embarrassment (or so it seems), is delightfully funny.

All clowns and magicians should cultivate the element of surprise, both to create humor and to keep an audience's interest. Keep them guessing even when performing serious magic. Don't tell them what you're going to do next—*show* them. Tell them only enough to build your story. Telling an audience, "I am now going to make this silk turn from blue to red" is boring. Instead say, "Watch what happens when I pull this silk through my fist." Not knowing what to expect will arouse curiosity and greater interest in your magic.

YOUR BAG OF TRICKS

Clown magicians get most of their business from children's birthday parties. It's not practical for the performer to show up at a party (or even a staged show) carrying an arm load of assorted props. They're too enticing for the youngsters. If they can see what you have, they will want to touch them. The props will also be a distraction as you perform. To avoid this problem, keep them out of sight until they are ready to be used, then put them away immediately afterward.

The best way to do this is to put all your props into a bag, suitcase, or trunk. In this way nothing is seen except what you pull out. The container also provides a convenient way to carry several things without losing them.

I personally transport my show in a small circus wagon that I constructed out of plywood and wagon wheels. This wagon holds all my props and magical apparatus. Not only is the wagon helpful in transporting and storing my equipment, but it is also a great selling point. After the party I usually pose for pictures with the birthday child on top of the wagon.

I have seen some clowns perform a full length show without the slightest bit of carry-on luggage in sight. They accomplish this by loading their pockets with small items that either unfold or pop open, giving the appearance of carrying more than they really are, almost like a magical effect by itself!

> Shopper: What's the price of your ground beef?
> Butcher: Ninety cents a pound.
> Shopper: Ninety cents a pound! But the butcher down the street sells it for sixty cents a pound.
> Butcher: Why don't you go there to shop?
> Shopper: I did, but he's out of it.
> Butcher: Well, when I am out of ground beef, I sell it for forty cents a pound.

CHAPTER 9

BALLOON SCULPTURING

Children love balloons! They like big ones and small ones, round ones and long ones, but most of all they like balloons that have been magically formed into cute bubbly animals. Magicians mystify their audiences by making coins disappear, silks change their color, or by restoring a torn paper to its original form. But when the nimble fingers of a clown transforms a skinny, lifeless balloon into a lovable, cuddly animal, that's magic!

A clown skilled in making balloon figures will always find a crowd of eager children gathering around in excited anticipation. Unlike magic, juggling, and other traditional clown skills, balloon sculpturing can be learned with just a few minutes' practice. Once you know how to make a few critters, you can delight an audience of kids. It doesn't matter that you may be able to make only two or three different animals. The fact that they're made with different colored balloon gives them variety, and you look like a master craftsman.

Balloons have other advantages. For one, they make an inexpensive giveaway. Usually a child has to settle merely for watching clowns perform, but with balloons they can take home a souvenir, a piece of the show. When you write your clown name on the balloon animal or attach your business card, a piece of advertising is taken home too. Balloons are also angle-proof. With children all around you and sometimes crawling over your shoulder, you don't have to worry about exposing the trick. Balloons make an excellent fill-in for walk-arounds, or can be expanded into an entire act.

Now that I've sold you on the idea of using balloons . . . read on.

DEWEY'S BALLOON BASICS

One of the questions I'm asked most often is "How can I get started in balloon sculpturing?" Short of having a personal instructor or a friend to demonstrate and critique, the best way to learn is by reading an instruction book. In that way you can follow the instructions and drawings at your own rate and find a wide variety of creations to choose from. This chapter is meant to be an introduction to the field of balloon sculpturing. It's only the tip of the iceberg. Dozens of balloon books and hundreds of creations are available. For the beginner I would like to suggest my book, *Dewey's New Balloon Animals*.

Balloon Types

Most balloons have a coded number which identifies their size and shape when fully inflated. The #260A's first number "2", for example, means that its inflated diameter is *two* inches. The "60" indicates that when fully inflated it will be approximately *sixty* inches long. The "A" denotes that it has a fairly thin wall strength ("A" for average) and is easier to inflate than the #260E. The "E" of the #260E means that the balloon has thicker walls ("E" for entertainer grade) and therefore is more difficult to inflate. Heat and sunlight soften balloons, thus increasing breakage. Though #260E balloons will withstand more exposure to the sun

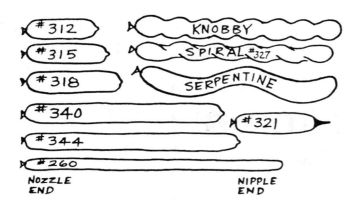

and more twisting, which is required for the more advanced animals, I recommend the #260A for the beginner.

Two main schools of thought exist on balloon sculpturing. One suggests making "single-balloon" animals; the other, the larger "multiple-balloon" animals. The "single-balloon" workers use #245, #260A, #260E, the Apple, the Bee body (#321), and other types. These small creations almost always use just one balloon. The popular #260A (sometimes called a "pencil" or a "twisty") is the basis for most single-balloon animals.

Easier to inflate are the "Airship" type balloons such as #312, #315, #344, and #340. These can be twisted together with other types to form the large multilple-balloon creations. Because these are large, they are more suitable for stage use than for the clown who mingles with the crowd.

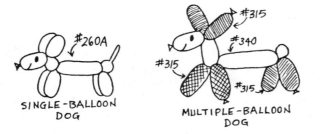

SINGLE-BALLOON DOG   MULTIPLE-BALLOON DOG

Balloon Care

Because balloons are perishable, you must take care of them if they are to last any reasonable length of time. Heat and ozone are the two worst enemies of latex balloons. Heat causes aging, and ozone eats tiny pinholes in latex. It's best to store balloons in airtight containers in a cool place, away from heat and sunlight. Tupperware brand containers or coffee cans with lids are good choices. (It isn't necessary to store them in the freezer or frigerator.) Old balloons tend to stick together and burst readily when inflated. If you need to store balloons for any length of time, a very light sprinkling of cornstarch all over your balloons is helpful. This will help prevent sticking as the balloons age. To increase your chances of getting the freshest product, always buy your balloons from a company that has a large turnover. If stored properly, balloons can be kept fresh for about a year. Otherwise their shelf life can be as short as a couple of months.

When sculpturing in winter, you may need to warm up the balloons just before using them. Either keep them in an inside pocket or warm them in your hands. Cold balloons are too stiff to expand and will burst easily.

Inflation

Inflating a #260A pencil balloon is difficult and takes practice and determination. There are a few tricks that will help. To soften the balloon prior to inflating it, some people like to stretch it a few times. I like to use my cheek muscles to start a bubble. Then I take a deep breath and use my chest and diaphragm muscles to inflate it to the desired length in one continuous effort.

Some people like to pull slightly on the nipple end of the balloon while inflating it. This motion tends to encourage the bubble to advance, thus helping with the inflation. Don't pull too much, though, or it will actually be *more* difficult to inflate.

Small diameter balloons (such as the #260A) tend to be difficult to inflate by mouth, while large diameter balloons (such as round, airship, and knobby) tend to be easier. Many beginners get dizzy when they first try to inflate balloons. I know I did. If you're like me, however, after a few weeks of light practice you won't get dizzy when blowing up these balloons. It's a good way to build lung power. If you're not in good

Jim "Dune Buggy" Russell

health, check with your doctor before trying to inflate balloons by mouth. If you have to struggle to blow up your balloons, you may need to consider a balloon hand pump. Most beginners need to give their lungs a rest now and then anyway.

After you have inflated the balloon, you will need to tie it off. There are many ways to tie a balloon. A simple, single knot is sufficient. Find the best way for you by experimenting. It isn't necessary to pull the knot extremely tight as some beginners often do; simply pull it snugly. This applies to any type of latex balloon you are tying.

Markings

Often clowns and balloon sculptors mark their balloon creations. A few strokes of a marking pen can turn a plain balloon animal into a cute pet with eyes, mouth, and whiskers, giving the creation a personality. After all, if it pleases the recipient, that's what it's all about. I like to use Sanford's "Sharpie" brand permanent black ink markers, which make a thin or broad line as needed.

MAKING BALLOON FIGURES

Basic Dog

Since dogs are frequently requested, it's best to learn the basic dog first. You will soon learn that by altering the proportions of the dog's body, you can make several spin-off sculptures. It will become one of your mainstay creations, and since many other balloon animals use the same basic body, it is important to master. By learning the dog, you can easily master about seven of his cousins. The basic dog and the remaining animals in this chapter use the #260A pencil balloon.

Before beginning to construct the dog you will need some basic information about bubbles and twisting them. When you are asked to "twist off a bubble," do it by holding one hand stationary and rotating your other hand. (In my case, since I'm right-handed, I hold with my left hand and twist with my right.) Rotate it at least two full turns as in the figure below.

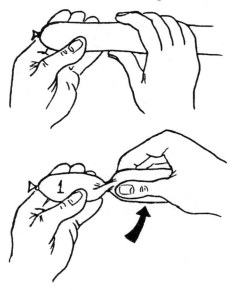

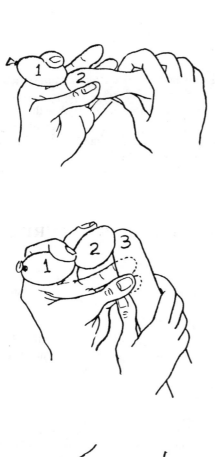

The two full revolutions are to ensure that the balloon will not untwist easily. When making three bubbles in a row, make sure that each twist for each bubble is always in the same direction. Make sure to hold on to the very first bubble as you are making the others until they are safely secured with a "twist connect." If you let go, they will all quickly untwist. To form the twist connect maneuver, follow the illustrations.

Form bubbles 1, 2, and 3 then fold bubbles 2 and 3 together. While holding bubble 1 and the remaining balloon, rotate bubbles 2 and 3 one full revolution. When they are released, they will remain locked together. Now with these preliminary instructions covered, let's start the dog.

First inflate a pencil balloon fully except for about five inches. "Burp" the balloon by releasing a small burst of air (this softens the entire balloon for easier manipulation) and tie a knot in the nozzle end.

Twist off three equal-sized medium bubbles (about two inches each) and then twist connect at points A and B to form the head and two ears.

Now twist off three more equal medium-sized bubbles and twist connect at points C and D to form the neck and front legs.

Twist off a long bubble, which will be the body, and two equal medium-sized bubbles; then twist connect them at points E and F to form the body and rear legs.

The remaining bubble (which is necessary to steady the rear legs) and the nipple end form the tail. All that's left to do is decorate the face.

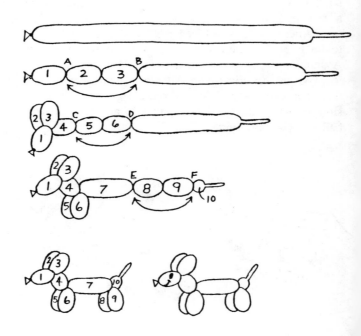

Giraffe

The giraffe is made exactly like the dog with a few modifications. The neck is longer (and decorated with spots), and the body and tail are smaller. To start the giraffe will require a little more air in the balloon than the basic dog. Inflate it fully except for about three inches. When you're finished with the twists, decorate it with a marker.

Dachshund

Another variety of dog, the dachshund, can be made simply by lengthening the body.

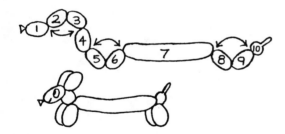

Horse

Shorter ears and a longer neck and legs change the basic dog into a simple horse.

Camel

Here's a chance to exercise your creativity. You can change the horse into a camel by shaping and bending some of the bubbles. Curve the face, the neck, and the body as shown in the figure below. To "bend" a pencil balloon, simply fold or bend it in the desired direction, squeeze its sides repeatedly, then release. Sometimes warming the balloon with your breath will soften the rubber and help it to form. Use a marker to add eyes and a mouth.

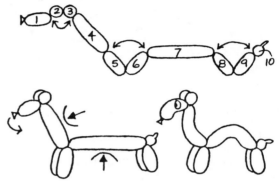

Rabbit

By giving the basic dog long ears and longer rear legs you can make a rabbit. The front legs will be tucked into the loop of the rear legs to make the rabbit sit. Enhance the face with eyes, mouth, and whiskers.

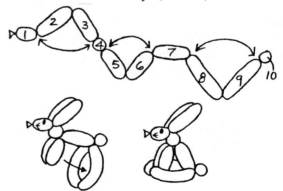

Mouse

The mouse requires only a small amount of air; about five inches is fine. The mouse is really the basic dog made with very small bubbles. It should have a long, uninflated tail remaining behind the "tail" bubble.

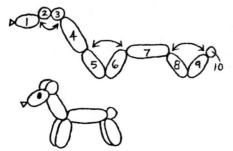

Squirrel

The squirrel is really a mouse with a long curved tail. Inflate the #260A balloon fully except for about three inches, and repeat the steps for making a mouse. Form the tail into a question mark shape by bending it as described for the camel.

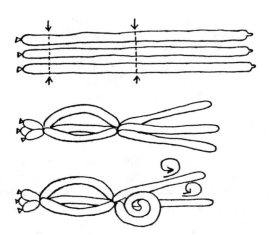

Party Hats

Children go wild over balloons . . . any kind of balloons. Including balloon toys or balloons that they can wear. Hats are especially popular. I know of one entertainer who specializes in balloon hats and does quite well with them. No two of his hats are the same.

Balloon hats are a way to express your creativity. I will show you one way to construct a balloon hat, but keep in mind that there are plenty of other ways to do it.

The "Wounded Wildebeest" takes three #260A pencil balloons (of different colors) which are inflated fully except for about one inch. Tie them off separately. Lay all three balloons alongside each other and twist them all together about three inches from their nozzle ends. Measure about one foot down from that point

and again twist them all together. Purse open the three foot-long bubbles to form the actual hat part. Then shape the remaining nipple ends of the three balloons into curls by rolling each balloon, then repeatedly squeezing its sides. When released, it will keep some of the curl shape. Position the curls randomly. When the "Wounded Wildebeest" is completed, place it on the happy child's head.

All kinds of loops, twists, curls, and zany shapes can be added to a party hat. Other types of balloons—knobby, serpentine, round, bee body (#321), spiral (#327)—can be used to enhance the decoration. Animal shapes can be sculptured into your creation. I have made a giant swan hat, a spider hat complete with dangling legs, and a Viking hat with horns. Animal heads with the remaining balloon made into a loop are also easy to make.

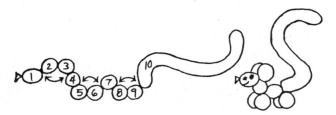

Janet "Jelly Bean" Tucker and Larry "Slowpoke" Tucker

BITS OF BUSINESS

Balloon Funnies

Many clowns use their balloon talents to do "mob" work. They mix and get mangled—oops, I mean mix and mingle throughout the crowd making balloon animals.

One of the biggest mistakes that new and even experienced clowns make is performing like a balloon vending machine. They appear to be in some kind of crazed race to crank out zillions of balloon animals per hour. These speed merchants hardly even notice when the bewildered child walks away slowly, mumbling something like, "What is it?" They don't take the time to do funny bits or tell jokes with their balloon creations; they don't entertain.

Understandably, there are times when a clown needs to work quickly, but people want to be entertained. People want to laugh, giggle, be surprised and amused. Take the time to joke, have fun, and perform for the crowd. These little fun ideas, jokes, or "bits of business" are one of the things that make the difference between a person in a clown costume and a real clown.

To give you an example and to get your imagination working, I'm going to share with you some of the bits of business I use. Usually I try to find at least one funny thing to go with every animal I make—more if I can. That way every animal I make has a built-in dialogue. Every time a child asks for an animal, no matter which one, I have a joke, story, or pun to fall back on. One of the tricks that balloon clowns use to keep their show going for hours is to repeat these bits of business. As the children select their choices for animals (hopefully alternating them), your jokes get recycled along with them. Even if the crowd has heard the joke, they're in the spotlight when it's their turn and they enjoy your personal attention. The following lines are a selection for the most commonly requested creations.

Dog. "It must be raining cats and dogs 'cause I just stepped in a poodle."

Mouse. "Did you hear about the mouse who was a louse? Yeah, his uncle was a rat."

Squirrel. "This squirrel likes you. He thinks you're nuts."

Horse. "I once knew a boy that wanted to be a pony. One night he stood out in the rain and by the next morning he was a little *hoarse*."

Rabbit. "I'm not so sure a rabbit's foot is good luck. The rabbit had four of 'em and look what happened to him."

Savers

Sometimes, halfway into making a creation, you discover that the balloon has a hole or that you put in too much air, or something else happens that makes it necessary for you to discard the balloon you're working on and start over. To save youself from possible embarrassment and to keep the audience's interest, you can use a saver.

Savers are jokes or gags you keep ready in case something unexpected happens. For example, if the balloon pops, don't apologize and look foolish. Turn the situation into a joke. Let the balloon drop to the floor then quickly stomp up and down on it and say, "There that'll teach you!"

Here are two ways I usually turn defeat into victory. If I've made several bubbles, I'll wad them all up and squeeze hard. The rapid pops sound like firecrackers.

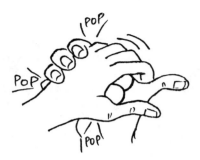

This is follow it up a comment about the Fourth of July.

The other "out" is what I call "divide and conquer." I pick a spot on a long section of balloon and twist it in half. Using the fingertips of both of my hands, I pinch the twist and tear it apart. I continue to hold

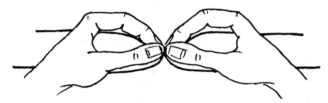

it to keep the air from escaping and hand one half to a child and ask him to hold it. Just as he reaches for it, I let it go and turn away. It will fly away quickly. Turning back around I ask "what happened?" Being a nice fellow as I am, I hand him the other balloon and warn him not to let it go as he did before. Again, just as he reaches for it, let it go. The older kids really enjoy this.

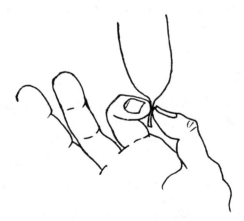

The Dog Act

In addition to jokes and puns, you can do other bits of business. The Dog Act is fun routine. Make the basic dog, leaving about two inches of uninflated nipple for the tail. Hold firmly near the end of the tail bubble with one hand. Grasp the very end of the uninflated

part with your other hand. Pull it sharply and snap it three times. That action will weaken the tip end of the tail. To make the pompon suddenly appear on the end of the dog's tail, cover the tail bubble completely with your hand, containing it, and squeeze a little. Don't let the bubble crawl. If you do this correctly, the pressure will make the uninflated end swell up miraculously. I like to pretend that I made it happen by blowing simultaneously on the thumb of my other hand. Of course the hand holding the dog is doing it but it appears that I inflated the tail through my body.

After sculpturing a poodle, you may want to show the audience how he is trained. He is able to bark on command. To make the poodle bark, hold him and rub your finger on the body of the balloon. Freshly washed fingers, which are oil free, will make a rasping noise when stroked across a balloon.

The dog can answer questions. "This is a poodle who uses his noodle, he wants all you kids to be kind to one another . . . isn't that right?" (By pushing the back of his head with your first finger the poodle will nod "yes.")

"Would you like to do a trick for the kids?" (Again he nods affirmatively.) To make him do a back flip through a hoop, you will need another balloon. Fully inflate a #260A pencil balloon except for about one inch. Tie it off, then tie the nozzle and the nipple ends together to form a hoop. With one hand hold all four legs of the poodle together. Have the hoop ready in your other hand. After the appropiate buildup, quickly open your hand. The poodle will jump up and flip over backwards. As it floats temporarily in the air, swoop the hoop around the dog. The poodle has just done a back flip through the hoop. Sure it's corny, but take your bow anyway. (Just a little practice will make his jump work smoothly.)

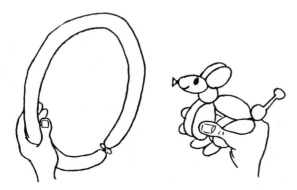

Next set the dog on the floor and quickly command it to lie down. (It will be about to fall over anyway.) Take a bow again. Now command the dog to play dead. (No response.) Again, tell the dog to play dead. Then out of mock frustration, step on him. (Pow, pow!) You can entertain the audience for hours with fun skits such as this.

The Invisible Balloon Dog

Balloons make great clown props. They are colorful, easy to construct, and economical. One such prop is the "Invisible Balloon Dog." It requires two #260A (or #260E) pencil balloons. Inflate the first balloon completely, tie it off and temporarily tuck it under your arm. Fully inflate the second pencil balloon except for about three inches and tie it off. Twist off a small bubble and a large ten-inch bubble and twist connect at points A and B.

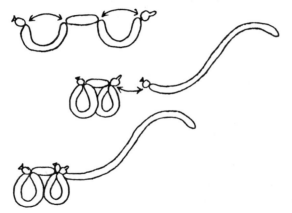

Twist off a four-inch bubble and approximately a ten-inch bubble and twist connect at points C and D. You should have a small bubble remaining. Shape and curve the first balloon (the one under your arm) into a lazy "S" shape. Twist a small bubble on its end then twist connect and join it with the other balloon. The first balloon is the leash and the second is the harness of the invisible balloon dog.

With your dog constructed, you have the chance to ham it up. The illusion of walking a dog is achieved by holding him about six inches off the ground. Weave him in and around the feet of the crowd while warning them "Watch out for my dog." Funny thing—he constantly tries to get up on people ("bad dog, BAD DOG") but luckily you get him under control. A few growls and barks (done ventriloquist style) add to the fun. And if the audience wonders why they can't see him . . . he's an *Airedale* of course!

Customer: Do you serve crabs here?
Waiter: We serve everyone. Sit right down.

Customer: Do you have pig's feet?
Waiter: Yes, sir.
Customer: That's too bad. If you wear shoes, no one will notice.

Customer: Do you have frog's legs?
Waiter: Yes, sir.
Customer: Well then hop in to the kitchen and bring me a hamburger.

Customer: This soup isn't fit for a pig.
Waiter: I'll take it back, sir, and bring you some that is.

Customer: There's a fly in my soup.
Waiter: Serves the cook right. I told him not to strain the broth through the fly swatter.

Customer: There's a fly in my soup.
Waiter: Don't worry, sir—he's a good swimmer.

Customer: There's a fly in my soup.
Waiter: That's funny, there were two of them when I left the kitchen.

Customer: What's this fly doing in my soup?
Waiter: I don't know—looks like the breaststroke.

CLASSIC CLOWN GAGS

Quiet Please

This is a good gag for jugglers working on a stage or platform.

The clown tells the audience that he needs absolute silence for his next trick. It must be so quiet in fact, that they can hear a pin drop.

After the audience is dead silent, the clown takes out a bowling pin (juggling club) which has been kept out of sight. Holding it high in the air he lets it drop to the floor with a loud crash!

Hole in the Head

The clown shows the audience a ping pong ball and places it in his hat. The hat is then put on his head. Immediately the ball emerges from the clown's mouth apparently haven fallen through a hole in his head.

The hat is lifted up off the head to demonstrate that it is no longer there.

Two ping pong balls are use. One is secretly put into the clown's mouth before beginning the stunt. The hat has also been prepared beforehand by placing a piece of double sided tape inside of it. The ball that is shown to the audience is secured to the hat by the tape. The hat can be lifted off the head without dropping the ball.

The Funnel Trick

One clown has another clown help him with a trick. The assistant clown is told to lean back and look at the ceiling. The first clown then places a coin on his assistant's forehead. A funnel is next placed in the front of his pants.

The first clown instructs his assistant to try to drop the coin from his head into the funnel. As the second clown attempts to do this, the first clown pours a picture of water into the funnel and laughs for having pulled a joke on his friend.

The assistant is angry and picks up a stick to club the other clown. The first clown begs him not to use it and offers to let the assistant try the same trick on him. The assistant agrees.

A coin is placed on the first clown's forehead and a funnel in the front of his pants. The assistant cheerfully pours a picture of water into the funnel.

While the assistant laughs the first clown straightens backup, pulls out the funnel, reaches inside his pants and pulls out a water bag with the water in it, smiles and exits.

The Big Squirt

For this gag the clown uses a bulb from a squirting flower or a small hollow rubber ball filled with water. He enters the stage holding the ball in the palm of his hand, under the third and fourth fingers, without letting the audience see it.

The clown appears to have a bad cold with a stuffy nose. To relieve the nose he grabs it with his thumb and first finger as if to blow it. Squeezing the ball a gush of water squirts out.

Quick Change Artist

A clown steps behind a screen to change his wardrobe. His hat is tossed up and over the screen followed by his coat, shirt, and trousers.

Accidentally he bumps the screen and it topples over revealing the clown—fully dressed just as he was before.

The Pocket

A clown reaches into his pocket to pull something out. The hand gradually goes deeper and deeper, going past the knee and finally pops out of the bottom of the trouser leg.

Clown looks puzzled, wiggles his fingers and pulls his hand back up.

CHAPTER 10

PUPPETS, PETS, AND PALS

While it may seem that clowns and puppets have nothing in common, this is far from the truth. The clown (or shall we say the person putting on clown makeup) is giving life to an alter ego and conceals his own personality behind the makeup. The puppeteer in placing his hand into a puppet and hiding behind a curtain (again concealed from the audience) gives life to the puppet. Both types of performers are creating a fantasy world for the audience that an actor just could not do.

Although puppetry dates back to ancient Greece and Rome (500 B.C.) today's style of puppetry can be traced back to early days of the Italian commedia dell'arte in the 1600s. The commedia dell'arte (comedy of professional actors) was a troop of traveling performers (magicians and stock characters). One of these stock characters was called Pulcinella, a character who became the bases for the English puppet, Punch. The term "slapstick"—a specally built club that made a loud slapping noise when hitting something—also comes from the commedia dell'arte.

The basic Punch and Judy story has its stock characters who are: the baby, Toby the dog, the doctor, the clown Joey (after Joseph Grimiadi, father of modern clowning), a policemen, the crocodile (or dragon), and the Devil. Within these puppets the "Professor" (a term given to Punch and Judy men) would improvise a play around a theme such as marriage, drinking, or breaking the law (usually after Mr. Punch has thrown the baby out the window!). "Breaking the Law" is still one of the most popular of the Punch themes. Punch later gained international fame under many different names: in Germany he performed as Kasper, in France Guignol, in Russia Petrouchka, but no matter what country the "Lazzi" (Italian for tricks or stunts) and character were the same. Throughout the years this style of comedy had evolved into what we today know as a "situation comedy" on television, with stock actors involved in a different story each episode.

PUPPET TYPES

Puppets, like people, come in different styles and shapes and are manipulated in different ways. Some puppets are worn on the puppeteer's hand or sit on his lap while others perform on a stage with the puppeteer hidden from view. In most clowning situations, both the puppet and puppeteer are in view of the audience. Let's look now at some of the puppets that are most adaptable for use by clowns.

Hand Puppets

Hand puppets are some of the most commonly used and recognized puppets in the world. There are three major types of hand puppets: finger puppets, mouth puppets, and hand and glove puppets.

Finger Puppets. The finger puppet is made up of a body and a head, with an unmoveable mouth. The puppeteer operates the puppet with two fingers (the second and third) in the head, the thumb in one of the puppet's arms, and the fourth and little finger in the puppet's other arm, (see illustration). The puppet Punch is considered a hand puppet, as is Kukkla, of Kukkla, Fran and Ollie fame from the 50's TV show. Smaller finger puppets can be operated with a single finger moving the puppet's head and each arm.

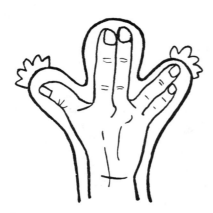

Since finger puppets do not have moveable mouths, to create the illusion that the puppet is real and can talk, movements are added to accent certain words. In the sentence *"I* am *happy* to be *here* today" three words are emphasized: I, happy, and here. When the puppet is speaking these words are accompanied by physical actions. The puppet would point to himself when

Royal Puppet Theatre

saying "I". When he says "Happy" he expresses delight by clapping his hands or bounces a little from side to side. Tapping or pointing to the floor can signify "here".

Finger puppetry is really all movement, but not movement for the sake of putting a puppet on your hand and jiggling it. Each movement or action has a purpose. Finger movements are used for positive ideas, thinking, clapping, pointing, crying, sneezing, and snoring. Using your wrist you achieve movements of rejection, bowing, looking around, or being shy. In using your arm you can show all movements of motion: running, hopping, walking, and falling. The concept of mime in puppetry is explored in detail in the book *Making Puppets Come Alive* by Carol Fijan and Larry Engler.

Mouth Puppets. With the advent of TV, mouth puppets have become popular because of how they move and act. The fact that a "creature" can talk and have proper movement, makes a child believe even more in the reality of the puppet. This is why today's most famous mouth puppets, are Kermit, Miss Piggy, Fozzie Bear—The Muppets. These types of puppets come as close to actual human lip synchronization as

Maher

possible and express more human reactions than the finger puppet.

In performing mouth puppets you must train your hands (both left and right) to always be in synchronization with that of the puppet. For each syllable that is spoken, your hand inside of the puppet's mouth opens and closes. For the moment, shape your hand as it would if it were inside a mouth puppet. Open your fingers and say the word "Hi" and then close the fingers (fingers are aimed down and stretched opened to pronounce the words). Now try it with the word watermelon. Remember on each of the syllables, your hand opens and closes. For the word wa-ter-mel-on your hand must open and close four times.

Hand and Glove Puppets. This type of puppet is really a mouth puppet with "real" arms. In perform-

ance one of your arms will operate the head and mouth while your other arm will operate the puppet's left or right hand. If you want the puppet to be able to move his head and both arms, you will need a second puppeteer to operate the other arm.

A hand and glove puppet has to be one of the best puppets for meeting and greeting children in walk-around entertainment because the puppet can shake hands or give gifts. Children can also touch them, which makes for nice entertainment and happy moments. If a child begins to cry, then move back or even away, don't try and tell them it's just a puppet and not to be afraid. Never spoil the illusion of a "living" puppet that you are trying to create.

Marionettes

Marionettes are the most complex and yet artistic of puppets. A Marionette usually is a wooden figure (sometimes just the head is wooden) whose body parts (back, legs, arms, etc.) are attached with loose joints

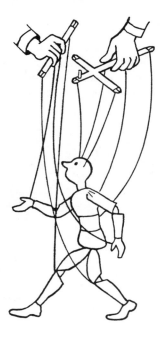

(hinges) and strung to a control rod. Usually this control rod has about eight or nine strings connected to the puppet, but more complex marionettes can have as many as 40 strings.

Because of the strings, marionettes require ample room for manipulation which limits the distance children can get to them. Many clowns build marionette clowns (usually with their own clown face) to walk along with them in parades or festivals. Animals and birds can be built as marionettes for parade or walk-around entertainment.

Ventriloquial Figures

The traditional conception of a ventriloquist's dummy or puppet is that of a little smart aleck boy. This figure made with wood, plastic or paper mache, has a movable jaw, a turning head, and possibly rolling eyes, and various other movements. The ventriloquist manipulates these movements with the use of strings or levers located inside the figure's chest cavity.

Most ventriloquists follow traditional roles, using a boy figure and pattering a dialog in which the ventriloquist assumes the role of the straight man and the puppet the comic. Other human figures that are also used are girls, grandfathers, grandmothers, drunks, and even speciality figures like Ronald Reagan.

Recently, with the growing popularity of Sesame Street and the Muppets, animal figures are being used more frequently, especially with clowns and other children's entertainers. The types and varieties vary drastically and include such creatures as: parrots, buzzards, monkeys, dogs, rabbits, ducks, turkeys, alligators, bears, and others. All of these are available from prop manufacturers or dealers.

Novelty Figures

There are other types of puppets that clowns can use which I would classify as novelty figures. Although in a strict classification, many of these could be grouped

with those already mentioned.

Figures do not have to be human or animal. A shoe, for example, could make a good companion for an interesting conversation; after all, it already has a tongue. Other figures that have been used include such things as talking socks, beer mugs, boxes, paper bags, walking sticks, balls, paintings, and hats. A pompon, like those worn on clown suits, with a couple of big eyes can turn into a cute little fuzzy bug. Attach a string and eight chenille stems (pipe cleaners) for legs to create a hairy spider. Put Velcro on the pompon and stick it on your costume. Kids love it!

Puppets are also made out of balloons and paper for short routines or gags. Many of these are easy to make and inexpensive so that they make an ideal give-away item. Kids will enjoy creating the figures themselves and making them talk.

The human hand can be made into a variety of interesting talking figures by decorating it with eyes, nose, lips, and hair. Moving the thumb manipulates the mouth and the wrist moves the head.

Most any object, whether it has a moveable mouth or not, can be used like a puppet. You can be creative and different by using a variety of props as puppets. Books can be rigged up so that the cover opens and closes like a mouth. A book entitled *English Language* would make a novel talking prop. A talking joke book can plague the performer with witty one-liners. Experiment with other props such as flowers, clocks, cupcakes, statues, and even rocks. Remember, your

Maher

puppet, pet, or pal doesn't have to have a movable mouth in order to communicate, so anything and everythilng can be used. This can lead to a lot of interesting and fun routines.

BRINGING YOUR PUPPET TO LIFE

When using puppets, you will need to give them a personality and make them come alive. One of the most important ways to do this is by giving your puppet the ability to communicate. This may be vocally as a ventriloquist would do, or the figure may not utter a word yet still maintain a conversation by whispering in the puppeteer's ear, "talking" softly so only the performer can hear, or using mime. We will now explore the different ways you can communicate with your "partners".

Teaching Your Partner to Talk

One of the major concerns many clowns have about using puppets and ventriloquial figures is developing a proper puppet voice. Logically you can't use your own natural voice when trying to create the illusion of the puppet speaking. Nor should your lips be obviously moving. In order to make it appear as though your partner was actually alive, possessing his own personality, you first need to give him a unique voice all his own. This skill has been used by ventriloquists for centuries and is extremely useful in making puppets appear real.

Many shy away from ventriloquism because they believe it to be a skill requiring a great deal of devoted practice in order to master. It does take consistent practice and experimentation to develop the skills of a professional ventriloquist, but that hasn't stopped many from trying and succeeding. Many successful ventriloquists began their careers with only a rudimentary knowledge of ventriloquism and perhaps only a few hours of practice.

Paul Stadelman, who stared with his partner Windy Higgins on their own TV show in the 1950s is one. He started out as a magician and was asked one day by his booking agent if he could do a "vent" act. He said "Sure" and was booked to do a show a few weeks later. With no experience in ventriloquism, he purchased a figure, wrote a dialogue, and began practicing. After his performance the manager, who was a friend of his, enthusiastically told Stadelman to junk the magic and stick to ventriloquism.

I believe many others have begun their careers much the same way, with little training. Their lack of skill did not prevent them from trying, and naturally their skills improved with experience.

What I'm trying to say is—you don't need to be an expert ventriloquist in order to put a voice into your puppet figures, especially if you are a clown. Clowns can get away with being a little less than perfect because that is what is expected of them. This does not mean you are given a license to do a sloppy job, only that you need not be perfect in order to experience the fascinating world of clown puppetry.

In order for you to accomplish the task of speaking for your partner without moving your lips, I am going to teach you some of the basic elements of ventriloquism that can be easily adapted by clowns. The method I will teach is easy enough for *anyone* with normal vocal cords to learn.

Labial Consonants. To start, get in front of a mirror and recite the alphabet speaking in a normal manner.

Notice the lip movement required to pronounce many of the letters. Keep looking in the mirror. Part your teeth and lips slightly, keeping your face relaxed. Now repeat the alphabet with as little lip movement as possible.

You will notice that most of the letters can be pronounced without much noticeable lip movement. Many of the letters which require movement in normal speech such as A, C, D, G, O, and U can be pronounced with the aid of the tongue, without using the lips. But a few, P, B, F, V, and M rely on the lips for clear pronunciation. These letters are referred to as the labial consonants.

If it weren't for the labial consonants, a ventriloquist's job would be easy. The key to mastering ventriloquism is being able to use words containing these letters without noticeable lip movement. Ventriloquists have developed several different methods to help them in this respect. Let's discuss some of the "tricks of the trade" for getting around labials.

Deletion. The simplest method for dodging labials is to carefully choose the words you use in your dialogue, avoiding all words containing labials. If you have a word with a labial replace it with a synonym. Instead of saying "mouse" which contains the labial "M" replace it with "rat". Practice several sentences which do not contain labials. The following list will get you started.

Hold your jaw still as you talk.
Talk without wiggling your cheeks.
Roses are red, grass is green.
How now little cow.

Completely avoiding words having labials can be difficult and although short conversations can be engineered, longer ones require a great deal of surgery. It is, therefore, best to learn to pronounce words containing labials. There are three methods used which allow the performer to speak any word desired, they are referred to as *false speech.* These are (1) substitution, (2) dropping the labial, and (3) decreasing volume.

Substitution. Of the three methods of false speech this is the one most commonly used. The substitution method, as the name implies, is used by substituting a labial with another letter. For example replacing the letter "B" with "G" pronounce the word "table" as "tagle." If you say the word naturally, it sounds like table. Used in a sentence, "tagle" becomes "table" in the mind of the listener. Repeat this sentence "Set the glass on the tagle." Listeners will mentally associate tagle with table without realizing it.

Below is a list of letters you can substitute for the labials.

Substitute G or D for B
Substitute T or E for P
Substitute N for M
Substitute H for F
Substitute EE for V

You may find that you prefer to substitute another letter than the ones listed; if it works, use it. Practice the substitution method with the following sentences.

In the zoo they have lions, tigers, and *bears.*
You have long *black* hair.
I like to eat *M & M's.*
I love *black*-eyed *peas.*
Open the *wrapper* and let's see inside.
He is a *very funny* clown.

Dropping the Labials. In this approach instead of substituting a easily pronounced letter for the labials, completely drop them out of the words you use. For instance "put" becomes "-ut" and "table" becomes "ta-le." If you speak as naturally as you can and use the words in a sentence to help the audience make a mental substitution, the audience will not notice the missing sounds. If you say "-ut the glass on the ta-le" they will believe you said "put the glass on the table."

Dropping the labials and letting the audience mentally replace them is in most cases more difficult to detect then when using the substitution method.

Decreasing Volume. This technique is best used in conjunction with the substitution method. When pronouncing the letter that has replaced the labial, decrease the volume of your voice. The "M" in monkey, for instance is replaced with an "N". When the word is said, "N" is spoken softly followed by a louder "-onkey".

Patient: There's something wrong with my stomach.
Doctor: Keep your coat buttoned and nobody will notice it.

Patient: Tell me the truth, am I going to die.
Doctor: Don't be silly, that's the last thing you're going to do.

In actual practice, all three types of false speech and the deletion method are used together. Practice using all these methods together using a mirror to help you out at first.

Modern Ventriloquism. False speech as I have described it has been used by ventriloquists and puppeteers for hundreds of years. Even today these methods are still frequently used. But most modern ventriloquists use a slightly different technique which allows them to actually pronounce the labials without lip movement. They position the tongue inside the mouth and mimic the sounds the lips make. This method of handling labials requires more dedicated practice but allows the entertainer to perform in close up situations where slight lip movement would be more noticeable.

If you desire to learn how to obtain a modern professional vent voice, I would recommend you take the course offered by Maher Studios. Their address is P.O. Box 420, Littleton, CO. 80160. Write to them for details.

Simple Ventriloquism. To use a puppet or ventriloquial figure as a clown does not require that you master all of the techniques of ventriloquism, be they traditional or modern. Although it is best to avoid moving your lips and jaw as much as possible, slight lip movement is not usually noticed. If the puppet you use looks and acts real and the audience is enjoying the show, they won't notice or even care if your lips move. After all, they know the puppet can't really talk.

As we have seen, only five letters out of the alphabet will give you trouble and even then you can pronounce words containing these letters with only slight lip movement.

Most people will concentrate their attention on the puppet when he speaks, allowing you to take the audience into your world of fantasy and make believe. In fact they want to believe that the puppet is actually alive. When they do, it only increases their enjoyment of your show.

Many people however, will look at your lips when you first introduce your partner, just to see how skilled you are. Once their curiosity is satisfied, they will focus their attention on your dialogue. Because of this the smart performer will avoid using labials for the first few minutes of the act.

Some kids will challenge you if they see your lips move. They will shout out something like "I saw your lips move." You are now caught in a potentially embarrassing situation. In order to save face and keep the show moving along smoothly, you will need to use

Fred Allen in his early vaudeville days. More of a juggler than ventriloquist, he was billed as "The World's Worst Juggler."

a "saver", a quick comeback, which will release the tension that may otherwise occur.

Reply to this type of question by saying "you did? Well would you like to see my nose wiggle?" Another comeback, "Of course you did, you didn't think this thing could really talk did you?" For the latter comeback, having the puppet break in to the conversation will help preserve the illusion of a living puppet. A sample dialogue is as follows:

Kid: I saw you lips move!

Vent: Of course, you didn't think a dummy can talk did you?

Puppet: Why not—you seem to be doing a good job at it.

Vent: I'm not a dummy . . .

In this way the challenge is avoided and you can continue with your routine uninterrupted. If your dialogue is clever and your acting good, the kids will forget about watching your lips and concentrate on listening to the act.

Finding the Right Voice

Once you have learned how to speak without moving you lips excessively, your next step is to give your partner a unique voice, one completely different from our own. This will give him a separate identity. Finding the right voice for your puppet may take only a minor amount of practice or perhaps several days of experimentation. Try raising and lowering the pitch of your voice. Experiment with all types of voices and do not rely solely on the pitch. Mel Blank makes most of the voices of the characters associated with the Bugs Bunny-Porky Pig cartoons, all of which sound uniquely different.

The first thing most beginners try to do when they bring out a puppet is to use a high-pitched squeaky voice. When you choose a voice for your partner, you will need to keep in mind that the voice must reflect the puppet's character. You must also be able to speak clearly so you can be easily understood. And you must be able to maintain a conversation without undue stress.

What type of character is your partner? Would a deep gruff voice be better than a mousy high-pitched one? Is the character happy, mean, rugged, gentle, dopey, intelligent, youthful, elderly or mechanical like a robot? The voice you choose should be consistent with your puppet's personality.

A voice can convey traits. When we speak of a large but gentle giant who is perhaps slow-witted, the voice that naturally comes to mind is deep and slow, with lot of pauses, such as "Ah . . . da . . . er" to show that he is thinking hard, even on seemingly simple problems.

Watch the children's shows on TV and listen to cartoon characters such as Porky Pig, Yosemite Sam, Elmer Fudd, Yogi Bear, Tweety Bird, Mickey Mouse, Goofy and others. Watch Sesame Street.

Try to define your puppet's character as much as possible with the voice you choose. A squeaky voice may be suitable for a mouse figure but would be out of place for a lion, alligator, frog, or a policeman.

A careful choice of slang or descriptive words and an accent can help out tremendously in giving your

> Woman: Doctor hurry please! My little boy just swallowed a fountain pen.
> Doctor: I'll be there right away. What are you doing in the meantime?
> Woman: I'm using a pencil.

puppet character. Be careful not to overdo it so as to become difficult to understand; audiences, especially young ones, get restless if they can't follow the conversation.

After you have chosen an appropriate voice, practice it using as little lip movement as possible. As you do this, it is helpful to use your puppet and think of yourself as teaching it how to talk, rather than just learning ventriloquism. It is more fun this way and you can start memorizing or creating new material.

Using a tape recorder will help you correct problems with speech, vocal clarity, and other bad habits.

If you have a desire to use puppets, yet don't know where to start in creating a dialogue, you can purchase ready made scripts from Maher Studios.

Animation

Having a unique voice for your puppet and using a clever dialogue will do a great deal in making your partner "real". Hearing a voice and seeing the puppet's lips move while yours do not will create the illusion that the puppet can speak. But even though your lips may be perfectly still, if your puppet's movements are unnatural or awkward, the illusion will be destroyed.

The most basic movement to master is the puppet's mouth (if it has a movable jaw). Each syllable must be synchronized with the opening and closing of the puppet's mouth. Practice synchronizing syllables with your puppet's mouth movements. Lips which are not in harmony with the sound look fake—even to the youngest viewer.

Movement of the puppet's lips will also draw the eyes of the audience away from you and towards your partner. This is another reason why slight movement of your lips is not usually noticed.

Sudden jerky moves always attract attention, even when done innocently. Jerking the puppet's head as it begins to speak or to emphasize emotion will draw everybody's attention. Ventriloquists often use this technique when pronouncing a word that requires lip movement. Quickly opening the puppet's mouth, moving arms, legs torso, etc. will produce a similar effect.

Once you've mastered lip synchronization, you should practice using body language. Remember you are trying to give the illusion that the puppet is a living, intelligent creature. To create this illusion, the puppet needs to reenforce his thoughts and words with physical movement. Just as people move their arms and body

Doris: Can you telephone from an airplane?
Daisy: Sure, anyone can tell a phone from an airplane. The plane is the one without the dial tone.

while in conversation, so should your puppet twist its body, lean forward and back or from side to side, jump, and move the head in all directions—even upside down if you can. Have him chew on props, mess your hair, or give you a hug. These actions will give your partner life and character. But avoid being jittery or too repetitious in the movement as this can be distracting.

One of the most common mistakes beginners make is ignoring the puppet's eye contact. When your partner speaks to you, he should be looking in your direction and not at the wall. You need to be consciously aware of where your partner is looking at all times. Would you look at someone's shoes and say "You look good in that hat?" If your partner says "Is it going to rain?" he should be looking towards the sky. Making your partner see is one of the most important principals in learning to manipulate a puppet properly.

The Muppets are very popular because they look and act like they are truly alive. The characters are well defined and move and act naturally so that the audience easily forgets that they are only puppets.

What if your puppet doesn't have a moveable mouth? You don't need the mouth to move in order to make him talk. Even without the figure's lips moving, you can create the illusion that the puppet is talking by careful manipulation. Moving the puppet's body while giving him a voice will make it appear as though he is talking. Give him full actions. Have him point to himself when he says "Me", rub his eyes when crying, shake the head "No" and nod "Yes." Have him act out as much of his dialogue as possible.

This brings us now to the next section on non-verbal communication.

Non-Verbal Communication

Not all puppets have to speak. Some puppets are not openly verbal but use mime or 'whisper' so that only the performer can hear.

This method works well if you're not good at ventriloquism or if you are using puppets that do not have a movable mouth. I have a routine in which I use "intelligent" juggling balls. They talk to me so only I can hear and we carry on conversations along with our juggling.

When this method is used, the performer must relate to the audience much of what the puppet is saying. Your dialogue would sound much like a telephone conversation with you repeating key words spoken by your partner. Here are some examples:

"What do you mean you don't like pickled fig jelly?"
"Yes, I know you want a motorcycle but I can't afford it."
"Don't tell me you're going to quit!"
"What—you didn't go to school today!"
"Stop crying, I can hardly understand you."

Most puppets have legs, arms, head, or torso that can move to indicate communication. Even simple objects like my juggling balls, which have no arms or legs, can communicate physically. I ask one a question and it can answer "Yes" or "No" by bobbing up an down or swaying back and forth while I hold it. It can demonstrate playfulness when I ask it to do something but does something else. It may show defiance or anger by hitting me on the forehead. When it tells a secret, it will whisper in my ear even though nobody can hear it talk. Juggling the ball gives it movement and direction. It can "run" off the stage, follow a pretty girl, do a double take, or stop to take a coffee break. The possibilities are endless.

CREATING CHARACTER

Just as the clown you portray must have a distinct character, so should your puppets. You are trying to make them act as living creatures, and, as such, they should possess distinct personalities. The puppet's personality should be consistent throughout the show. The audience expects the "performers" to have separate and consistent personalities. If they don't, the audience becomes confused and the figures lose their appeal, appearing more like objects than living characters.

What type of personality traits should your partner have? Use the following list to help define your partner's character. Is it male, female; young, old; happy, grumpy; rude, well mannered; clumsy, skilled; smart, dumb; mischievous, kind; brave, or cowardly?

To help build an interesting character, you should give your puppet likes and dislikes on subjects such as music, clothes, sports, books, friends, and food.

What about his education and background? Where was he born? Was it in the city or country? Did he graduate from high school, clown college, law school, or a military academy?

What does he do for a profession? Is he a singer, acrobat, dancer, farmer, student or hobo?

Use these ideas to help define your partner's character and keep each puppet in character when you perform.

CLOWNS AND PUPPETS IN PERFORMANCE

You have a puppet, how would you use it? There are those clowns who just put a puppet on their hand and have it say "Hi boy and girls, how are you?" After showing the puppet, it is put away just like it were another magic trick. Well any child with half an imagination will tell you that "You just had a puppet on your hand!"

Your puppet should come to life for your audience the same way you come to life for them behind your clown makeup. Always relate to the puppet as a co-star and not a doll or a toy. It does no good to be a skilled puppeteer and have a convincing puppet voice and character if you treat it like a puppet. It's a fantasy character just like your clown. Make it as real as it can be and react to it just as you would a pet or a pal. If it's a dog puppet, it might always want to lick you in the face like a real dog, which you may or may not enjoy. Or it could be continuously hungry, always bagging for a dog biscuit. By reacting to your puppet as if you believed it were alive, you make the audience believe the fantasy you've created.

Puppets can be used as partners or assistants in a variety of ways. Routines may consist of a simple comic conversation or can involve a demonstration of talents and skills like magic, singing, and juggling.

Magic and Puppets

Depending on the type of puppet that you use, you can perform many different magic tricks. In doing magic with a puppet, you will need to scale the size of the props to the puppet. Never use a trick which is so large that it is difficult for the puppet to manipulate properly. An example of this is a hand puppet trying to use a professional size Square Circle Box. The box is much to large for the puppet to even show that it is empty. Buy and use smaller props or make your own to the size you need.

With a mouth puppet, all manipulation of the props or tricks are done with the puppet's mouth. Ordinary tasks such as picking up a magic wand and waving it can appear humorous when done by one of these puppets. You, as the magic clown, might show a box to be empty then have the puppet reach in the box with it's mouth and pull out silks or ribbons. The use of mouthcoils are just perfect for a mouth puppet if assisted by you or a second puppet.

In performance with a hand and glove puppet, you can really perform any magic trick that you can do with one hand (or two if you're using an extra puppeteer). This type of puppet can even palm a coin (if the puppeteer already knows how to palm objects) and produce it from a child's ear.

Some of the popular magic tricks I have found that work well with puppets are listed below. Most of these can be purchased in any magic shop.

Finger Puppets:

- Flower Wand
- Egg Vase
- Production Boxes (scaled to size)
- Prayer Vase
- Silk Blow
- Metamorpho Spots
- Mini Chicken Pan
- Mini Rice Bowls

Mouth Puppets:

- Metamorpho Spots
- Hold That Tiger
- Dove Pan
- Foo Can
- Mouthcoils
- Sponge Ball
- Hippity-Hop Rabbits
- Paper Fir Tree

Hand and Glove Puppets:

- All the tricks listed for finger and mouth puppets
- Wilting Flower
- Clippo
- Sammy the Seal
- Rigid Hank
- Skeleton in the Closet
- Snake Foo Can
- Cagey Canister
- Chained Lighting
- Rabbit Wand

Because of certain limitations (strings) marionettes are rather hard to use for magic tricks. This is not to say it's impossible, but you'll have to work around the strings. Having a puppet perform magic adds to the world of fantasy that the clown creates.

Juggling and Puppets

I have previously described how I use talking balls as puppet-like partners in my juggling act. Other juggling props such as clubs, rings, bean bags, and cigar boxes work equally as well. Any of these props can be used like a pal or pet having their own personality which will lead the juggler into many comic situations.

Stuffed animals or bean bag animals can make interesting juggling companions. The Chasley company sells several animal shaped bean bags, such as bears and dogs, just for jugglers.

Puppets can also be used like a juggling partner to help juggle other props. Hand puppets (particulary mouth puppets) can be easily adapted by the juggling clown to manipulate most any juggling prop. Mouth puppets fit on the juggler's hand much like a glove so that the puppet's mouth is used to catch and toss the balls or clubs.

Whether you juggle balls, balance poles, do magic, sing, or make balloon animals, you can use puppets or talking props in your act. Use your imagination and experiment. How about a talking unicycle or kazoo?

Third Arm Puppetry

When puppets perform on small stages, the puppeteer is hidden from the audience. Clowns, on the other hand, perform in full view with their puppets so that everyone can see how they are manipulated. By hiding the hand that controls the puppet, the clown reenforces the illusion that his companion is alive. This is where "Third Arm Puppetry", as I call it, comes in.

Third arm puppetry is the illusion that your hands and arms are holding a box or bucket in which the puppet lives in. I would like to introduce you to a device called a "third arm jacket" (see illustration). This device can give you that extra hand and create a magical illusion.

Take a jacket or shirt and attach a long opera-length glove that has been stuffed with either cotton or foam into one of the sleeves. Carefully, cut a hole in the chest of the jacket on the same side which has the fake arm so that your real arm can enter the prop to work the puppet. On each of the fingers of the fake arm,

attach either Velcro or snaps which will secure the arm to the prop. Now you have a third arm jacket, complete with a fake arm which can go around any prop that you wish the puppet to perform from. On the hand which is not operating the puppet, wear an identical glove to match the fake hand.

In any performance with puppets, always give proper action-reaction. Your action or the puppet's, deserves an equal reaction. If the puppet is misbehaving and you give it a reprimand, it might act good for awhile but then acts even worse and ending up hitting you. Comic timing between you and the puppet will make the audience believe even more in the reality of the puppet. The following are some clown-puppet walk-around gags which use the principal of the Third Arm Jacket.

A Dog Catcher. Armed with a net and a box of dog biscuits, you play the part of the evil town dog catcher. Look for stray dogs, calling "Here doggy" and waving a giant dog biscuit. All this time the dog keeps popping out of the box of biscuits—to the audience's delight, but you never notice.

Arnold "Giggles" Firine

College Professor. Dressed as a college professor in cap and gown you are carring a stack of books (fake stack, really boxes glued together and painted to look like books). The fake arm is attached to this stack of books. Have a puppet book worm (or snake) pop out of the top of the stack. Comic ideas could be that the worm shoots out water or baby powder (looking like smoke).

A Magician. Enter carrying a giant top hat. Wave a magic wand over the top hat, and a rabbit puppet pops up. Seeing the magic wand, the rabbit takes it away and disappears. You try to get the wand back by reaching inside the hat. Then the rabbit pops up again and hits you on the head with the wand.

A Plant Salesman. As you carry a tray full of lovely looking plants which you are trying to sell, one appears to be alive. Sometimes it stands straight up and other times it acts as if it is thirsty. So you water the plant with a watering can and it appears happy. Then it begins to spray water back at you and the audience.

All of these clown puppet gags have a hole in the rear of the prop so that your real arm and hand can operate the puppet or the squeeze bulb (containing water or baby powder). These gags work best in most parade/circus type walk-around situations.

BEING A CLOWN PUPPETEER

There are many types of puppets available on the market to choose from or you may also create your own. In building and designing your puppets and props, keep the look simple. It makes no sense to build a puppet or gag which is too complex or heavy to work. In creating a puppet, always give the character a cartoon look which makes it a lovable.

For points of reference in building your puppets, Props Unlimited (P.O. Box 3440, Reno, NV 89505) supplies a package of 14 different puppet patterns (dog, cat, dragon, chickens, etc.). These puppets are created out of fake fur and have the look of the puppets see on TV. Other sources for puppet patterns come from Simplicity (the clothing pattern company) although these puppets don't look as professional. If you are choosing to build, do not use those shaky eyes such as the ones sold in the arts and crafts stores. They just don't look real, ping pong balls cut in half (or used whole) are much more convincing.

Again keep in mind the design of the puppet and what you may want it to do. Less is best, but build it to last long. Create the most realistic puppet that you can. Look at other puppets, art books, comics to get the best features.

Being a clown puppeteer means that you will always have a comic partner to work with. Treat your puppet a loving pet or intelligent pal and the comedy and fun will happen for you and your audiences.

CHAPTER 11

HOW TO JUGGLE FUNNY

Juggling . . . just the thought of the word brings visions of performers having great physical dexterity and skill as well as exhibiting scenes of buffoonery and nonsense.

The art of clowning and the skill of juggling have gone hand in hand for centuries. Our present day concept of the medieval clown or court jester is that of a juggler.

Juggling still is one of the basic clown skills. In fact, a clown who can not juggle is considered unusual by most people. In my opinion every clown should know at least the basics of this skillful art.

JUGGLING AS AN ART

For clowns, juggling is more than just tossing around three balls or performing spectacular tricks. The ability to make an audience laugh by mixing juggling and clever dialogue is an art.

In this chapter I will not only explain how to juggle, the easy way, but I will describe several ways to make your juggling funny and to stimulate your imagination.

The things a juggler can do even with just three balls is limitless. An endless variety of tricks (and jokes) can be conceived and mastered with practice.

Fancy juggling tricks alone will not make a juggler funny. For this reason I have included a section on funny juggling, in which I describe some of the things

jugglers can do to get laughs. This section is provided to give you some ideas which I hope will inspire you to create humorous jokes and routines of your own.

JUGGLING AS A SKILL

Some people are hesitant to learn juggling and others are easily discouraged because they don't know the "secret" to keeping three moving objects in the air. After only a few minutes practice, they give up in despair.

Juggling is as much a skill as it is an art, and like any skill requires a certain amount of time and effort to learn. Many people have learned to juggle on their own, usually very determined people who learn by pure repetition, trial and error. This method is discouraging because it wastes so much energy and takes a great deal of time.

I have taught many students to juggle over the past several years and have developed what I feel is a sure fire system for learning to juggle. I explain the "secret" of juggling so that anyone, no matter how uncoordinated they think they are, can learn. If you were able to learn to ride a bicycle, then you can learn to juggle.

The advantages of learning how to juggle are tremendous. In my opinion every clown or future clown should learn enough about juggling to be able to perform the "cascade," the fundamental three object pattern used by all jugglers. Most new jugglers start by practicing this pattern because it is the easiest movement to learn. Jugglers use it as a "rest position" between the more difficult tricks.

THE JUGGLER'S TOOLS

Let's begin with the tools or props best suited for a beginner. Jugglers use a variety of props ranging from ordinary balls to knives, axes, rings, clubs, plates, torches, and even chain saws.

Small balls have traditionally been used as the standard juggling prop. Because of their spherical shape, they are relatively easy to catch and control. Bean bags, which also are basically spherical, have become increasingly popular.

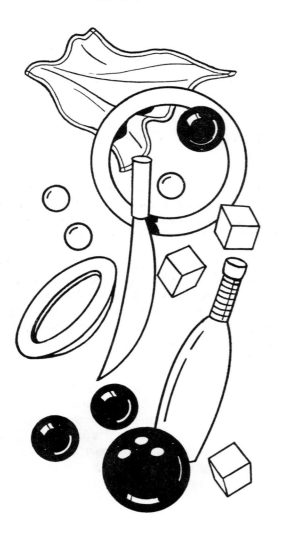

Objects which are not round, such as clubs and rings, require an added spinning motion to keep them in balance. Before attempting to juggle nonspherical objects, you should first learn to juggle with balls or bean bags.

The best type of ball to use is one that is small enough so that two can fit comfortably in the palm of your hand; about two to three inches in diameter.

The heavier a ball is, the more manageable it becomes. Lightweight balls such as racquetballs have a tendency to bounce a bit in the palm of the hand when being caught, which increases the difficulty of juggling.

The best balls are those which are easy to grab and relatively heavy. Lacrosse balls have these properties and make excellent juggling balls. If nothing else is available, tennis balls will suffice.

For a beginner I highly recommend bean bags. They are heavier than ordinary balls and don't bounce around in the hand, making them easy to catch and control. Another important feature of the bean bag that beginners will appreciate is that it won't bounce or roll away when dropped. This saves the time and effort of crawling under the sofa and around chairs to retrieve stray balls.

JUGGLING—THE EASY WAY

I will describe in detail the steps used to learn the cascade juggling pattern. The system I use stresses a gradual progression of skill development, requiring six steps. Each step must be mastered before moving on to the next. The first step teaches how to throw and catch one ball correctly. The other steps build on this and gradually two and three balls are used.

Learning to juggle in a progressive manner like this is the real secret to juggling. If you started out at the beginning with three balls, as many people attempt to do, you would be overwhelmed and more likely than not would become discouraged.

Step One

Before doing anything else, imagine two spots about at forehead level, one just to the right of your head and the other just to the left. Both spots should be about a foot in front of your face (Figure 13-1). These will be your control points and are VERY IMPORTANT!

Figure 13-1

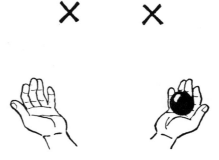

Figure 13-3

Take one ball into the palm of your right hand and hold it at about stomach level in front of you (Figure 13-2). From the juggler's point of view it would look like Figure 13-3. Toss the ball up and across to the imaginary spot on the left side of your forehead. When it comes down catch it in the left hand (Figure 13-4).

Toss the ball from your left hand up to the imaginary spot at the right side of your forehead. As it falls, catch it with your right hand (Figure 13-5). The ball has now made one round trip in a figure-eight pattern (Figure 13-6).

Practice this pattern with one ball, making sure it hits the imaginary spots on each side of your head. Don't throw the ball too high or too low. Focus your attention at these spots and make your throws as consistent as possible. Right now it doesn't seem to be a problem if you don't get the ball to hit the spots exactly, but it will become vital as you work up to three balls, so practice it right.

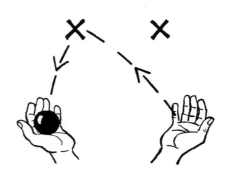

Figure 13-4

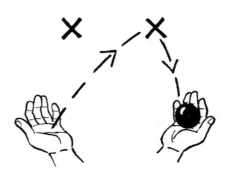

Figure 13-5

Figure 13-2

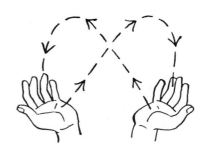

Figure 13-6

As you're practicing, make sure not to reach up to grab the ball as it comes down. Let the ball fall into your hand. As you are learning make it a point never to raise your hands above chest level when either throwing or catching. Continue to practice this step until you feel comfortable with it.

Step Two

Now that you have mastered juggling one ball, you can try two. Put one ball in each hand. Keep your elbows bent, and your hands away from your body but at stomach level.

Throw the ball in the right hand up to the imaginary spot on the left side of your head (Figure 13-7). When the ball reaches this spot, toss the ball which is in your left hand toward the imaginary spot on the right side of your head (Figure 13-8). As soon as you release the ball from your left hand, quickly catch, with your

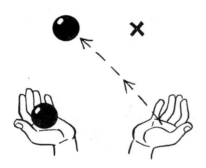

Figure 13-7

Figure 13-8

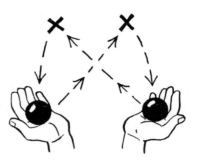

Figure 13-9

left hand, the ball thrown by the right hand. Finally, the right hand will catch the ball thrown by the left hand (Figure 13-9).

You have just made a simple two-ball exchange. The ball which started in the right hand, is now in the left and vice versa. Repeat this sequence, starting with the right hand until you can catch the balls every time.

It is important that the balls are thrown as close to the imaginary spots as possible. Don't watch your hands or follow the movement of the balls; keep your eyes focused at the two imaginary points. I cannot emphasize this point enough. A ball that is not tossed correctly will throw off your timing, causing you to drop it. This will become more evident when you start to use three balls.

To help keep your timing consistent you might want to throw the balls as you say "right-left." Throw the ball in the right hand as you say "right." When it reaches the imaginary spot, say "left" and throw the left hand ball.

Step Three

Repeat the procedure in Step Two, except this time start by throwing the ball that is in the left hand first. This sounds easy, but at first it's a little more difficult than you might think. Continue to practice this step until you can catch the balls every time. When you can do this consistently, move on to Step Four.

Ed: Do you have holes in your underwear?
Fred: What an insult! Of course I don't have holes in my underwear.
Ed: Then how do you get your feet through?

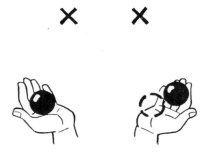

Figure 13-10

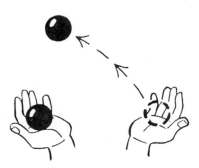

Figure 13-11

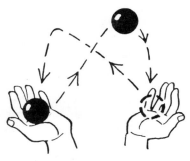

Figure 13-12

Step Four

Take one ball in each hand. Imagine an invisible third ball in your right hand along with the real one already there. You now have one real ball in your left hand, and one real ball and one invisible ball in your right hand (Figure 13-10).

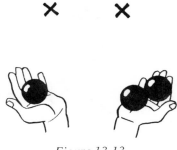

Figure 13-13

Begin by tossing the real ball from your right hand in the normal figure-eight pattern. Continue as you did in Step Two. When the first ball reaches the imaginary spot on the left side of your head, toss the second ball from your left hand toward the imaginary spot on the right (Figure 13-11). Quickly catch the first ball with the left hand.

Up to this point you have been doing the same thing as you did in Step Two. But now here's the difference: as the second ball reaches the imaginary spot on the right, go through the motion of tossing the invisible third ball from the right hand before you catch the descending second ball (Figure 13-12).

This exercise gives the beginner practice in throwing a third ball without the added worry of catching it or getting the throw exactly right. Practice until you feel confident with it.

Step Five

In this step you do the same thing as you did in Step Four, except this time replace the invisible ball with a real ball (Figure 13-13).

Proceed as you did in the last step. When you get to the point of throwing the third ball, concentrate on the accuracy of the throw. Make sure it goes to the imaginary spot on the left side of your head. Don't worry about catching it right now, let it drop to the floor.

The purpose of this step is to give you some practice in actually throwing the third ball and making the throw correctly. Check yourself as you practice this, making sure each of the three balls hits the imaginary spots.

For some people this step will come easily and they will naturally move on to Step Six.

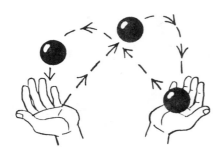

Figure 13-14

Step Six

Here it is, the final step. If you have practiced Steps One through Five and can perform them with confidence, this step will come much easily.

Pick up all three balls. Hold one ball in your left hand and two balls in your right. Do the same thing that you did in Step Five, but this time catch the third ball as it comes down. Make sure you throw the ball that is already in your hand before catching the next one.

Continue by tossing and catching each ball in succession. DON'T STOP! Keep tossing the balls in the figure-eight pattern (Figure 13-14).

After the first two throws, the right hand is doing exactly the same thing as the left, catching and throwing the balls, that's all there is to it. If you can do this without stopping, you're juggling!

The jump between Steps Five and Six is a big one, and generally will require more practice than the other steps. Expect to spend some time on this. If you feel you're having more difficulty than you should, back up a step or two and practice that step some more. I guarantee that if you follow these steps and don't give up, you will learn to juggle.

JUGGLING TRICKS

The reason juggling attracts attention and interests people is because of its apparent difficulty. The average person cannot juggle. People look at jugglers with amazement and admiration for being able to do such a difficult thing. If learning to juggle were easy, it would lose its audience appeal. Once you have crossed over the barrier and are able to keep three balls going

at the same time, juggling seems very simple. Like walking or riding a bike, once you learn how to do it, you never forget.

As you practice, your skill will improve and you will gradually want to add tricks and variations. Jokes can be told with most any type of juggling pattern. Many creative routines using physical comedy and slapstick, need a certain degree of juggling proficiency.

In order to bungle juggling, as clowns are often expected to do, they must know what it is they are attempting to bungle. They need to be skilled enough to juggle correctly and to make the bungle look spontaneous, realistic, and funny.

A good way to learn a new trick is to break it up into smaller pieces and practice it a step at a time, just as you did when learning the cascade. Let's take the knee bounce as an example. This trick consists of bouncing one ball off the top of the knee while juggling in the cascade pattern.

The hardest part of this trick is hitting the ball with the knee and having it rebound up to a position in which it can be easily caught. The bounce must be made directly on top of the knee. If it is not, the ball will rebound off to the side, where it may be almost impossible to catch.

The ball must also be hit with just enough force to send it up where it will blend back into the cascade pattern. Hitting it either too hard or too softly will blow the trick.

Start by using just one ball. Toss it up as you would when juggling and hit it with your knee. At first it will be rather difficult to control, but with a little practice, you will begin to get the feel of it.

When you can do the bounce correctly, try using two balls. Put one ball in each hand and do a simple exchange. Toss the ball in your right hand to the left side, then toss the left-hand ball to the right. Catch the first ball with the left hand, but let the second ball come down and bounce off the right knee.

When you can do this without problem, move on to three balls. Juggle in the cascade pattern and attempt the knee bounce. It will take some practice, but you've built a good foundation by taking gradual steps.

Many tricks are best learned using this simple step-at-a-time method. Take the hardest movement and practice it first with one ball, then two, and finally three.

There isn't room enough in this book to explain in detail all the possible tricks you could do, but with the ideas I have presented, you can experiment on your own. Use the method described above and try these tricks: under the leg, under the arm, behind the back, bounce the ball on the floor, head bounce, arm bounce,

Patrica "Pokey Patti" Gonsalves and Donald "Dee Gee" Gonsalves.

foot bounce.

Once you have learned a trick with one hand or on one side of the body, learn how to do it on the other side. Jugglers should be ambidextrous; every trick they know with one hand can be performed with the other. To limit yourself to one hand greatly reduces the variety of tricks possible. Once you learn a trick on one side, it's easier to learn on the other, and you can add other tricks by combining the right and left sides of your body. For example, the knee bounce should be learned so that a ball can be bounced back and forth between each knee.

GREAT SKILL NOT REQUIRED

Make 'Em Laugh

Learning to manipulate three or more objects in the air, although interesting for a time, is not entertaining. Sure you'll attract a great deal of attention and get people to look at you, but if you don't do anything funny, extremely difficult, or dangerous, people will become bored. Because of this, you will need to work in material that will entertain the audience.

Juggling is only a tool used by the clown to get laughs. The humor comes from the way the clown presents himself, regardless of his juggling skill. Just learning to juggle will not make you funny, but it can provide opportunities for you to be funny.

Getting Attention

One of the distinct advantages of juggling is its ability to attract attention. You don't need to be an accomplished juggler to do this. Just the sight of a juggler sparks interest and draws crowds, an obvious advantage for any clown who works malls, fairs, and other places where there are many distractions.

Knowing the basic three-ball cascade is enough to grab and hold an audience, if combined with some clever dialogue or actions. Once a crowd has gathered, the juggling can be replaced, if necessary, by other talents to entertain the audience.

In this instance, the juggling was used only to draw a crowd and was not meant to be the main part of the act. In a more formal setting, such as in a circus or on stage, where the audience is seated, juggling can be used as a warm-up before the main act.

Warm-ups need to be only a few minutes long and help the audience loosen up for the coming acts. They are used as an ice breaker, so to speak, and tell the audience to get ready for some fun and laughter.

In some places, such as parades or walk-arounds, the most elementary juggling movements are all that's needed.

Non-Juggling Juggling

You don't have to be an expert juggler to entertain an audience. Some of the juggling routines I perform contain no real juggling at all; I use mime and verbal expression to act out the juggling. Surprisingly, these have been some of my most successful routines.

I have one routine where I juggle three mosquitoes. Since the mosquitoes are too small for the audience to

Ed: Did you hear about the man who lives on onions alone?
Fred: No. But any man who lives on onions ought to live alone.

Doris: Our dog is just like one of the family.
Daisy: Which one?

see, I fake it. After introducing my little helpers to the audience, we move into a conversation which includes funny dialogue and mime juggling. As I juggle, they do a number of humorous things. I can pretend to be a very competent juggler by performing the most spectacular juggling tricks (it's easy to do hard tricks when you don't have anything in your hands).

Many different types of juggling can be devised without props. One way is to use very tiny objects, such as my mosquitoes, which are too small to be seen. Other small objects of this sort could be flies, peas, rice, tiny space creatures, germs, and daffagoyals . . . Daffagoyals? What's that? . . . I don't know, but use your imagination and invent things like this.

Another idea is to use invisible objects. These can be most anything that has been exposed to atomic radiation or shot with an invisibility ray. It's much easier to balance an invisible bowling ball on the tip of your nose than a real one, and you can still make all of the funny faces that a trick like this might cause.

You can also use imaginary objects and only pretend to juggle something. I have another routine in which I find myself on stage without any juggling props. I tell the audience I'm going to juggle for them but can't find anything suitable.

The problem is solved when I remove my eyeballs and juggle them. Each eyelid is closed as I remove the eye to show that it's no longer in my head. When I juggle, the audience must use their imagination and follow my actions. Be creative, use your imagination.

A great deal of juggling skill is not needed for these types of acts. However, knowledge of juggling gives me a base on which to build a non-juggling juggling routine and gets my mind thinking from a juggler's perspective. By knowing how the tricks are supposed to look, I can make them appear realistic.

Non-juggling juggling routines can be very effective but don't limit yourself to them. The more skill you have as a juggler, the more variety you will have and the more jokes will be available for you.

Whenever I do routines like these I always add some real juggling, either before or after. People like to see juggling, and if I tell them I'm a juggler, they would be disappointed if I didn't do any real juggling.

HANDLING DROPS

Dropping a prop is probably the biggest problem jugglers have to face. For some, an occasional drop is not very serious. Besides, clowns are supposed to be clumsy, aren't they? Yes, to some extent, but a good performing clown drops on purpose, not by accident.

All jugglers even the best, drop a prop now and then; it's unavoidable. A dropped prop can have a damaging effect on your act. If done during routine juggling, it may not be too serious, but if a drop occurs at a critical point, say just before a punch line, it may ruin the joke or even a string of jokes to come.

For this reason it's wise to practice a new trick thoroughly before presenting it in front of an audience. As a rule of thumb, you should be able to do the trick 90 percent of the time before including it in an act.

Even with this precaution, drops will still occur; if not handled wisely, you could begin to lose self-confidence. The audience, instead of laughing with you, will begin to feel sorry for you.

Turning Drops Into Jokes

Since an occasional drop is unavoidable, you need to prepare for it in advance. Memorize jokes associated with dropping props. For instance, you could be

Comic juggler John R. Mallery working with devil sticks.

juggling three balls when one drops. Instead of looking embarrassed and building up tension, frown and yell, "YOU'RE FIRED!" This keeps the act running smoothly and saves you from unneeded embarrassment.

The audience will soon forget that you ever dropped anything. If done well, they will believe the drop was part of the act. I have purposely dropped props just so I could use some of my dropped prop lines.

Plan ahead and think of three or four different dropped prop lines you could use. Memorize these and use them whenever the occasion arises. To give you some ideas of the of things you might say here is a list of a few dropped prop lines.

(1) Point your finger to one side of the audience and shout, "E-GAD! . . . Look at that giant hairy tarantula!" As the audience turns to look, quickly pick up the dropped prop. "Oh no, my mistake, it was just the man with the beard in the front row."

(2) While bending over to pick up the prop say, "This act is picking up."

(3) After dropping the prop, quickly grab something else, such as a hat or a handkerchief, and continue juggling as if nothing happened.

(4) Sew a small ball inside a handkerchief and stick it in your back pocket or some other easily accessible spot. When a drop occurs, take out the handkerchief and wipe your brow saying, "Phew, I must be getting tired." Now bounce the handkerchief on the floor to get a laugh.

(5) After dropping a prop, continue to juggle as if nothing happened. Suddenly notice that you only have two objects in your hand and say, "Why didn't you tell me I dropped one?"

(6) If you're juggling bean bags or non-bouncing balls, stop after the drop and look confused. Stare at the prop as if something was wrong. Pick it up at arm's length and let it drop again. "Yep, it's got a flat." Pretend to pump or blow it up with air, then test it by bouncing it off your knee, arm, or foot to show that it's working again.

(7) Have a foam rubber hammer concealed nearby. When the prop is dropped, take out the hammer and hit yourself over the head. If you drop the prop two or three times, this can be used as a running gag throughout your act. The second time you can hit yourself again, but the third time get mad and take out your frustration by vigorously hitting the dropped prop.

(8) "Quick! Everybody close your eyes . . . are everyone's eyes closed?" Frantically pick up the prop and start juggling as if nothing happened and continue, "For my next trick . . ."

(9) "Wasn't my fault; there was a sudden gust of gravity."

(10) When the prop falls, let out a scream: "Yahhhh—stop that!" At the same time drop the rest of the props and jump back. "Sorry about that." Rub an apparently sore hand, "I've only had these things for a couple of months and they just started teething."

Interruption Method

Another way of saving yourself when a drop occurs is what I call the interruption method. When the prop falls, stop, look at the audience, and tell a joke. Any funny joke will do, it doesn't have to relate to juggling or to anything you're doing.

As an example, after your mishap step toward the audience and say "Did you know that the first real cure for dandruff was the guillotine?" Then pick up the props and continue as if nothing had happened.

Dropping a prop creates a break in the performance, which is distracting and harmful to good showmanship. Using the drop as a means to tell a joke or a funny story fills this gap and lets the act run smoothly. The fact that the joke has nothing to do with juggling or with what you're doing adds to the humor of the situation. Memorize a few jokes or stories for just such occasions.

CREATIVE JUGGLING

Funny Juggling

I believe that most clowns who juggle only occasionally don't juggle more often because they can't think of anything funny to do or say. If they had a lot of funny juggling material, they would use it. The problem is that they don't juggle enough. You can't expect to create funny material if you don't put some effort into it.

As you continue to practice and as your skill improves, you will get urges to try new juggling patterns or tricks. Gradually you will add more variations to your bag of tricks, which will open up many new opportunities for jokes.

When I practice my juggling, I make it fun by doing silly things and attempting things I can't do. This activates my creative juices and leads me to create new comic material and new juggling tricks.

The tricks you use don't have to be difficult in order to be effective. I have some very simple tricks(?) I like to use, such as juggling on one foot (either mine or someone else's), jogging in place while juggling (joggling), stretching one leg at a time in the air (Richard Simmons juggling), and many others. My body is doing something while I juggle in the cascade. These tricks are some of the easiest any juggler can do, yet the audience gets a kick out of them because I put life into them and make them look silly. I always get laughs with them. These tricks and others were dreamed up just by fooling around while practicing.

By making your juggling practice fun and by goofing around as you do it, you will stimulate your imagination. The time you spend practicing will be more enjoyable and will help you create new comic juggling material.

Use of Props

The type of props you use has a dramatic effect on the type of jokes you create and use. The standard juggling props are balls, clubs, and rings. These props are popular because they are so versatile and much can be done with them. You shouldn't restrict yourself just to these however. Other objects can add a whole new appearance to your act and provide a change of pace. Experiment with shoes, hats, rubber ducks, electric razors, and other objects. Just attempting to juggle new things will lead you to create new jokes and gags.

Take an apple, a cigar, and a shoe for example. A routine can be worked out with these props which would not be possible with standard juggling props. The juggler tells the audience he will perform the famous apple eating trick while juggling these three objects.

As he juggles, he attempts to take a bite out of the apple. Grabbing the cigar by mistake, he sticks it into his mouth and bites off the end. He begins chewing, makes a sickly face, chokes, and swallows.

He attempts the trick again, but this time he sticks

Bettmann Archive

Tramp juggler W.C. Fields performing a vaudeville act, May 1900.

the shoe into his mouth, followed by comical reactions and facial expressions.

He tries it one last time. Finally he is able to bite the apple, but unfortunately his finger is caught between his teeth and he can't remove it. This can then lead into more comical situations. Other such gags can be created with similar props.

Many specially prepared props are available from novelty shops ranging from rubber eggs and chickens to toilet plungers and giant fly swatters. Inserting a dowel rod into a rubber chicken to stiffen it creates a comic club. One common prop sold is a set of three billiard eight-balls. The clown asks the audience, "Would you like me to juggle eight balls?" He then proceeds to juggle the three eight-balls and gets a laugh.

Bean bags made specifically for juggling are available in a variety of shapes ranging from teddy bears to whales to dinosaurs. Some clowns make their own bean bags and fill them with rice, aquarium sand, or plastic pellets. Using appropriate comments with such props can be very funny, toss a dinosaur and announce, "This is my friend Dino . . . watch Dino soar." If you drop one, explain, "Now you know why they are extinct." An effective bit when any animal is dropped is to give it artificial respiration.

Some props, such as juggling scarves and balloons, require very little juggling skill. Lightweight scarves made especially for juggling can be purchased in novelty shops. Because they are so light, scarves and balloons float to the ground giving the juggler plenty of time to grab and toss them back into the air. Even non-jugglers can learn to do this with relative ease. Many tricks which cannot be performed with regular juggling props can be easily accomplished with scarves and balloons.

The slow motion effect of these falling props adds a degree of humor to the juggling action, especially if combined with a frantic, quickly moving juggler. My scarf juggling routine is one of my most successful stunts. It has never failed to bring me thunderous roars of laughter from the audience.

Use your imagination and make your own props. I have many homemade juggling props, such as my spaghetti. It consists simply of spaghetti-colored yarn glued onto a couple of brown painted golf balls (meat balls). I use this for my spaghetti juggling trick.

A whole meal can be juggled by using plates, celery sticks, carrots, and other veggies. You can even eat while you juggle, but be careful not to eat the spaghetti, golf balls don't digest well.

A sense of humor is a form of creativity; it's the uncanny ability to make ordinary things funny. Whether

the clown uses juggling, puppets, magic, or some other medium, the success of the show depends his performance.

Most juggling acts are made up of a series of jokes and gags. These isolated bits of humor are often related to each other only by the clown's personality and the juggling theme. This type of act works well, especially in walk-arounds and fairs where the audience is mobile. Don't limit yourself to this, tell a story using a theme and add rhymes, music, and other elements to create a complete juggling act.

Combining Skills

Use your imagination and do more than simply juggling. Clowns can use all their skills to make juggling entertaining and funny. No great physical talent is needed, but a good imagination is. To get a new slant or to stimulate new ideas, try combining juggling with unicycling, stilt walking, magic, ventriloquism, or music. Have fun and explore the possibilities.

Some of my favorite juggling routines involve talking props. I use both the standard balls and clubs, and specially prepared hand puppets and stuffed animals. The props in essence become my juggling partners. I can either wear a hand puppet and have it juggle with me, or juggle talking stuffed animals, bean bags, balls and other props.

Customer: Waiter, what kind of soup its this?
I ordered pea soup but this stuff tastes like liver.
Water: I'm sorry sir. I gave you tomato soup by mistake, the pea soup tastes like soap.

The following is an example of one of my juggling hand puppet routines. The "H" stands for Harry, a mouse puppet, and "J" for juggler.

J: Hi, this is my furry little friend Harry. We're the dynamic duo of juggling, man and beast.

H: That's us, that's me, that's him.

J: Don't say "That's me, that's him." You'll get the people mixed up and they won't know which one is the rat.

H: It is hard to tell, isn't it?

J: I'm no rat, dummy!

H: You're right. You're only a dummy.

J: Don't say that. I don't want the people to think I make a living by acting dumb.

H: No, you do it for nothing.

J: Oh, pipe down. You're not so smart; your grades in school are terrible. What's wrong with you?

H: Nothing's wrong with me; they just don't know how to read.

J: Who doesn't?

H: My teacher. Every time I write something, she says she can't read it.

J: Maybe you need some spelling practice. Let's have a test. What does C-A-T spell?

H: Dog.

J: Wrong. Try this, D-O-G.

H: Cat.

J: Wrong again. Try this, P-I-P-E.

H: Cat.

J: No, I'll give you a clue, P-I-P-E is something I smoke.

H: Grass.

J: NO! . . . Let me give you another hint. We have a P-I-P-E in our kitchen that runs along the wall and into the sink.

H: Oh, I know . . . roaches!

J: Harry, if I were a drinking man you would drive me to drink.

H: Do you have a driver's license?

J: Yes, I do.

H: Well, then, drive yourself.

J: Cut that out. Let's do some juggling now. (Turning to the audience.) Harry here is the world's only juggling mouse. He can juggle balls, clubs, apples, and all sorts of stuff. Here, Harry, show them what you can do. (Juggler gives Harry two balls.)

H: OK, here goes. (Harry juggles both balls catching them in his mouth, which is actually the juggler's hand.)

J: That was good, Harry. Now let's add another ball and juggle as a team. Ready?

H: Ready.

J: Here goes. (Harry and juggler do a three-ball cascade and a few simple tricks.) All right, let's do some bouncing tricks.

H: How about the elbow bounce, where we bounce the ball off your elbow.

J: OK, I'll do it first. (Juggler does an elbow bounce.) Now it's your turn. You try it Harry.

H: OK, here goes. (Harry tosses ball up and it comes down on juggler's head.)

J: OUCH! . . . Hey, what's the big idea?

H: It slipped.

J: Oh, all right, let's try it again, the elbow bounce . . . OUCH! (Ball hits juggler again.) You knucklehead, why did you do that?

H: I thought it was funny so I did it again.

J: Well I didn't, so don't do it anymore! I want to try another trick. Let's use this apple and do the apple eating trick.

H: Oh good, I like that trick. (They start to juggle. As the apple lands in Harry's mouth, juggler takes a bite and holds it there, struggling with Harry who is also trying to take a bite.)

J: Hey, what are you doing?

H: You said we were going to do the apple eating trick.

J: That's right, but I'm going to eat the apple, not you.

H: But I'm hungry, and you always get to eat the apple.

J: That's because it's my apple, and besides I'm the leader of this troupe and what I say goes, so I'm eating it. Now let's try it again. (As they are juggling Harry grabs the apple in his mouth and begins chewing. The juggler continues to juggle the two balls in his other hand.) Harry, what are you doing?

H: I'm eating the apple.

J: I told you I was going to eat that apple—now give it here . . . Harry, did you hear me? HARRY! Give me that apple!

H: OK loudmouth. (Harry shoves the apple into the juggler's mouth.)

J: (The apple is stuck in his mouth and he can't pull it out because his other hand is still juggling the two balls. The apple should not be so far in the juggler's mouth as to prevent him from talking in the puppet's voice. Juggler's eyes open wide, his face turns red with anger, he mumbles violently.) Mumble . . . gereggle . . . erg.

H: Are you trying to say something?

J: Mumble . . . errrg!

H: (Harry pulls the apple out.) What's that? I can't hear a word you're saying with this apple in your mouth.

J: WHY YOU LITTL—(Harry sticks the apple back into his mouth.) MUMBLE GERGLE GEEK! (Juggler stops juggling and removes apple.)

H: Didn't your mother ever tell you it's not polite to talk with your mouth full? Tee hee.

J: Harry, what's the big idea?

H: I just wanted to do a trick. You always get to do the good tricks.

J: That's because I'm the star of the show and you're just my dumb assistant.

H: I'm YOUR dumb assistant?

J: Yeah, I think so too. Ha ha—I got you that time.

H: Sticks and stones will break my bones but names will never hurt—

J: That reminds me, our next trick will be to juggle these. (Juggler holds up sticks and stones.)

H: Hold on now, wait a minute—

J: What's the matter?   Are you afraid?

H: Well, ah . . . those stones are really hard . . . and every time we juggle sticks I get hit in the head.

J: I tell you what, I'll even let you do a trick all by yourself.

H: You'll let me do a trick by myself?

J: Yes, that's what I said.

H: Can it be any trick I want?

J: Yes, it can.

H: OK, I'll do it.

J: What's the name of your trick?

H: The name?

J: Yes, what do you call the trick you are about to perform?

H: I call it . . . two rocks down, one stick up.

J: That's an unusual name for a juggling trick.

H: It's an unusual trick.

J: OK, let's see it.   Oh, and be careful, don't break any of your bones.   Hee hee.

H: Don't worry, I won't.   (They begin to juggle two rocks and one stick.)   Here goes, two rocks down and one stick up.   (Harry tosses both rocks onto juggler's foot and tosses stick up so it comes down and hits juggler on the head.)

J: Ouch, ouch . . . ow! . . . Why, you little rat.

H: Ha ha.   How did you like my new trick?

J: I'll show you a new trick.   (Juggler takes puppet off his hand.)   I call this mouse juggling.

H: Hey! (Juggler tosses puppet in air and juggles with him.) Whoa . . . hey . . . yeekes . . .

For additional ideas on novel ways of creating humorous juggling routines read the book *Dr. Dropo's Juggling Buffoonery* by Bruce Fife.   Another good source for comedy juggling material is Rich Chamberlin's *Comedy Juggling*.

CHAPTER 12

BALANCING BUFFOONERY

One of the most popular skills associated with toss juggling is balancing. In fact, one who is skilled at balancing is also referred to as a juggler, jugglers commonly use the two skills in combination.

Balancing is a basic skill jugglers have used for thousands of years. The audience is filled with wonder and amazement at the sight of a performer balancing pool cues, tennis rackets, balls, plates, juggling clubs, swords, and other objects, often while juggling three or more other props.

Professing to have the skill to balance objects, yet never able to do it quite like the "professional juggler," is a source of amusement any clown can use. The clown, who portrays a clumsy showoff, never manages to do the tricks right. He may perform some fine balancing tricks and movements, but appears to be out of control and looks like a goof. All of which makes the clown a hilarious success.

A clown can create much humorous material with the art of balancing; unfortunately, few clowns have actually used this skill to its fullest potential. In this chapter I will explain the types of balancing popular with jugglers and other circus performers. I will describe the different types of balancing methods and how to accomplish them. Most important, I will show you how to present this skill in such a way as to impress and delight your audience. Like juggling, balancing can be combined easily with comic patter and physical humor in an endless variety of ways.

Before you learn the funny side of the art, you must know its fundamentals. I will describe the serious side of balancing first, looking at it from a juggler's point of view, and then will explore the creative humor that can be derived from this skill.

Like toss juggling, this is a skill that can be learned with practice. Learning to balance simple objects is relatively easy and requires much less effort to learn than juggling. Also it's not nearly so physically demanding, although it can be if you plan on balancing bowling balls and truck tires.

BASIC PRINCIPLES

There are four basic types of balancing methods used by jugglers: (1) vertical balancing, (2) horizontal balancing, (3) set balancing, and (4) gyroscopic balancing. The first three are stationary methods; the fourth, gyroscopic balancing, requires that the object be in motion.

To understand balancing, it is helpful to know the concept of *center of gravity*. Every object has a center of gravity, a point in which the entire weight of an object appears to be centered. A fulcrum or support placed directly under this point, called the *equilibrium point* or *rest point*, allows the object to maintain a stationary position. An object is said to be in balance when it is supported at this rest point. When attempting to balance any object, you must find this point first.

The location of the center of gravity varies with the shape of the object and the density of the material it is made of. A sphere made of a single material, such as a cannon ball, has its a center of gravity at its geometric center. A long thin pole has its a center of gravity midway between its two end points.

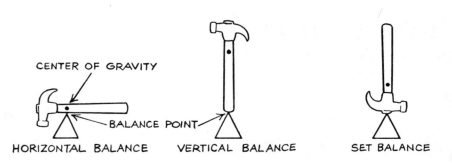

CENTER OF GRAVITY

BALANCE POINT

HORIZONTAL BALANCE   VERTICAL BALANCE   SET BALANCE

Objects with more complex shapes, such as a chair, the center of gravity isn't as easy to locate. It may not even lie within the object itself. A hoop, for example, has its center of gravity in the hole at its center and not on the rim, yet to make a hoop balance vertically you must position the balance point directly below the center of gravity.

The basic difference between the three stationary forms of balancing is the location of the center of gravity in relation to where the object is supported. A hammer has its center of gravity on the neck of the handle just below the head. Its balance point can be located by balancing the hammer horizontally, as shown in the illustration above. In a vertical balance the heaviest end is placed up. For a set balance the heavy end is down.

In each method of balancing, the support is placed directly below the center of gravity. This concept is most important when balancing any object. The support is usually some part of the body; the palm of the hand, a finger, chin, nose, or forehead. Balancing can also be done on other objects, such as the end of a long stick or pedestal. Often both methods are used together, as when a pool cue is balanced vertically on the chin with a ball balanced on top of it.

much experience with balancing but an object with the center of gravity at the upper end moves more slowly if it begins to fall, so it is easier to balance. A four-foot-long broom, for example, balanced with the bristles at the top, is easier to control and keep erect than a four-foot dowel with a lower center of gravity.

If the support is stationary and there is no air movement, an object, once balanced, will remain in balance. Air is seldom stagnant and the human body which is used as the support is never completely motionless. For these reasons the stick is continuously subjected to forces that may cause it to fall. The performer must constantly keep the object in balance by maneuvering the base of the stick so as to keep the balance point directly under its center of gravity.

The best way to accomplish this, and the real "trick" to balancing, is to fix your eyes to the top of the stick and keep them there. Don't look at your hand. The key to vertical balancing is detecting the slightest sway in the stick and correcting for it before the stick falls.

The biggest mistake beginners make when learning this type of balance is not watching the top of the stick. If the stick leans off balance, the first noticeable

VERTICAL BALANCING

Vertical balancing can be described best by using a long linear object such as a pool cue or a yardstick. I will use a yardstick in this explanation, but you can use almost anything of similar shape.

Stand a yardstick or some other linear object on end in the palm of your hand. Align the stick so that its center of gravity is directly above the balance point on your hand. If one end of the object you are using is heavier then the other (mop, baseball bat, tennis racket, pool cue), *place the heaviest end up*. That's right—up. This may sound strange if you haven't had

movement will be detectable at the very top. If you're constantly watching this point, you will be able to see the first sign of movement and will be able to correct it with the least amount of effort. As you practice, you will develop a feel for the balance and will gain greater control, and the movement of the stick will become less perceptible.

Correcting the position of the stick is done by moving the hand forward, backward, left, right, or some combination these. Moving the entire body in the proper direction will accomplish the same thing. A common problem you may encounter is combining both body and arm movements, thus over compensating the correcting force and pushing the stick out of balance in the opposite direction.

Practice Techniques

As you practice you may want to try some of the following subtle techniques, which will help improve your balancing ability.

Low Support. Keeping the balancing point low and close to your body will give you greater control. It will also lower the top of the stick, bringing it closer to eye level where movement can be perceived sooner.

Adjusting the Height. Raising or lowering the hand will also affect the stick. Lowering the stick when it begins to lean to one side will tend to straighten it back up. Lifting the stick up, will only accelerate its fall.

Side-to-Side Motion. Movements from side-to-side are more readily detectable by the eye than those going forward and backward. For this reason you should move the base of the stick sideways whenever possible. You may want to use this idea when purposely trying to move the stick around during your clowning so you will have better control over it.

Minimize Movements. Use the fewest movements possible to keep balance. Move either the hand or the body, but not both. If you move, do so only in one direction; for instance, go left but not forward and left. Make corrections with a single movement if possible.

Balancing Long Objects

What size object is best to balance? Try this. Take a pencil, stand it up vertically in the palm of your hand, and try keeping it in balance. You'll discover that the pencil is much more difficult to control than the stick is. The longer an object is, the easier it is to balance. A two-foot-long stick would have to lean twice as far from the vertical position as a four-foot stick would in order to be detected by the eye.

This is important in terms of showmanship. To most people longer sticks look harder to balance. The performer will gain greater respect from an audience by balancing longer objects, even though they require less skill. Balancing an eight-foot pole on your hand or head looks impressive yet is much easier than trying to the do the same thing with a three-foot stick.

Variations

Once you feel confident balancing an object with your dominant hand, learn to do it with other parts of your body. First train the other hand, then try the top of your foot, a raised knee, an arm, your shoulder, finger, chin, nose, forehead, even your ear. One thing you must keep in mind with any of these positions is to place the object where you will be able to see its top. You must be able to see it lean in order to correct it. That's why the vertical balance is virtually impossible to do from the top of the head.

When you are able to balance the object on more than one hand, you can start tossing it from hand to hand, or from hand to foot, knee, or arm. When tossing a balanced object, keep it as vertical as you can and your eyes focused at the top. When you toss it from one place to another, don't physically throw it over, simply toss it straight up and exchange the base upon which it will balance. For example, if you have it in your right hand gently toss it up a few inches, keeping it as vertical as possible. Move the right hand away and replace it with the left hand. The object will come down on the left hand into a balance giving the appearance that it was actually thrown from one hand to the other. Try catching it in a similar manner with the knee, foot, and elbow.

> ### Daffy Definitions
> Bacteria: The rear portion of a cafeteria.
> Wino: Opposite of "Why yes."
> Bar Stool: What Davy Crockett stepped in.
> Bigamy: Large pigmy.
> Polygon: Dead parrot.
> Fungi: A comedian; the life of the party.
> Quadrillion: Dance requiring four million
>   participants.

Add some life to a simple balance by moving around. While holding the balanced object, step forward and backward, adjusting your hand as needed. Try sitting down on a chair or even on the floor, maintaining the balance the entire time. Some accomplished performers have been able to keep spinning balls and other objects in perfect balance while turning somersaults and doing headstands.

Balancing Odd-Shaped Objects

So far I have referred only to linear objects, but objects of different shapes can also be balanced ver-

tically by using the same principles. Things such as picture frames, chairs, suitcases, saxophones, small tables and even ten speed bicycles can be vertically balanced by standing them up diagonally or along their longest axis, heavy end up.

HORIZONTAL BALANCING

Generally the easiest position in which to balance an object is on its largest side, as when you place a yardstick across the edge of your finger, or the center of a plate on your fingertip.

It is relatively easy to find the center of gravity in thin, linear objects such as yardsticks and pencils. Most

everyone has at some time in their life toyed w balancing of this sort. Balancing objects like th requires only locating the center of gravity. This po is found by sliding the hand along the length of object and testing the balance, in other words, by tr and error.

The same process is used to balance a disk-shap object, such as a plate, although the balance point somewhat more difficult to find. A stick can be divic into two halves, one on each side of the supporti point. A plate, however, is continuous all around support and has more "sides" to balance.

Try balancing a plate (don't use your good chin on your fingertip. As long as you keep the support finger steady, you can move the plate up and do and from side to side without dropping it. If the fin leans to one side even slightly, the plate will l balance and begin to slide off.

In vertical balancing, the supporting point m constantly be repositioned to keep under the center gravity. In contrast, horizontal balancing requires supporting point to remain as rigid as possi Balancing a book on top of the head is a horizon balance. To keep the book off the ground, the h must be kept as still as possible, even while mov other parts of the body.

Balancing objects horizontally is unimpressive for most part, mainly because it looks too easy. For reason horizontal balancing is not often used. Balanc spinning plates, a common trick used by m performers, is similar to horizontal balancing but actually a form of gyroscopic balancing, which will discussed later.

SET BALANCING

Set balancing combines attributes of both the verti and horizontal balance. It may look very much vertical balancing, but in actuality it functions more a horizontal balance. Although objects are stood end as in a vertical balance, they are not balancing a single point, but on a flat or semi-flat surface, in horizontal balancing.

To perform a set balance successfully, the perfor must weight the object heavily at one end. This is then placed or "set" on the head or some o balance surface.

Balancing a bottle, a small pedestal, or a lamp a heavy base on top of the head is a set bala Most of the weight of the object is located at

bottom, the performer is merely setting the lamp on top of his head. All he has to do to hold this balance is to keep his head steady and horizontal.

A partially filled drinking glass, vase, or bottle can be balanced in this manner on the palm of your hand, your forehead, elbow, raised knee or any other part of the body that can be made horizontal. The juggler is simply providing a flat surface, like a table, upon which it can rest.

Since a set balance requires only a motionless horizontal surface, the performer does not need to keep the top of the object in sight, as is required in vertical balancing. This is why it is the preferred type of balancing used in combination with toss juggling. By feel alone, the juggler can tell if the object is in proper balance while keeping his eyes on the jugging props.

A bottom heavy pedestal, as illustrated on this page, is favored by jugglers. These pedestals are specially designed so that they are remarkably stable in an upright position. The bottom portion is filled with lead shot so most all of the weight is located at its base. This gives the appearance of a vertical balance but works as a less difficult set balance.

Usually a lightweight rubber ball is placed on top of the pedestal for added effect. Keeping a small ball in the socket on top generally requires no more skill than balancing the pedestal itself, but it looks more impressive.

> A man walkes into the doctor's office with a toad growing out of his foot.
> "When did you first notice it? The doctor asked.
> "It started as a wart," replied the toad.

GYROSCOPIC BALANCING

Balancing which is assisted by rotating an object around a central axis is referred to as gyroscopic balancing. Spinning a ball, tray, or plate and balancing it on a finger or at the end of a stick are examples of this.

Any object which is spun freely will rotate around a central axis, and the entire object becomes perfectly balanced around this axis of rotation. The rotating motion creates a force physicists call "torque" which keeps the axis in a vertical position. This torque is what causes a toy top to stand up on end when spun. The force, which overcomes the gravitational forces trying to upset its balance, continues to exist as long as the top spins fast enough. Pushing sideways on the top does not knock it over as in the other balancing methods, but merely moves it sideways. Because of torque, a spinning balance is considerably easier to maintain than the other forms of balancing. Tricks which are almost impossible with stationary balancing can be accomplished with relative ease with gyroscopic balancing.

Gyroscopic balancing is not necessarily easy to learn. Although maintaining the balance is relatively easy, giving the proper amount of spin and positioning the axis of rotation directly over the finger (or other point of balance) can take a great deal of practice.

Balancing a Ball

Most everyone who has seen the Harlem Globetrotters is amazed at the extraordinary ball-handling skills of some of these players. Balancing a spinning ball is one of their favorite tricks and is always an audience pleaser, especially when combined with clever moves.

If approached properly, gyroscopic ball balancing is relatively easy to learn. Start with a large round ball, such as a basketball. Some people prefer to deflate the ball slightly to flatten it out on the supporting finger, they feel this makes it easier to balance. To make learning the balance as easy as possible, I would suggest locating the heaviest side of the ball first. All balls, no matter how well they are made, have some variation in weight. By finding this side you will be able to position the ball with the heaviest part down. Although not necessary, this step will make the ball somewhat more stable when you try to catch it on your finger. To find the heavy side of the ball, float it in a tub of water. The heaviest point will turn to the

bottom. Take the ball out of the water and make a small mark on the bottom of the ball for later reference.

Take the ball in the palm of your right hand, heavy side down, fingers spread evenly around it's base (see illustration). With a quick twisting motion toss the ball *directly upward* about five to ten inches.

Your hand should follow the ball up without touching it. Extend your index finger under the mark you placed on the ball. As it comes down, ease the landing onto your finger by dropping your hand slightly.

How the ball spins on your finger is regulated by personal preference. Some like to point the finger straight up or even on the fingernail. Others prefer to balance it on the fleshy part of the finger.

Once balanced, the ball will remain where it is until the spin slows down to a point at which gravational forces can pull it down. As long as you can keep it rotating, it will stay balanced (provided you hold it correctly).

You can add more spin by lightly brushing the ball with the other hand. When doing this, make contact with the ball at or below its equator, not above. A second method for adding spin is to use the second finger on the balancing hand and gently tapping the ball in the direction of the spin.

To work up a routine and add variety, you should also learn to balance the ball on your other hand. When you can do this, you can start tossing the ball from hand to hand or around your back, over your shoulder, under your leg and catch it with either hand. Adding a second ball opens up even more possibilities.

One easy trick is to simply transfer the ball from the right hand to the left without tossing it. This can be accomplished in a variety of ways, such as under the leg or behind the back.

Balancing Spinning Plates

Spinning a Plate on the Finger. The techniques used to spin plates can be applied to any flat or disk-shaped object, such as pie tins or trays. The method is similar to ball spinning.

Find yourself a plate, not a paper plate, the heavy ones work best. As you practice, you will drop it many times, so use a plate that will stand up to the abuse, and practice on the lawn or over a soft carpet.

Start with your hand under the plate, fingers spread out around its base. Toss it straight up with a twisting motion, just as you did with the ball. Follow the plate up and extend your index finger. It should contact the plate slightly off the axis of rotation. As the plate touches your finger, lower the hand slightly to ease the landing and immediately begin to move the hand in a circular motion in the same direction as the spin. This motion will accelerate the spin of the plate. As you do this, slide the finger to the axis of rotation. Once your finger is under the center of the plate, let it spin freely. You can keep the plate spinning indefinitely by shifting the finger off the center and again swinging the plate around.

This is not an easy skill to learn using ordinary plates, and it will take many hours of practice to become even moderately confident with it. For this reason, most clowns opt to learn the less difficult ball spinning or spinning a plate on the end of a stick.

Spinning Plate on a Stick. Spinning a plate on a stick looks just as difficult as spinning a plate on your finger, but with the use of specially made plates it's an easy trick that can be learned in minutes. These plates have a rim around the bottom and a deep depression or dimple at the center. The rim around the bottom prevents the plate from sliding off the end of the stick and aids in swinging the plate to build up rotational speed. The dimple allows the juggler to find the center of the plate easily and to keep the stick there.

Basically the same method is use to spin a plate, whether you use your finger or a stick. To spin the plate, place the dimple in the center, on top of one end of the stick. With your free hand give the plate a spin. To build up speed, start turning your wrist and rotate the stick. The stick will come out of the dimple and press against the rim on the bottom of the plate as you do this. Once you've built up speed, hold the stick rigid, and the plate will slide back to the center and spin even faster. Each time the plate needs more rotational speed, you can repeat these steps.

Props such as balancing plates and sticks can be purchased at local magic shops or by mail from Jenack Circus Corporation; Brian Dube, Inc.; The Juggling Arts; or Jugglebug, Inc. Their addresses can be found in Appendix B.

Helpful Hints

The Three I's. Some objects or shapes are easier to balance than others. Laws of physics indicate that gyroscopic balancing can become more stable by doing one or more of the following:

1) Increase the diameter of the object
2) Increase the object's density
3) Increase its rotational speed

A ball with a large diameter, such as a basketball, is easier to balance than a smaller tennis ball. A heavy porcelain or metal plate is easier to balance than a lighter plastic one. Obviously the greater the spin, the more stable the object will be; as it loses speed, it becomes wobbly and eventually falls.

Combination balancing. You can hold the stick with the plate on top in your hand, or better yet, balance it on your hand, chin, or forehead. This type of balance is a combination gyroscopic-vertical balance. The plate is balanced by the gyroscopic method and the stick by the vertical method. You will notice that by adding the spinning plate to the top of the stick you have given the stick a very high center of gravity, actually making the balance easier than the stick alone would be. This is a standard balance that you should learn if you plan

---

Father: Who was that you were talking to on the phone?
Son: I don't know, they just said it was a long distance from Tokyo and I said it sure was.

---

on doing any balancing.

For variety you can even balance the plate and stick on top of a second stick, or use both hands to hold several sticks and plates. Try tossing the spinning plate straight up in the air and catching it on the end of the stick as it comes down.

Peacock Feathers. Peacock feathers are ideal objects for a clown to use for balancing. Very little practice is needed to balance one vertically on most any part of the body, as long as you can see the top. Because they almost stand up by themselves you can balance one on your nose, chin, or foot and even toss it from place to place with relative ease, which makes you look great. Many seemingly difficult tricks can be performed with a peacock feather; combined with clownish physical expression and humorous dialogue you can get a lot out of it. Florists' shops usually sell these feathers. Buy one and experiment with it, you'll discover what I'm talking about.

Kids from the audience can be invited to come up and perform balancing tricks using a peacock feather. They will enjoy this because they, too, will be able to do many tricks themselves.

Rudy Horn

ADVANCED BALANCING SKILLS

Many creative jugglers have sharpened their balancing skills to what seems to be the limit of physical possibility. Balls, hats, vases, dishes, and other objects balanced at the top of a pool cue which rests on the juggler's chin have been popular advanced skills.

Strong-arm or heavyweight jugglers have been able to balance extremely heavy objects on their heads and chins, such as cannons and carriages (minus the horses).

The following are a few examples of what accomplished jugglers in the past have done.

Mac Morland would balance a saxophone on his forehead while juggling a violin, a bow, and a top hat.

Waldemar Paetzold would balance a bicycle on his forehead while his left hand held a spinning hat on the end of a stick and his right hand juggled two other hats.

Vittorio Ferroni, while standing on the back of a horse, would balance a bottle upside down on the edge of a plate, which he held vertically. He would then toss the bottle up in the air, it would make a full spin and come back down into a perfect balance on the edge of the plate.

Paul Cinquevelli seemed to defy gravity with his balancing skills. One of his most famous tricks was to hold a goblet in his teeth, in which a ball rested. Vertically balanced on top of this ball was a pool cue. On the top of the pool cue were two more balls, one balanced on top of the other! This amazing trick has never been accomplished by any other artist.

If Paul Cinquevelli could balance three balls and a pool cue on top of each other, there's no telling what is physically possible. Many such ideas can provide material for balancing gags and routines useful to clowns.

SHOWMANSHIP

Balancing is one skill that can be performed with the appearance of great difficulty while actually requiring moderate skill. This illusion is created by using showmanship. Let me illustrate what I mean by using trained animals as an example, lion taming in particular.

All cats, including lions, are unpredictable. Working with these large cats has its dangerous moments, which makes lion taming intriguing to circus audiences.

When you hear the word "lion" what picture pops into your mind? If you're like most people, you envision a large feline beast with a shaggy mane. This, however, is only the male lion, the female lion lacks the male's bushy head of hair and looks more like an overgrown cougar.

The female lion is much more temperamental than the male and is thus a much more difficult (and dangerous) animal for trainers to work with. Animal trainers have learned that using trained female lions does not gain as much awe or respect as using males, even though they are more difficult to manage and train.

People want to see the king of beasts, the one they have seen all their lives and visualize in their minds. Therefore lion tamers know that the effort put into training female lions is not rewarded; the public would rather see the more manageable male. This basic fact is true not only for animal training but with balancing or any other skill.

Performers of all types have learned that good showmanship involves giving the audience what they want and making the most of it. During an interview in 1893 Paul Cinquevelli stated, "The public always likes best the showiest tricks, and they are generally the easiest." Jugglers, clowns, and other variety artists are in fact actors. The showy tricks which audiences believe are very difficult are handled with fanfare to fulfill audience expectations. Making an easy trick look difficult brings a more favorable response from an audience than making a hard trick look easy.

The purpose of learning a trick for theatrical purposes is to impress and entertain an audience. It makes more sense to spend time perfecting a simple trick than waste effort practicing one which, although harder, will not be appreciated as much.

When I first started to do shows for kids, I had only a handful of juggling tricks down solid. I also did a few other tricks which, although not perfect, I was able to do 75 percent of the time. Being a clown, I didn't worry too much if I dropped a prop now and then. Tossing a ball around my back while juggling was one of these tricks. When I first started to do this trick, I threw the ball, at times, with a little less accuracy than I had wanted and had to make an obvious effort to reach out and recover it and still continue juggling. The kids could see this effort, and believing the trick to be very difficult, they yelled with delight and applauded. At other times I would do the same trick with all the finesse of a seasoned juggler, making it look easy. The kids would then look at it as an interesting trick but nothing to get excited about, and I received very little response. What was wrong? I had made the move look too easy, that's what. In the kids' minds it was easy.

People are impressed by how difficult a trick looks, not by how difficult it really is. In regard to balancing tricks, a long pole looks harder to balance than a short one, so use a long pole and look impressive. Also an object with one end larger and heavier than the other looks hard to balance heavy end up. But in a vertical balance this feat is relatively easy. Balancing is a skill that with a little practice can make anyone can look impressive.

Not all balancing tricks are easy and some may require years of practice to become even moderately proficient. Still there are many tricks a clown can learn easily and build into clever routines.

COMEDY BALANCING

Now that we've discussed the serious side of balancing, let's see how a clown can use balancing to create laughter and amusement. Balancing is much like juggling, magic, or any other clown skill in the way it can be used humorously. Funny dialogue and physical and slapstick humor can be used.

Perhaps the best way to describe how to make balancing entertaining is by giving you some examples. The following short routines will give you an idea of the type of things that can be done. Use these examples as a springboard for creating your own original material.

Balancing Cups and Saucers

This is a classic stunt that clowns have used in a variety of ways. To work the trick, you need three or four cups and saucers. Using a drill, screws and glue, attach the cups and saucers to one end of a dowel or broom handle.

The clown can walk out on stage acting as if he is balancing the stack of cups and saucers on the end of the stick. He goes through several different balancing moves with carefully controlled movements, exchanging hands, balancing the broom on his foot and his chin, and passing it around his back.

During this apparent display of extraordinary skill, he trips and stumbles toward the audience. Balance is lost, and the cups and saucers come tumbling down over the audience. They will duck, perhaps let out a scream, but the cups and saucers remain safely on the end of the stick. The clown's trick is exposed, and he gets a laugh.

Balancing A Balloon

In this stunt a round balloon is made to balance on the end of your nose. To prepare for this trick inflate a round balloon, but don't tie it off. While it is inflated, put some rubber cement on one spot and let it dry for a couple of minutes. Deflate the balloon. Apply a coat of rubber cement to the end of your nose and let it dry. You are now ready.

The balloon can be inflated in front of an audience and "balanced" on the nose with ease. The cement holding the balloon to your nose will keep it in place until you pull it off (the balloon, not your nose). Don't worry about putting the cement on your skin; the glue will peel off without any trouble.

The following routine is taken from *The Wonderful Father Book* by Richard Mann (Turnbull & Willoughby) © 1985.

Begin with balloon deflated. "Ladies and gentlemen . . . You are about to witness an incredible feat of skill and daring never before attempted by a rational, clear-thinking individual." With this ballyhoo, blow up and knot the balloon.

"And now I The Great Daddo, will balance this balloon on this nose, and I will do it while standing on one foot." Pause. "I must ask for complete silence please." This last request, of course, will invite the opposite.

Now stand with your head tilted back. With the utmost concentration, place the balloon on your nose, making certain not to connect the glue spots. Hold your hands away and let the balloon fall.

Again, go through the motions with the same result. "This is not as easy as it looks," you explain. "Please bear with me once more."

This time, connect the glue spots. Slowly take your hands away. Move from side to side as if you're trying to maintain balance.

While the kids are applauding, lower your head. The balloon will remain stuck in place and the kids will come unglued.

As you exit, pull at the balloon as if it is permanently stuck to your face.

The Talented Clown

The clown comes on stage carrying a bag of props and announces, "I will demonstrate for you several different types of balancing."

He pulls out a cane. "This is called cane balancing." He balances the cane in his hand.

"This is foot balancing." He balances the cane on top of his foot.

"This is arm balancing." The cane is placed on his arm.

With lots of facial expression he says, "And this is happy balancing—ha, ha, ha." He smiles and laughs.

"Sad balancing." He frowns and lowers his eyes, greatly exaggerating his expression.

"Crazy balancing." The clown sticks out his tongue, makes a funny face, and looks stupid.

"This is called balancing my mother's broom." A broom is picked up and balanced.

"Upside down balancing." The clown turns the broom around and holds it by its bristles.

"Plumber's helper balancing." A toilet plunger is held in palm of clowns hand, heavy end up.

"Sideways balancing." He sticks the handle between teeth and holds it horizontal.

"Double balancing." Keeping the handle in his mouth, the clown stands on one leg.

"Balancing on one finger." Clown places plunger on his finger.

"Now on my nose." He turns the plunger over and stands it up on his face, suction side down.

"Cough—cough—choke!" Ripping the plunger off, he gasps for air, makes an ugly face, and sticks out his tongue. "I think my brother-in-law has been fixing his plumbing again—pew."

A very large half-filled bean bag is pulled out. "Now I'll show you bean bag balancing." He puts the bag on his nose letting it cover his whole face.

"Last time I did this trick my mother-in-law thought I was a bean bag chair and sat on me—you laugh, she weighs 300 pounds and looks like Hulk Hogan! Do you know what it's like walking around with your nose stretched over to where your ear should be?" He makes a face by bending his nose sideways.

"Now I'll do handkerchief balancing . . . it's safer than bean bag balancing." The clown lays a handkerchief over his face, with his eyes barely showing.

"I learned this trick in Egypt." Putting one hand on his head and the other on his hip, he acts like an Arabian beauty queen.

"Now I'll balance it upside down." The clown sticks one end of the handkerchief between his fingers and lets it dangle freely.

"You ain't seen nothing yet. For my final and most spectacular trick, I will attempt to juggle three balls while balancing this large ring on my chin. Watch closely while I perform this unbelievable trick."

The clown sets the juggling ring on top his chin. "All right, here we go." As he lets go of the ring it drops backward, falling on his face.

"Hmm . . . Let me try that again." He sets the ring on his chin again.

"I'll just have to start juggling a little faster." As he lets go of the ring, he tosses a ball in the air; the ring balances for a second than falls onto his face.

"I don't understand it . . . maybe I need to toss the balls faster."

Again he puts the ring on his chin. As he lets go, it starts to lean; he moves to keep the balance and quickly tosses all three balls into the air in a vain effort to juggle before the ring falls—but no luck.

In frustration he takes the ring, sticks it between his teeth, and starts juggling. "Ta—da." As the final trick, he juggles the balls while tossing them through the ring in his mouth.

Elmo the Magnificent

"I have a very special pet I would like to show you—his name is Elmo. Elmo is my pet stick. Now I know what you're thinking—what's a pet stick? I'll show you. Elmo here isn't just an ordinary stick, he is a highly trained performer and can do some amazing tricks—let me show you . . . Are you ready Elmo?"

Elmo shakes his head yes.

"OK Elmo, stand up." The clown balances the stick vertically in his hand.

"Now play dead." He balances the stick horizontally across his index finger.

"OK boy, now roll over." The clown twirls the stick around through his fingers like a baton twirler.

"Good boy." The clown pats the stick on head.

"See what I mean? He does all sorts of tricks. Watch this—stand on your head Elmo." The stick is turned upside down and balanced again in the clown's hand.

"Now balance on my head."

The clown stops and looks inquisitively at the stick. "What was that Elmo? You're afraid to balance on my head? Why? . . . It's too high off the ground and you're afraid you might slip and fall. Oh don't be such a big ninny, get up there you chicken-livered stick."

The clown starts to lift the stick up to his head, but the stick refuses and jerks his hand down.

"Hey stop that! Come on, get up there." A struggle ensues, with Elmo bouncing up and down as the clown tries to put it on his head. A great deal of physical comedy can be added here.

Elmo grabs hold of the clown's chin as the struggle continues.

"Let go!" Finally the stick is pulled free.

"OK, OK, how about my shoulder? It's not so high up. Will you balance on my shoulder?"

Elmo nods his head yes. The stick is placed at the base of the clown's neck, just inside his shirt.

"Ya ready, Elmo? . . . Here goes." As he lets go of the stick, it slips down the back of his shirt, out of sight.

"HEY! Where did you go? Hee, hee, Elmo? Hee hee ha ha, stop that. Elmo, come out of there, hee hee ha ha ho ho hee, stop it, stop it, get out of there . . ." Clown grabs his side, back, and legs trying to catch Elmo before finally pulling him out.

"Elmo you tricked me—you're always doing that, you know how ticklish I am. You made up that whole business about being afraid of heights just so you could embarrass me. Now stand up on my chin, and *no tricks this time!*"

The clown places the stick on his chin and faces sideways so the audience can see only one side of him. As he lets go of Elmo, the stick slips off the far side of his face and out of sight from the audience. The clown grabs the top end of the stick before it falls to the ground. The stick should be positioned so as to appear to the audience as if it has fallen into the clown's mouth. The clown yells with a muffled voice, "Hey what are you doing? Get out of my mouth! You want to choke me?"

He pulls the stick up slowly. Hidden in his sleeve are three scarves tied end to end. At the base of the stick is a very small nail which hooks the first scarf. As the stick is withdrawn from the clown's mouth, it pulls the scarves out with it. The arm with the hidden scarves is positioned up at his mouth in such a way as to make it look realistic.

"What's the big idea? I said *no tricks.* Now cut it out . . . Let's continue—Elmo will now balance a spinning plate on his head for you."

The clown uses a special plate with a large dimple in the center for easy balancing and performs the stunt.

"That was good Elmo, now try it with this custard pie" The clown places the pie on top of the stick.

"OK—steady, Elmo steady." As the clown removes his supporting hand, the pie tips over and falls, landing right in the middle of his face. Clown exits.

When performing balancing routines such as those described here, don't rely only on the dialogue for laughs. Your actions will add humor and enhance your dialogue. For the best results use full physical expression: exaggerate movements, make a variety of facial expressions, and show emotion.

For additional ideas on balancing comedy read *Dr. Dropo's Juggling Buffoonery.*

CHAPTER 13

THE MAGIC OF MUSIC

Anyone who is around children for any length of time can testify to the fact that kids and noise go together; you can't have one without the other. In fact, the intensity and frequency of the noise in a group of children increases proportionally with the addition of each child. It seems as if kids can't be happy without an assortment of squeaks, cries, screams, and giggles.

Can you imagine a dozen kids in a room, all being absolutely quiet and enjoying themselves? Goodness, no! They could be restrained from making noise, but it wouldn't be fun.

Ask a kid what he's doing as he blows unmercifully on a whistle, beats a stick on the table, or slaps the top of a toy drum with his hand, and he'll tell you he's making music. To many children noise is music. But transforming noise into music, using rhythm and harmony, the sound is enjoyed even more. Because music appeals to both kids and adults, it can be used to great advantage by entertainers.

THE POWER OF MUSIC

Sound in the form of music has a magical effect on all of us. Who can resist the overwhelming desire to tap their foot in time to a catchy tune, or to sing, hum, or whistling along? Music has the power to conjure up thoughts and influence our emotions. It can create a variety of moods and feelings.

The influence of music has been known for many years, and is the reason we hear musical accompaniment in TV and movies. Almost all professional performers use music in their staged shows. Music leads the listener to experience emotions and to taste the atmosphere the performer is trying to create. Depending on the performer's theme, he can choose a piece of music to set the stage. An old western song brings thoughts of cowboys and gunfighters; the sound of a calliope stirs up images of carnivals, clowns, cotton candy, and fun. Synthetic or mechanical music projects the mystery of space travel, alien creatures, and robots.

Music can have a significant effect on an otherwise ordinary clown act. It can add life, making the act more professional and more enjoyable for the audience.

MUSIC AS A TOOL

Recorded Music

Music is a tool that any clown can use, and should accompany any formal staged show. If electrical outlets are available, sound equipment and recorded music can easily be set up and played. Where electricity is not readily available, portable battery operated equipment might be considered. If you do use portable sound equipment, the music must be clear and sharp. Music cluttered with static or other noise is difficult to hear and can be more of a distraction than a help.

The music need not be played continuously; it can be used as part of an introduction. This will announce to the audience that the show or the next act is beginning, and will draw the entire audience's attention toward the stage and you.

Descriptive music will also prepare the audience for the type of act they are about to see. Melancholy organ music may send shivers up their spines and tell them that the show will involve a Halloween theme. They will prepare mentally for spooks and monsters rather than cowboys, the milkman, or some other topic.

The mood you initially set will last until you're able to grab the audience's attention and lead them along with your clowning. Different types of music can also be played throughout the skit to accentuate a particular scene. For instance, a fast or busy old piano tune like those from the Keystone Cops movies may be interjected during a silly chase sequence.

Clowns who perform offstage will have to use slightly different methods. At carnivals and fairs where the clown is down in the audience, he may wish to carry along a cassette recorder or, better yet, play his own musical instrument. In most any setting—parades, birthday parties, picnics, or stage shows—clowns can use music effectively by playing their own instruments and/or by singing.

You may be saying, "But I don't have a good singing voice." Who cares? You're supposed to be a clown, not Bruce Springsteen or Crystal Gayle. "I can't play a musical instrument either, I haven't any musical skill." Doesn't matter, read on.

Playing Your Own Music

Clowns can use a multitude of instruments effectively: guitar, banjo, ukulele, piccolo, accordion, harmonica, flute, tuba, saxophone, and portable organ, to mention just a few. For a more unique or novel approach, you could learn to play less common instruments such as bagpipes, xylophone, harp, Chinese lute,

> Wise man says:
>
> "When everything's coming your way, you're probably in the wrong lane."
>
> "Learn from the mistakes of others because you can't live long enough to make them all by yourself."

or Yugoslavian gusle. Learning to play any of these instruments will take time and effort, but the rewards can be well worth it.

Don't let the idea that you are tone deaf or lack musical talent stop you. Music can be used in many types of clown acts. If you don't know how to play a musical instrument, you can always learn. If you don't want to spend the time and effort required to play a standard instrument, you have other choices. There are several easy to play instruments that require little, if any, musical ability, such as drums, tambourines, whistles, Jew's harps, and kazoos.

COMEDY THROUGH SONG

Everybody loves to laugh and everybody loves to listen to music. It seems only natural that combining comedy with music would be an instant success and indeed, many successful performers have used this combination. I will describe four basic methods that have been used successfully by professional comedians and clowns. Use them as a guide to develop musical routines that suit your clown character and personality.

Sour Notes

This method is the most natural with clown comedy. The performer attempts to play a beautiful tune or sing a song, but plays off key or sings sour notes. Jack Benny, although an accomplished violinist, made audiences roll with laughter with his "terrible" violin music.

I will always remember a singing clown I saw many years ago. The fact that he had a lousy singing voice was bad enough, but every few seconds he would blow on an old bugle and rattle a tambourine. The music was so awful that it was hilarious.

This type of music (if you want to call it that) can be performed by talented musicians, such as Jack Benny, or by those who have absolutely no musical skill, as the clown described above.

Humorous Lyrics

Songs with funny lyrics are a long-standing favorite. Many old folk songs have humorous or nonsensical lyrics. Unlike the sour notes method described above, most humorous songs are played skillfully; the lyrics make them funny.

Allen Sherman made a name for himself by singing this type of song. Most of us are familiar with his classic "Hello Muddah, Hello Faddah." Spike Jones, Tom Lehere, Ray Stevens, and more recently Barry Polsar are just a few of the performers who have become popular by using funny lyrics.

There are many songs available you can use. Visit your local music store or library and see what song-books they have. Two excellent books are *The Silly Songbook* and *The Funny Songbook*, both by Esther L. Nelson. They contain many old favorites with both old and new lyrics. The songs include "Ain't It Great to be Crazy?," "I'm a Nut," "Five Little Monkeys," "Fooba Wooba John," and "I'm being Eaten by a Boa Constrictor." Most of the songs use familiar folk tunes we all learned as kids, and are easy to play or sing.

If you like really off beat music, write to Rainbow Morning Music, 2121 Fairland Rd., Silver Spring, MD 20904 and inquire about their book *Noises Under the Rug* by Barry L. Polsar. He has written many original songs such as: "Never Cook Your Sister in a Frying Pan," "I Got a Teacher and She's So Mean," "One Day My Best Friend Barbara Turned into a Frog," "My Brother Threw Up on My Stuffed Toy Bunny," "I'm a Three-Toed, Triple-Eyed, Double-Jointed Dinosaur," and "My Brother Thinks He's a Banana."

The Interruption

This is the method the Smothers Brothers have used so effectively. They begin to play a song, but before they get very far, the song is interrupted by Tommy, the clown of the duo. He always comes up with unusual lyrics, noises, or something else to make his brother Dick angry. For instanc,e their song "John Henry" starts off like a normal folk ballad with Tommy

singing, "When John Henry was a little baby, sittin' on his daddy's knee, his father picked him up and threw him on the floor and said 'This babe's done wet on me'!" Dick then jumps in, "Stop, that's not the way it goes . . ." and a comical discussion follows. The song resumes only to be stopped again with another discussion. The entire song takes several minutes to complete.

This is an excellent technique to use if you perform with another clown or even with a puppet. Songs can provide a lot of good springboards into comic dialogues.

Talk and Song

The distinguishing feature about this method is the talking between songs. The songs can be of any type: comical, sing-a-longs, or serious, but the discussion between the songs is where the real comedy is.

Between a series of songs the clown can tell stories about the songs, how they came to be written, what they mean, and so forth. Any topic can be discussed, then capped off by a song with a similar theme. The

Sign on a pet shop window:
Great Dane puppy for sale. Housebroken, faithful, will eat anything. Especially fond of children.

clown can discuss birthdays, tell some humorous stories, and finish the discussion with a birthday song.

Simple dialogues explaining how a song came to be written can be funny. For example I'll say, "I would like to play for you a couple of songs I wrote myself. This first song was written as a result of getting my lips stuck in the mouthpiece of my kazoo. It's titled 'Please Release Me'." The song is then played with a lot of wild blowing, mixed with mumbling pleas for help to release my captured lips.

"This next song I wrote when I got my tongue stuck between the strings of my guitar. . . don't ask me how the guitar strings got in my mouth, they just did, OK? . . . Actually, I spilled some gravy on my guitar as I was eating and when I tried to lick it off, I got stuck. Let me pass along a little advice to you—don't ever lick gravy off your guitar. Your tongue might get trapped for hours, and besides—guitar strings taste terrible."

In many instances a performer will use a combination of the four methods just described. It may even be difficult to identify a routine as belonging to any single category. Although you should have a distinct style, use each method and work out the combination that functions best for your clown character and your own personality.

WRITING YOUR OWN SONG

There are many humorous songs available that can be used successfully by clowns. All the clown has to do is to find a funny or potentially funny song and design a short routine around it. Many excellent routines have been developed in this way.

When working with another person's song, however, you are bound by the composer's words and music. In many cases your act will involve a certain subject for which no suitable song is available. You may need a song on bicycle safety, eating vegetables, yellow lizards, or three-toed hairless giraffes, but finding one to fit your needs could be nearly impossible. Writing your own songs can give you the freedom to explore any subject. Your songs, being original and hopefully unique, will give the audience something new and different.

Few people are talented enough to compose their own music. If you are one of the lucky people who possess this talent, by all means use it. If not, don't be discouraged. There are thousands of old songs which you can write new lyrics to. Folk songs have changed continually over the years with the addition of both new lyrics and notes.

If you can make up simple rhymes, you can compose your own lyrics. Clowns have a keen sense of humor and the ability to create funny statements. Writing lyrics is really no harder then telling a funny joke.

The easiest types of lyrics to write are ballads and parodies. Ballads are stories told in song; parodies are comical imitations of popular songs.

Practice writing a new song by taking a well known song and changing a few words here and there to give it a humorous slant. You can use most any type of music: folk songs, ballads, marching songs, hymns, rock and roll, opera, country western, or foreign songs. The most difficult part of writing your own lyrics is finding a suitable song to work with. Gather a bunch of songbooks containing well known tunes. Look at the titles and change a word or two to make them funny or different. Here are some examples:

"Dancing in the Dark" becomes "Dancing in the Mud."

"A Bicycle Built for Two" becomes "A Unicycle Built for Two."

"Raindrops Keep Fallin' on My Head" becomes "Bubble Gum Keeps Stickin' on My Shoe."

"Swing Low Sweet Chariot" becomes "Swing Low, Then Kick Him in the Knee."

"I'm Forever Blowing Bubbles" becomes "I'm Forever Doing Homework."

"I Found a Million Dollar Baby" becomes "I Found a Hair in My Gravy."

"My Wild Irish Rose" becomes "I Have to Itch My Nose."

"Yankee Doodle Dandy" becomes "Spaghetti Noodle Doodle."

Once you've created a new title, look at the rest of the song. Can it be rearranged or rewritten to make it funny? You will have to determine if the change you made to the title can be carried through to the rest of the song. Unfortunately, you'll find that some funny ideas expressed in the titles may not be easily carried throughout the entire song. If not, try another song.

Here are a few things to keep in mind when choosing a song and writing lyrics. First, the best songs to use

Daisy: Did you hear about the kidnapping down the street.

Doris: No! What happened?

Daisy: Nothing much. After a while his mother woke him up.

are fast and lively. Kids are full of energy and slow songs tend to bore them unless the lyrics are very clever.

Second, when you begin writing the words to a song, use topics that kids are involved with today. Most of the funny folk songs floating around are old fashioned. Although enjoyable, kids don't relate to them. Use subjects involving school, troublesome brothers and sisters, riding on the school bus, eating all their vegetables—topics of everyday experience to a child.

As you write the words to a song, think like a kid. For most clowns this is easy. What are a child's likes and dislikes? What's important to them? You should also use subjects, characters, and heroes that are popular now.

Singing a song about subjects that the children are familiar with or can identify with will greatly enhance the song's appeal. Any humor you add will be met with greater acceptance and enjoyment.

SAMPLE SONGS

The following lyrics are sung to familiar tunes. Each song involves subjects that concern kids: ice cream, playing in the mud, homework, and eating pizza. Kids like these sorts of songs because they're part of their world. Plus the tunes are familiar—it's like having fun with something they know and feel comfortable with.

"On Top Of My Pizza" (sung to the tune of "On Top Of Old Smokey").

On top of my pizza
All covered in sauce,
I saw an anchovy
Who thought he was boss.

When I took a big bite
He poked me in the eye,
I screamed for my mother
And started to cry.

My barefoot brother
His name was Ralph,
He picked up my pizza
And stuck it in his mouth.

I grabbed for my pizza
But he ran out the door,
He dropped all the olives
And slipped on the floor.

He laid in the hallway
with olives between his toes,
And my poor little anchovy
Was stuck up his nose.

"I've Been Workin' On My Homework" (sung to the tune of "I've Been Workin' On The Railroad").

I've been workin' on my homework,
All the live long day;
I've been workin' on my homework,
Just to get a stinkin' A;
I'd rather be out playin' baseball,
Fishing or chewin' gum;
I'd rather be out playing baseball,
But then I'd grow up dumb!

"My Ice Cream Fell In The Mud Puddle" (sung to the tune of "My Bonnie Lies Over The Ocean").

My ice cream fell in the mud puddle,
Now my ice cream is covered in goo.
My ice cream fell in the mud puddle,
And I stepped on it with my shoe.
Get off, get off,
Oh, get off my brand new shoe, you goo,
Get off, get off,
Oh, get off you yucky old goo.

MAKE YOUR SONG COME TO LIFE

Just playing or singing a funny song isn't enough. That may be all that's needed to get some chuckles and smiles from the kids, but you can go a step farther. By using vocal fluctuations and sound effects you can add life to a song. Don't just sing or play an instrument—add character by emphasizing certain points in the song. Shout, whisper, cry, giggle, sound like

Fred: Have a piece of candy—sweets to the sweet.
Doris: Oh, thank you. Here have some of these nuts.

Galina, Slava, and Paul Polunin in the Leningrad clown-mime theatre.

a car engine, a rocket ship, or a cow. All of this will make the song more enjoyable and funnier.

Clowns are actors. To be a good actor requires the ability to speak with tonal variations and emotions. A speaker or actor who talks in a monotone may say the most interesting things yet still lose the audience's attention. Songs too, although they involve several different notes, can still come across like a person who speaks in a monotone. Without feeling, a song is half dead.

The songs you play and sing must be fun, lively, and full of life. Insert emotion and sound effects wherever you can. Look at the song "Greasy Grimy Gopher Guts." It's sung to the tune of "The Old Gray Mare."

Great green globs of greasy grimy gopher guts,
mutilated monkey's meat,
decapitated donkey's feet,
Great green globs of greasy grimy gopher guts,
And I forgot my spoon!

What emotions can you incorporate into this song? The first four lines can reflect a yucky, sickly feeling. The last line ending with sour disappointment because there is no spoon. For practice sing the song putting full feeling into it.

Physical Expression

In addition to vocal sounds, use as much visual expression as possible. Tone of voice and facial expressions communicate feelings that words by themselves cannot. Make funny faces at appropriate times and use body language. Make your whole body tell the story.

Go back to the song "Greasy Grimy Gopher Guts" and sing it again adding visual expression as well as vocal expression. As you sing the first four lines contort your face as if actually seeing the sickly greasy grimy gopher guts. In the last line change your expression to to grief. Shake your your head slowly back and forth and give a disappointed snap of the fingers.

Special Effects

Incorporate any type of sound effects that would fit with the song, such as laughter, crying, rattling a chain, or stamping your foot. Use your voice to imitate musical instruments, animal sounds, the roar of an airplane, the cheers from a crowd of people.

Look over some songs of your own choosing. Sing them using all of the vocal and visual aids you can think of.

A wide variety of props can be used to accentuate the visual effects. Use pictures, balloons, toys—anything that relates to the song. Simple tunes can take on new meaning and interest with the use of props, as in the following:

Peas porridge hot,
Peas porridge cold,
Peas porridge in the pot
Nine days old.
Some like it hot,
Some like it cold,
Some like it in the pot
Covered with green hairy mold.

A good visual complement to these lyrics would be to juggle three pea-green bean bags. Stick one bean bag in your mouth after singing the third line. Pull it out, make a sour face and continue with "Nine days old." At the end of the song, pull out a fourth bean

bag made out of green fake fur, "Covered with green hairy mold." Combined with appropriate vocalizations, this simple song can bring a good audience response.

For songs involving animals you can use balloon figures or hand puppets. Use as much visual assistance as you can. Combine talents in other areas such as magic, puppetry, and dance. Visual aids give the kids something to focus on during the song, keeping their interest high.

Activity Songs

Combining movement and dancing with the music gets everyone involved, so activity songs are fun.

Kids love to be involved. They have a lot of stored up energy and are always ready to use it. When they become involved in an act by singing or acting, they can come away with a feeling that they took part in the show.

There are several ways of involving the audience with a musical clown act. The simplest is a sing-a-long. Avoid trying to teach new songs unless they are extremely simple. Stick with familiar tunes that won't be confusing.

Another technique is to have the audience interject sound effects as you sing the song. The sound effects can be a word, a phrase, clapping of hands, or stamping the feet.

Most any song can be used in this way, but those containing nonsense words, animal noises, and unusual

MUSICAL GAMES

Some songs can involve a great deal of physical activity: jumping, skipping, yodeling, or clapping. These songs turn into games and should be saved for the end of an informal show. The adrenalin builds up in the kids as they participate in these highly active songs so that in most cases it's hard to calm them down afterward.

A number of games can be played with music. The rhythm and melody of the music instills the desire in both kids and adults to tap their toes, move their bodies, or dance. For picnics or birthday parties, musical games can be a good way to finish off a clown act.

When we talk about musical games, the first game to come to mind is the old favorite—Musical Chairs. This is an easy game that will end up with one or two winners. The winners usually get a prize, which the clown can supply.

There are dozens of other games that are just as much fun. Musical Freeze is one of these. In this game some lively music is played while the kids wiggle and dance. The music is stopped intermittently and each time it does, the kids must stop dead still, as if instantly frozen. Those who move are out, and the game continues until only one person remains.

There are several variations to this game, and you can invent some of your own. One variation is to choose a leader; as the music plays, all the kids must follow the leader and do as he does.

You may decide not to have a single winner—instead of eliminating kids as the game progresses, let them stay in and just have fun. This can avoid some friction.

To add excitement and make the game more lively, the clown can occasionally toss a few pieces of wrapped candy among the kids and let them chase after the treats. When the music stops, however, no one can move. Those who continue to chase after the candy or happen to be jumping in the air at the time are out. The amount of candy dispersed can be controlled so that the winner will wind up with the most as his reward.

Bob Gibbons as Skoopy the Clown.

sounds work best. Take the classic "Old McDonald's Farm" for instance. Before singing the song, tell the audience they're going to help you out with the animal sounds. Take a few minutes and have fun practicing sounds such as moo, cock-a-doodle-do, bow-wow, baa baa, and the rest. Once they have practiced and know what to do, sing the song having them insert their part on your signal. The song doesn't have to be funny, but the kids will have fun. They get a kick out of making the sounds.

The audience can also participate by using physical movement. As the song is sung, the kids can act out certain parts. Some songs are especially well adapted for audience participation. The children's song "Do As I'm Doing" is an excellent activity song. As the clown sings he taps his foot, wiggles his chin, bobs his head up and down, and whatever else he can think of. The children follow along, copying everything he does.

Daisy: Do you really love me?
Ed: Yes! I would die for you.
Daisy: You're always saying that, but you never do it.

A good source for over 50 different musical games is *Musical Games for Children of All Ages* by Esther L. Nelson. This book can be purchased in your local music store or checked out of the library.

THE KAZOO AND YOU

No Experience Necessary

Although most any musical instrument can be used effectively by clowns, the kazoo is a traditional favorite. It requires no musical training and only a little practice is needed to learn how to use it. Anybody, no matter how unskilled in music, can play it.

The kazoo itself has no musical capabilities; it has no holes to plug or keys to press. The tones it delivers depend totally on the kazooist. If you can hum or sing (even off key), you can kazoo.

The kazoo produces its unique sound from the vibrations of a thin membrane in the turret, the round appendage on the instrument. The membrane vibrates when the kazooist hums on the mouthpiece.

Kazoos can be tricky. When I picked up a kazoo for the first time, I thought it would be easy to play. After all, I said to myself, it's just a funny looking whistle. When I blew into it, nothing happened. I tried it again, thinking maybe I hadn't blown hard enough. Still nothing happened.

I must be blowing at the wrong end, I reasoned, so I turned it around and tried it that way. Still no sound. I was getting frustrated. Even blowing on the turret didn't work.

Son: Dad, what makes the wind blow?
Father: I don't know.
Son: Dad, what makes water?
Father: I don't know.
Son: Dad, why is fire hot?
Father: I don't know.
Son: Dad, you don't mind if I bother you with all these questions do you?
Father: Absolutely not, son. How are you ever going to learn anything if you don't ask questions?

I was discouraged and thought I had purchased a defective kazoo. Admitting defeat, I resorted to the only thing I could do—read the instructions. It clearly stated, "Don't blow—hum." When I stopped trying to "blow" on the kazoo and began to hum, it worked beautifully. Blowing does not vibrate the membrane in the turret but humming does, a subtle but important point.

Any song you can hum, you can play on the kazoo. It's as simple as that. The kazoo gets its range of tones not from the instrument itself but from your own vocal cords.

Sound Effects

Beside playing music, you can use the kazoo to create animal sounds and unusual noises. Donkeys, roosters, cows, sheep, and pigs can all be imitated with surprising realism on a kazoo. This could be a handy aid with songs such as "Old McDonald's Farm."

Experimenting with different sounds, blowing the air both in and out, or fluttering the tongue and changing pitch can lead to a variety of sounds. You can imitate space ships, robots, laser rays, and neutron torpedos. Simply talking into the kazoo can give a good impression of a robot or Darth Vader.

Styles

Several different styles of kazoo are availble on the market, all of which sound much the same. They come in shapes that range from round to elongated. Some mimic band instruments such as trombones and clarinets.

You can create your own kazoo band instrument by replacing the mouthpiece of the original instrument with an ordinary kazoo. Combining a tuba with a kazoo creates what is called a "kazooba." A bugle and kazoo forms a "kazoogle." You can create many others. It looks like an ordinary musical instrument but sounds like a kazoo.

A Word of Caution

Playing the kazoo has hazards which you must be aware of. Never eat garlic or other spicy foods before performing. The pungent exhaust from the end of a loaded kazoo can be overpowering to your audience.

CLASSIC CLOWN GAGS

The Big Sneeze

Clown has concealed a handful of confetti in one hand. Slowly he builds up a big sneeze. "Ah . . . ahh . . . ahhh . . . " Quickly he brings his finger up under his nose to prevent the blast from occurring (using the hand holding the confetti).

The sneeze continues "Ahhh . . . CHOOO!" As he sneezes the confetti is tossed out of his hand towards the audience.

Four Leaf Clover

One clown is standing staring down at the ground when a second clown comes walking by. The second clown asks what the first one is looking at. "It's a four leaf clover," he replies.

The second clown smiles and says, "A four leaf clover brings good luck. I'm going to pick it."

As he bends over the first clown smacks him in the seat of the pants with a paddle and runs away.

The Tie

The end of the clown's tie is tucked underneath his belt. Wanting to hang the tie outside his trousers he gives it a little pull. But the end is still inside his pants. He pulls more out. The more he pulls the longer the tie becomes. Eventually he reaches the end.

The tie is so long that when the clown walks, it drags on the floor. Stepping on it he trips and falls. Annoyed he shoves the tie back into his pants and walks away.

Put Out the Flame

One clown has a lighted candle or large burning match. To extinguish the flame he doesn't blow it out but pulls out a toy water pistol and begins to shooting it with water.

A second clown becoming curious approaches and looks closely at the flame. As the flame goes out he gets squirted in the face.

You're Pulling My Ear

Two clowns get into an argument. One clown grabs the other by his ear and begins tugging on it, stretching it several inches from his head, while the second winches in pain.

To perform this gag, the clown who gets his ear pulled conceals a flesh colored balloon or rubber glove in his hand. He then claps this hand over his ear as if to protect it when his companion grabs for it.

The first clown grabs hold of the balloon and pulls. The victim responds with obvious discomfort. When the torture is over the ear-puller lets the ear snap back. The second clown runs away howling.

CHAPTER 14

THE ART OF STILT WALKING

Giants . . . man has always been fascinated by them. Literature is full of tales of extremely large human beings. We have Goliath from the Bible, Paul Bunyan from American folklore, the giant from Jack and the Bean Stalk; we find them in fables, fairy tales, folk stories, and history. Stories of giants have always sparked interest and made intriguing tales.

One reason for the fascination we have with giants is that true giants are a rarity. Some people, such as professional basketball players, approach a height we often consider gigantic, but people over seven feet tall are unusual and consequently exciting.

Just as real giants and storybook figures draw our interest, it can be thrilling to see someone impersonating a giant by wearing stilts. The sight of a stilt walker dressed in colorful costume immediately draws attention and curiosity. Who can resist watching one of these long-legged creatures amble by?

The art of stilt walking extends back to the ancient Egyptians. In those days stilts were used by carpenters and other craftsmen in place of ladders, as they often are now. These unique tools were later adapted by clowns or jesters to amuse audiences. Even now they are used by clowns with much success.

HOLD-ON VERSUS TIE-ON STILTS

When we think of stilts, the first thought that comes to most people is the hold-on type many of us toyed with as kids. These stilts were long, often extending above our heads. We would hop up onto the two wooden foot supports and awkwardly control our movements with both hands and feet. When we lost our balance and began to fall, we just jumped off and started over.

Hold-on stilts are basically toys and are not generally used by clowns. The stilts clowns prefer are the tie-on type which have no handles to grab a hold of. These stilts reach no higher than to the top of the knee. They are strapped securely to the feet and legs, acting as extensions of the lower leg. When you lose your balance with tie-on stilts, you can't just jump off, an obvious disadvantage, but the benefits of tie-on stilts far outweigh this inconvenience. With the stilts attached snugly to the legs, the hands are left free to do other things such as shaking hands, making balloon animals, and working props.

More importantly, these stilts are easy for clowns to disguise as their own legs. A pair of specially made long-legged baggy pants can be pulled up over the stilts, hiding them from view. The pants must be loose enough in the legs to allow the feet to fit inside without showing any unnatural bulges. This gives the clown the appearance of a long-legged giant. This disguise can be so convincing that many younger children actually believe the clown to be a giant.

TYPES OF STILTS

Footed Wooden Stilts

As the name suggests, footed stilts have a wide base or foot. These feet vary in size, some are large while others are no wider than the stilt leg itself. The size of the foot is important because it has a pronounced effect on the stilt's function.

The longer the foot, the easier it is to balance. Large feet, however, make walking difficult. Big feet are great for standing still and balancing but can be lousy for getting around on. Stepping on a very small stone or on a slight incline could be all that's needed to topple you over. Ouch!

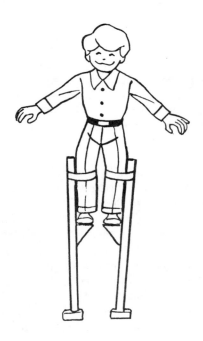

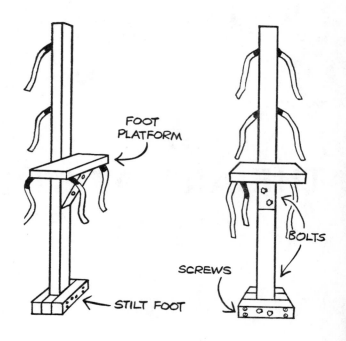

Although you can buy a pair of stilts, most beginners start out on a homemade set. These can be made relatively easy and inexpensively. The figure above shows a pair of footed stilts which you can make in your own workshop. This is a basic design which you can modify to your liking.

These stilts can be made from standard sized wood available at a hardware store or lumberyard. Cut the pieces to size and bolt or screw them together using glue wherever possible. I strongly advise you to use long bolts in the foot supports, as shown in the diagram. They will hold much better than screws or nails.

The knee and foot straps can be tied or buckled, but I prefer to use Velcro. With Velcro I can adjust the tightness precisely as I want, which isn't always possible with other types of straps. For the best support and control, you can bolt a pair of lace-up shoes directly onto the foot platform.

The height of the foot platform determines how high you will stand above the ground. The farther up you go, the more difficult it is to control the stilts and keep balanced. To start, I recommend that the foot platform be placed only 8 to 12 inches above the ground. As your skill improves with practice, you can increase your height. Most stilt walkers use stilts that lift them only 18 to 30 inches above the ground, a height sufficient to make an ordinary person look like a giant.

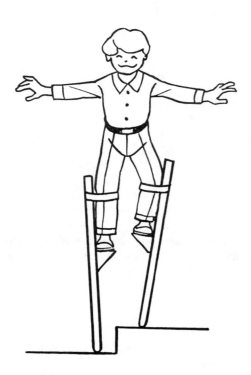

Remember as you build your stilts that a large foot on the base of the stilts makes them more stable and easier to balance, but less manageable. A short base allows much more freedom of movement.

Chinese Stilts

In contrast to footed stilts, Chinese stilts have no protruding foot. The legs of the stilts go straight to the ground. These types of stilts are not for the beginner. Because of their narrow base, they require a greater amount of practice and sense of balance to control. Balance is not maintained by keeping the legs steady as with footed stilts, but by continuously shifting the weight of the body from one foot to the other.

Even though the stilt walker must constantly be shifting the weight of his body from side to side, these stilts have some definite advantages over their big-footed cousins. Once you get the "feel" of using them, they actually become easier to control. They can be manipulated over obstacles, or made to go uphill or along uneven ground to an extent unobtainable with footed stilts. Because of their greater mobility, they are also better suited for activities such as running or dancing.

Mechanical Stilts

If you plan on doing a lot of stilt walking, you should use the best pair of stilts you can find. Mechanical stilts made of lightweight aluminum are unquestionably the best type of stilt available. These stilts are manufactured specifically for use by drywall workers, painters, and other tradesman, but clowns can use them just as well.

The illustration below shows a pair of Shujax Walking Stilts. They weigh approximately 15 pounds per pair and are engineered for comfort and mobility. The biggest advantage these stilts have over homemade stilts is the mechanical ankle. Combined with a special spring to supplement the leg muscles, this ankle allows a walking action that makes the stilts easy to use and control. It also allows the stilt walker to bend his leg without lifting the foot off the ground, something other tie-on stilts can't do. Because of this movable ankle, the walking action is very similar to normal walking and reduces muscle fatigue, a distinct advantage in parades or whenever extensive walking is required.

Some mechanical stilts can be adjusted in height from 12 to 36 inches so that one pair can be used either by a beginner or by a more advanced stilt walker. They are relatively easy to use and ideally suited for use by clowns, but they are not cheap. Several styles are available ranging in price from $140 to $235 a pair. If you would like more information write to Goldblatt Tool Co., 511 Osage, P.O. Box 2334, Kansas City, Kansas 66110.

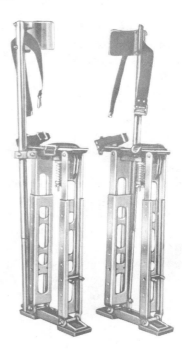

HOW TO RIDE A PAIR OF STILTS

The Joy of Stilt Walking

Who me, on stilts? . . . You've got to be kidding! Learning to walk on stilts is not as difficult as it first appears. Using short, big-footed "beginner's" stilts, you can learn to stilt walk in a matter of minutes.

The key to learning is to progress in steps (no pun intended). Start with a pair of short stilts, with the foot platform only 8 to 12 inches off the ground, and gradually work up to taller ones.

Most stilt walkers limit their stilt height to 18 to 30 inches, but some have gone much higher, five, six, fifteen feet and even higher. The tallest stilts I have ever heard of being used with any degree of control were worn by Harry Sloan in Great Yarmouth, England. He was able to manipulate a pair of stilts 21 feet tall!

To get an idea of how high this is, go to a multistory building and look out a third-story window—the height he was walking around on using tie-on stilts. As you can imagine, a fall from a height this great would be rather painful if not discouraging. For me 30 inches is enough. If I go any higher than that my nose starts to bleed, either from the altitude or from falling on my face.

Although interesting and definitely eye catching, stilts of these heights are generally impractical and awkward. The addition of five or six feet to a person who is already six feet tall would make him an enormous 13 to 14 feet in height. Such a height can inhibit motion in many places and requires a great deal of leg strength and control.

It is not necessary for you to learn to walk on stilts greater then two or three feet in height to look like a giant. Basketball players who are rarely over seven feet tall look like giants to us. You can clown around wearing stilts which are only 12 or 18 inches high and still look like a giant. A person who is naturally six feet tall will become seven feet tall with just the addition of one extra foot of height. As your skill and confidence improves, move up to the more common 18 to 30 inch range.

When you begin to practice, you will find that stilt walking is fun. Perched up above the heads of everyone else and being able to move around provides a new perspective that only giants have. And just like other clown skills, once you have mastered the basics you can begin to explore the multitude of variations and really enjoy the art. Not only that, stilt walking adds a real boost to your ego as kids squeal in delight over the sight of you.

Safety Equipment

After making yourself a pair of beginner's stilts you should do one more thing before attempting to practice with them, that is, prepare for falls. Protective padding is strongly suggested and is particularly important for beginners. Go to a sporting goods store and buy some knee, shin, and elbow pads. Thick gloves may also be of some help. You may even want to wear a motorcycle helmet as you practice, especially when you increase your stilt height.

Knee and elbow pads should always be worn; they are easily concealed under the costume and are unnoticable. If you fall, you'll be glad to have the protection.

The First Step

Find a location with a level surface to walk on: a driveway, porch or whatever. Get a table, bar stool, car, or anything else you can sit on and hang your legs over while you put on your stilts.

Before sitting down, put on your protective equipment. Climb on top of the table (or what have you) and hang your legs over the edge. Strap each stilt onto your legs and bind all the straps tightly so that there is no slack.

With both legs firmly secured to the stilts, bring your legs close to the edge of the table. Place the bottoms of the stilts flat on the ground and stand up slowly. It would be helpful at first to have an assistant stand in front of you to hold your hand. Try taking a few short steps. You will undoubtedly be a bit shaky until you develop the feel for keeping your balance. Extending your arms out to the sides will help. Practice walking until you feel comfortable and can keep your hands down at your sides.

Beggar: Lady, please help me. I haven't eaten for four days.
Lady: Gracious! I certainly wish I had your willpower.

Beggar: Mister, I haven't tasted food in a week.
Man: Don't worry, it still tastes the same.

Falling Down

Falling down with a pair of tie-on stilts can be an unpleasant experience if you don't prepare yourself. Besides wearing protective padding, you need to learn how to fall to lessen the chance of injury. Whenever you feel yourself begin to topple over, bend your knees and crouch down as low as you can get. This will lower your body and lessen the impact of the fall.

Always fall face forward, landing on your arms and knees. Knee and elbow pads will protect these parts of your body. If you begin to fall backwards quickly twist your body around so as to land forward. Landing on your back can be dangerous!

Once you have fallen down on the ground you are faced with another problem—getting up. If your assistant tries to pull you up by your hands this can be a most difficult task and an awkward experience. You may wind up getting more laughs this way than from your jokes.

To stand up, first get on your knees. Your assistant should stand in front of you, bend down and grab hold of your knees or the upper part of the stilts. Now hold onto your assistant's shoulders to balance yourself as your assistant lifts your knees. In this way you and your stilts are easily(?) lifted back into walking position and ready to go again.

Solo Training

Your assistant will be a great comfort to you as you take your first few steps, but you may not always have an assistant to help you. In my opinion, one of the best training devices for stilt walkers is a long pole—no, this is not a tall person from Poland, but the wooden kind sold in hardware shops and lumberyards.

Poles are used by rope walkers and others to increase their control and balance. Held horizontally, as a rope walker does, can improve balance. In this respect, however, a pole has a limited use for stilt walkers. Its real value is as a third leg, much like a cane. While walking you can either lift the pole off the ground or let it hang down vertically to touch the ground.

If held like a cane don't put any of your weight on it, just hold it ready to use if you begin to lose balance. You should use it only when you feel as if you're going to fall. If you rely on it too much, you may become dependent on it. Use the pole only to help you as you first begin stilt walking, then get rid of it.

Although using a pole will help you maintain your balance, there will be times where you may still occasionally fall. The pole will come in handy to replace your assistant in getting up. After a fall, get into a kneeling position. Hold the pole vertically in front of you. Using your arms, pull your body up, lifting your legs until you're again in an upright and balanced again.

As with any skill it will take some practice before you feel comfortable. Believe it or not, stilt walking is much easier to learn than many of the other traditional clown skills, such as juggling or unicycling. Unlike these other skills, you will be able to walk on stilts with your first attempts, if your stilts don't lift you up more then 12 inches or so and they have a fairly large foot.

USING STILTS FOR CLOWNING

A Real Eye Catcher

A clown on stilts is "eye catching". The mere sight of a stilt walker immediately draws attention from most any observer. A long-legged giant is an unusual creature. The novelty of a clown on stilts stirs curiosity and amusement. Just the clown's appearance is enough to interest onlookers at parades and other places where his exposure is brief.

At a business promotion, such as a grand opening, the purpose of the clown is to attract attention and draw customers. Clowns on stilts are ideal for this, and they can still perform the normal meet-and-greet activities: shaking hands, telling jokes, and pulling off gags.

A clown that can walk on stilts has a far greater chance of getting a job than another clown. Skills such as stilt walking can persuade a manager to use you instead of his nephew Elwood, who may have never worn a clown suit in his life. A few pictures of

Don't let the attractiveness of the stilts go to waste; once you've drawn an audience, entertain them. What can stilt walkers do? Anything other clowns do: juggle, sing, shake hands, perform stunts and gags, and do magic. Balloon sculpturing is a good skill to use in combination with stilt walking. The stilt walker's height makes it easy for everyone to see how the balloons are twisted and pulled into recognizable animal shapes.

Putting Life in Your Step

Experiment with your stilts and practice moving your body around into different positions. Bend over as if trying to touch your toes. Hold another stilt walker's hand and lift your leg high into the air. Lift it forward, backward, and sideways. Try hopping and running. Twist your body, combining different types of movements with comic dialogue or music. Put some life in your step.

Want to attract even more attention or add a novel twist to your stilt walking? Try stilt dancing—that's right, stilt dancing. What type of dance can be done? Most anything is possible except perhaps break dancing. For starters stick with the easy dances, like the fox trot. Dance with other stilt walkers, clowns, or even spectators. As your skill increases, you can move up to the cotton-eyed joe, polka, or imaginative modern dancing. How about tap dancing or clogging on stilts? Is it possible? If people can jump around and do the polka on stilts, I think nearly anything is possible.

Needless to say, you can't be stiff-legged to dance on stilts. You must have control of every movement and be confident in yourself. The type of stilts you use are important also. Stilts with small feet, such as Chinese stilts, are most adaptable.

Mechanical stilts have been used successfully for dancing even though they have a rather large base. The ankle movement of these stilts allows stilt walkers to be much more mobile than with ordinarily stilts.

yourself on stilts can help impress the store manager of the appeal and visibility such a gimmick provides.

Stilt walking is fun to watch but that alone will not retain an audience's interest. The clown must do something beside stand around on stilts if he wants to keep their attention for any length of time. For parades and grand openings, where exposure is brief, there isn't much time for the stilt walker to do anything extra, but at fairs, carnivals, malls, and other places a pre-planned routine or well-rehearsed set of jokes and gags is essential.

PROPS FOR STILT WALKERS

Stilt walkers have an elegance about them, much like the giraffe, that is entertaining in itself. But why stop there? A stilt walker's appearance can be enhanced by incorporating the same types of props that other clowns use, making him that much more entertaining and unique. An additional element of humor enters the act when long-legged clowns perform these silly stunts.

For instance, take the classic invisible dog on a leash gag in which the clown holds a stiffened rope with a leash, but no dog at the end. The clown walks around as if he was walking an invisible dog. The stilt walker can use the same gag with a longer leash. Picture the scene in your mind, a very tall clown being pulled along by some tiny invisible dog. Even a real dog (if very small) would be humorous because of the contrast in size.

Musical instruments make a good accompaniment to stilt walkers. Since both hands are free, you can strum a guitar or ukele, blow a bugle or kazoo. You don't even have to know how to play an instrument to use it, just blow or strum and sing off key. Add funny lyrics and dialogue and you'll make yourself a hit with the audience. Everyone will want to see the silly singing giant.

Try inventing some props. Use standard props and lengthen or alter them slightly. A yo-yo with an extra long string for example, has an interesting effect. Obtain a good-quality yo-yo and replace the string with one that matches your stilt height. Create some tricks that may be impractical with an ordinary yo-yo. Tell and perform yo-yo jokes or *tall* yo-yo jokes; your audience will think you're a yo-yo! They'll love it!

Combining other skills with stilt walking is a novel way to present what otherwise would be an ordinary act. Magic is entertaining, but if you don't do anything spectacular or elaborately funny, you become just another magician or magic clown. Perform magic on stilts, and you'll be unique and remembered as the giant magician.

Puppets are a great complement to all clowns. The contrast between a seven or eight foot giant and a small hand puppet is humorous in itself. The puppet can be animal, human, or extraterrestrial. It can be smart or crafty, setting up the clown for the jokes. It may be a somewhat more serious creature like Walt Disney's Jiminy Cricket, and the clown may be his less intelligent companion, as Pinocchio was.

Juggling and other manipulative skills may also be successfully combined with stilt walking. Can you picture the interest a juggling giant would stir up? Try some of the old standard tricks and gags; they'll take on new life when combined with stilts.

The kidney swing is a juggling gag that has been around for years. Combined with stilts, it could be very funny. This trick uses three balls, one of which is attached to a thin nylon fishing line or string. One end of the string is tied to the juggler's belt, the other end to one of the balls. The ball on the string should be able to swing freely through the juggler's legs.

The gag works when the prepared ball is thrown down or dropped during juggling. It will swing down between the legs and then swing back up. As the ball swings back it is caught, and the juggling is continued. Stilt walkers can add longer string for greater effect.

A variation of this trick is to attach the string to your wrist instead of your belt. In this way you can control the swinging ball and add some new movements. You could even try using an elastic string to give the ball some rebounding capabilities.

Giant Props

Since giants are bigger then life, they must do things in a big way, such as using larger than normal items. Oversized or disproportionate props complement the bigness of a stilt walker. Such props are available in novelty shops and include such things as, giant fly swatters, sandwiches, hot dogs, hats, and hammers. Disproportioned props, such as an umbrella with a very long handle and a very small top, look good with clowns on stilts.

A giant juggler can use several kinds of oversized props. Juggling rings 12 inches in diameter are large and easy to see.

Extra large 16 inch rings are also available. Beach balls can be juggled, and so can balloons; small 12 inch balloons are easily obtainable. Giant balloons which expand to two or three feet can add a lot of fun to clown antics.

Don't restrict your props to just those things you can purchase in magic shops; try making some of your own. What would look funny enlarged or disproportioned? You might try wearing an extra long tie or coat, using a long walking stick, blowing on a long trumpet or other musical instrument. Use your imagination and create some funny, original oversized props.

TALL FUNNIES

Most any of the typical clown gags can work well for stilt walkers. The fact that the clown is doing them on stilts, adds a novel twist to the presentation.

When my kids saw a stilt walker for the first time at a young age, they truly believed him to be a giant. With wide eyed excitement and curiosity they were magnetically drawn toward him. His comic presentation and terrible singing voice drew a large circle of amused spectators. This unusual clown act was fascinating to me and I knew my kids were delighted.

All clowns must have a personality which is consistent with their costume. Stilt walkers have a distinctive physical appearance; because their bodies are disproportioned and odd, the clown character should also be odd or goofy.

Stilt walking clowns readily adapt to the less intelligent roll when acting with other performers. Remember Herman Munster from the TV series *The Munsters*? He wore elevator shoes to make him look taller then he really was and he played the buffoon. The character he played fit his odd shaped body and mannerisms to a tee.

Stilt walkers can be whiteface, auguste, or character clowns. I have seen some excellent character clowns who have combined tallness extremely well with their character, portraying characters ranging from Uncle Sam to the Jolly Green Giant.

Since the tall clown's physical features are so prominent, the clown should capitalize on this and make reference to it. Create a relationship between the jokes and physical appearance. The visual effect will enhance ordinary jokes and give them greater impact. Use jokes involving tallness or shortness; tell a "little joke" or a "tall tale"; "stretch" your imagination. Go up to the tallest person in the audience and call him "Shorty."

Tell stories, jokes, and riddles using a tall theme such as the following:

Q: Why does a tall man eat less than a short man?

A: Because he makes a little go a long way.

———————

Q: Why isn't your nose twelve inches long?

A: Because then it would be a foot.

Start a conversation with another clown or even a puppet. Work the dialogue using tall and short jokes. In the following examples String Bean represents the tall clown and Shorty represents the short clown or hand puppet.

Shorty: As tall as you are, String Bean, you must be heavy and your feet must get awfully tired and sore after a long day.

String Bean: You said it. I bought this new pair of shoes this morning and they've been killing me all day.

Shorty: Well, no wonder, you have them on the wrong feet.

String Bean: I do? . . . But I haven't got any other feet!

———————

Shorty: You're such a big guy.

String Bean: Yep.

Shorty: You must weigh an awful lot?

String Bean: More then most.

Shorty: Ya know, most things get heavier with size, just as you're heavier than me. But there's one thing that weighs the same no matter what size it is. Can you guess what it is?

String Bean: Ahh . . . a frying pan?

Shorty: No.

String Bean: I don't know. What weighs the same no matter what size it is?

Shorty: A hole.

_____

String Bean: I may be tall, but at least I have two legs and two feet.

Shorty: Nobody has more than two feet. If ya got two legs, ya got two feet; it's as simple as that.

String Bean: I know something that has four legs and only one foot.

Shorty: Yeh, what's that your Aunt Mildew?

String Bean: No.

Shorty: Come on, nothing can be like that.

String Bean: Ya give up?

Shorty: Yeh, what has four legs and only one foot?

String Bean: A bed.

_____

Jokes don't have to be specifically "tall" or "short." Other jokes can be modified slightly by adding a lead-in which deals with height or bigness. The following examples are all older jokes which I have altered by adding an appropriate lead-in.

Shorty: You're so tall and far away from everything, can you smell things down here, like flowers?

String Bean: I can't smell a lot of things you can down there.

Shorty: That can be an advantage around some places, like a fish market.

String Bean: Stinky fish never bothers me. I have a secret method which keeps fish from smelling.

Shorty: Yeh, what's that?

String Bean: I stick cotton up their noses.

_____

String Bean: I think tallness grows in our family.

Shorty: What?. . . How can tallness grow?

String Bean: You remember my little nephew Billy?

Shorty: Yeh.

String Bean: You wouldn't know him since you last saw him, he's grown another foot.

Shorty: What? You mean he has three feet?

String Bean: No, he's growing so fast it's just not normal.

Shorty: Nobody in your family is normal.

String Bean: What do you mean by that?

Shorty: Well, take your Aunt Mildew for example.

String Bean: What's wrong with my Aunt Mildew?

Shorty: She sees with her mouth.

String Bean: Sees with her mouth? What are you talking about?

Shorty: Last time I was at her place for dinner, she had to taste the soup to *see* if it was hot.

———————

String Bean: Hey Shorty.

Shorty: Yes?

String Bean: How come everyone calls you Big Bill?

Shorty: 'Cause I'm a doctor.

———————

Shorty: You're so tall and your arms are so short, how do you ever put your socks on in the morning?

String Bean: It isn't easy. (He pulls up pants legs to show a blue sock on one foot and a red sock on the other.)

Shorty: That's strange, you're wearing one red sock and one blue sock.

String Bean: I know, and the funny thing is, I've got another pair just like it at home.

———————

Shorty: Hey String Bean, where were you born?

String Bean: In California.

Shorty: Oh yeh, which part?

String Bean: All of me of course . . . I may be tall, but I'm not *THAT* tall.

———————

Shorty: How's the weather up there, String Bean?

String Bean: I don't know, let me check. (He pulls out a short piece of rope and holds it up.)

Shorty: What are you doing?

String Bean: I'm checking out the weather with this weather gauge.

Shorty: Weather gauge? . . . That's just a piece of rope, how can that tell you the weather?

String Bean: It's simple, dum-dum. When it swings back and forth, it's windy. When it gets wet, it's raining.

———————

Shorty: What makes you grow so tall anyway?

String Bean: Sandwiches, lots and lots of sandwiches.

Shorty: Is there any particular type of sandwich you like best?

String Bean: Yes, peanut butter and jelly. I have one with me . . . Here, would you like to try it?

Shorty: Sure . . . UCK! This sandwich tastes awful. What type of jelly did you use?

String Bean: Jellyfish.

These jokes originally had no relationship to being tall, but after I altered them they seem very natural as tall jokes. These jokes were included not to give you source material, but to provide examples to spark your imagination and help you create tall jokes of your own.

Stilt walking is a versatile skill that adds variety and is relatively easy to learn. Perhaps even more important, it's just plain fun.

CHAPTER 15

CLOWNING ON ONE WHEEL

Unicycling and clowning make an interesting and fun combination. Many unicyclists add clowning to their skills and performances, and clowns often incorporate unicycling into their routines.

The sight of a clown perched on top of such an unlikely form of transportation is one that commands an audience's attention. Although interesting as it is to see a clown dressed in full attire riding a unicycle, the real joy comes from watching how the silly thing is handled. Riding a unicycle is relatively simple, but a considerable amount of practice is required to make clowning on one wheel effective. Before going into clowning while unicycling, we will first consider learning to ride a unicycle.

HOW TO RIDE A UNICYCLE

Many people have learned to ride a unicycle by trial and error, without any instruction. This isn't the easiest, fastest, or safest way to learn, and it often leads to poor riding habits. Before starting the learning process, you will first need a unicycle.

The Unicycle

The logical starting point is with a standard unicycle. This type of unicycle has the crank arms fixed directly to the hub axle, unlike a giraffe unicycle, which usually has a chain drive.

Manufactured standard unicycles are available in two basic types: tricycle and bicycle. The tricycle type lacks strength and precision and is unsuitable for children, let alone adults. These unicycles will not be considered further here.

The bicycle type standard unicycles have cottered or cotterless bicycle type crank assemblies. These unicycles are often called "professional models," although they are also best for beginners.

The bicycle type standard unicycles are available in a range of prices from about $75 to $165 or more. They vary in quality and features, but most are suitable for learning to ride. Advanced riders usually prefer one of the higher priced models.

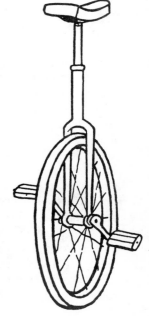

A standard unicycle with a 20-inch wheel is usually recommended for learning to ride, except for children who are too small for this size at the lowest saddle height. In that case a 16-inch wheel is recommended.

The saddle height should be adjusted so that your legs are nearly extended to reach the pedal in a downward position without twisting your body to one side.

The most common mistake is to set the saddle too low, which makes learning much more difficult. If the forward/backward angle of the saddle is adjustable, it usually works best to have the saddle an inch or so higher at the front. When everything is adjusted properly, there should be no feeling that the saddle will slip out from under you forward or backward. It's also important to have the right pedal (usually marked with an "R") on the right side so that riding forward will tend to tighten rather than loosen the pedal threads.

Riding Basics

Unicycling is possible because the rider has control of the wheel and thus controls the relationship between the unicycle frame and the wheel. For example, if the wheel falls behind while you're riding forward and you start to fall forward, increasing the pedal action will make the wheel catch up to you. Or if the wheel gets ahead, then you slow the pedal action so that you can catch up. It all boils down to keeping the base of support (the area of contact between the wheel and the riding surface) under your center of gravity. Forward and backward balance while riding forward on a unicycle is similar to walking. It's balance in motion.

Of course it's also possible to lose balance to the side, but I've found that once the forward/backward balance on a unicycle is mastered, most riders automatically can keep side-to-side balance. The first thing you will want to concentrate on is the forward/backward balance.

Good posture, with the body upright and the head and shoulders in line with the unicycle frame, is extremely important and should be practiced from the start. The main principle to keep in mind is that balance is controlled by pedal action rather than by movement of the upper body or arms.

Learn on a hard, smooth surface. Begin with two helpers. Place the unicycle wheel against a curb or a block of wood. Stand behind the unicycle on the curb or behind the block of wood and tilt the unicycle back toward you. Have one pedal back toward you so that placing weight on it will force the wheel against the curb or block. Straddle the saddle while the helpers stand at your sides. Hold their hands and mount the unicycle by stepping with the other foot from the ground to the free pedal and allowing the saddle to come up over the wheel. Keep most of your weight on the pedal that is toward the curb or block so that the unicycle will not roll forward and out from under you. Your helpers should hold their hands flat, with the palms upward. Apply pressure downward on their hands.

Practice riding forward while holding hands with the two helpers. The helpers should remain directly to your sides as you move along. They will keep you from twisting and falling to the sides so you can concentrate on the important forward/backward balancing.

Doris: How come your nose is swollen?
Daisy: I bent down to smell a brose in my garden.
Doris: You mean rose, not brose. There's no "B" in rose.
Daisy: There was in this one.

Make half pedal revolutions at a time and try to keep the unicycle saddle moving forward at the same speed as the unicycle hub. Allowing the unicycle saddle to lag behind is a common problem. After each half pedal action, freeze the pedals in the horizontal position and straighten your legs while squeezing the saddle between the legs. This will make it easy for the helpers to get you back in balance. Always sit back down on the saddle before starting the next half pedal action.

Here are some tips: (1) look forward rather than down; (2) maintain good posture so that the saddle is directly over the axle; (3) when you pedal forward, make sure that the saddle moves forward at the same speed as the hub.

Dismounting should be controlled, and should be learned both forward and backward. First, come to a complete stop with one of the pedals in the lowest position. To dismount forward, release one hand from a helper and grasp the saddle behind you. Then take the foot from the upper pedal and step down forward.

Catching the unicycle should become a habit, as dropping it can cause damage.

To dismount to the rear, release one hand from a helper and grasp the front of the saddle. Step from the upper pedal to the ground behind you.

Continue with the two helpers until you master the forward/backward correction pattern and require only light hand holding from the helpers. Also, make certain that you're riding with good posture and making the balance corrections by pedal action. It may take less than an hour or it may take a month or more of daily one-hour practice sessions to progress to this stage. In any case, don't go on until you can do these moves with control and confidence.

Next, mount, ride forward, and dismount with one helper. Gradually use less and less hand pressure until you can ride alone.

Once you can solo, you should not experience much difficulty in making turns. All that is required is a slight lean in the direction you want to go and a slight twisting action of the body.

Using first two helpers, then one, and finally working alone, learn the following skills: (1) mounting in the open without a curb or block of wood, (2) riding backward, and (3) rocking back and forth in one place with half-pedal cycles in alternating directions. You will also want to try riding with only one foot on a pedal while the other foot is extended forward or propped against the fork at the base of the saddle tube. Hand-holding patterns and formations with two or more riders can also be performed. For example, two riders can hold hands and ride along in the same direction, or face opposite directions and go in a circle.

Intermediate and advanced skills, such as wheel walking, gliding, spinning, coasting, riding off the saddle, and bouncing, as well as riding giraffe unicycles, are detailed in my book, *The Complete Book of Unicycling*, by Jack Wiley, Solipaz Publishing Company, P.O. Box 366, Lodi, California 95241.

Father: Son, be good while I'm away.
Son: OK, I'll be good for a quarter.
Father: For a quarter? Why when I was your age I was good for nothing.

Doris: I suppose you think I'm a perfect idiot?
Daisy: No, no one is perfect.

Ed: What time is it?
Fred: Can't tell ya, my watch is on the bum.
Ed: Yes, I can see that.

CLOWNING ON THE UNICYCLE

Two phases of clowning are considered: skill on the unicycle, and special cycles and props. Although I treat these separately, they should be combined for the best effect.

Unicycling Skills

Successful clowning on a unicycle requires considerable riding skill. It's definitely not for a beginner. Much of clowning on a unicycle is a deliberate violation of the so-called correct exercise of unicycling skills. A

Tom Murphy and Benji Marantz

basic unicycling skill is to ride smoothly in a straight line. For clowning, a wobbly motion can be used with greater effect. An artistic unicycle stunt is done with control. The clown will do the same stunt with what looks like complete loss of control.

A basic clowning move is to ride forward and allow the unicycle to wobble with the pedal action. Try to exaggerate the action by making it appear that all control has been lost. Add twisting and leaning actions to the riding. To add to the effect, look in the direction opposite the turn. This creates the effect that the unicycle is going the wrong way, out of control.

Next, create the impression that the rider and the unicycle are not working together. Try turning in one direction with an exaggerated lean while looking in the opposite direction. Make it appear as if you have lost balance to the point of no return, then recover at the last possible instant.

Keeping the back straight and the head up are stressed in basic unicycle riding. For clowning, however, ride bent forward so that the unicycle fork and your body form a curve. In this way the unicycle fork will be angled backward while you're riding forward. Instead of keeping your body in line with the unicycle, angled it off in one direction. It's particularly effective to arch backward while riding forward. Also try leaning to the side so that the unicycle fork is angled in the opposite direction. The arms can be worked in an awkward manner.

A good sequence is to ride forward, lose balance sideways, then spin around quickly to recover balance and then ride on. Or ride forward, do a half spin, ride backward, do a half spin, ride forward, and so on. The movement should be made so that it appears that the half spins are falls. Recovery should be made at the last possible instant. By looking away from the direction of the fall, you can magnify the effect. Much of the humor in clowning is achieved by acting with the whole body; this is true when riding a unicycle. Learn to use your body, including facial expressions and eyes.

Next, try an uncontrolled-looking loop-the-loop ride. To do this, ride forward. Start to fall sideways. Make a quick complete circle to recover. Ride forward and repeat the loop motion.

Comedy actions and maneuvers while riding backward are even better. An uncontrolled-looking wobble will serve as a starter. Use the same principles to achieve effects as was done in forward riding.

Many clowning stunts involve fake falling. A problem here is that the unicycle and/or stage floors can be damaged. If you perform these stunts, use a unicycle that has a seat protector and plastic pedal ends

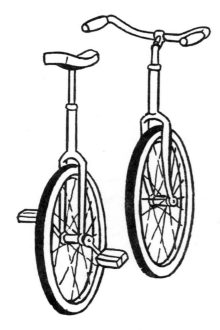

so that no metal parts can touch the floor.

A typical movement of this type is to ride in an uncontrolled manner and then fall forward. Land on the feet with as much forward lean as possible. Immediately go into a forward or side tumbling roll. In the meantime the unicycle crashes to the floor.

Clowning can also be added to many group stunts. For example, two clowns can start by doing various double stunts, with each clown on a unicycle. Then they can begin trying to throw each other off balance. (Of course, all of this should be rehearsed.) For example, the two riders come toward each other at a rapid pace. They start to clasp hands and go into circles, but one rider spins the other instead and continues on forward.

Follow-the-leader type stunts also work well in clowning routines. Another possibility is for a clown to mimic stunts done by a "serious" rider.

A "plant" in the audience always seems to work well. Ask if there are any volunteers in the audience who would like to try to ride a unicycle. The plant waves his hand in the air, yells, and runs up to the stage, tripping on the stairs on the way up. The unicycle clowning stunts described above can follow. This routine works especially well when used with a giraffe unicycle, with the plant being "tossed" aboard the unicycle. Some of the props, described later in this chapter, can also be used.

A clown drill team on unicycles is another possibility. Especially when following a regular drill team demonstration. The clown team tries similar patterns, only they get mixed up and bump into each other, cross

---

What do you get when you cross . . .

a lion and a parrot?
I don't know, but when it talks you'd better listen.

a bumble bee with a doorbell?
A hum dinger.

an owl and a goat?
A hootennany.

poison ivey and a four-leaf clover?
A rash of good luck.

a hen with a banjo?
A self-plucking chicken.

a shark and a parrot?
An animal that will talk your ear off.

An old hobo living in New York hears that his brother is very sick in Los Angeles. By working day and night for a week he is able to beg enough money to buy himself an airline ticket to California. Rushing down to the airport he dumps all his money down at the ticket counter. The clerk slowly counts each coin then says to the hobo, "I'm sorry sir, but you're a nickel short."

"I'll be right back" the hobo tells him and runs out in front of the terminal.

Stopping the first man to walk by he says, "Mister, can you let me have a nickel so I can get to California?

The man flips him a quarter and says, "Here—take four of your friends."

Doris: How can you tell if there is an elephant under your bed?
Daisy: I don't know. How?
Doris: You can touch the ceiling with your nose.

Ed: I can lift an elephat with one hand.
Fred: I don't believe that.
Ed: I'll prove it to you.
Fred: How?
Ed: Get me an elephant with one hand, and I'll show you.

the wrong way, end up without a partner, and so on. This works well for parade riding.

A clown band on unicycles also works well for parade riding. Breadbox drums and other improvised music instruments can be used to give a terrible yet comic blend of noise.

Special Props and Cycles

A number of simple props can be used for clowning. The old water bucket routine always seem to work well on unicycles. Start with two clowns on unicycles, one chasing the other. The one who's doing the chasing carries a bucket of water. He catches up with the lead rider and throws water on him. The wet clown rides off, returns with a bucket filled with paper confetti, and chases the clown who threw the bucket of water. The lead clown falls off his unicycle near the audience and the chasing clown throws the bucket of confetti, spraying it over the audience.

Another good clown stunt requiring only a simple prop is the pole balancing sequence. A tray is securely fastened to the end of a pole. Several light plastic items, such as cups and a pitcher (select the type that looks like ceramic), are connected to the tray by short lengths of string. The containers are placed on the tray and filled with confetti.

The clown then rides the unicycle and balances the pole on his hand. As he rides towards the audience, he stumbles and lets the pole fall toward the crowd. At the last instant he catches the pole. The containers end up hanging by the pieces of string and the confetti falls over the audience.

A toy push-unicycle clown (available from Solipaz Publishing Company) is ideal for clowning when used by a clown riding a unicycle. The toy clown pedals and moves his arms up and down as he is rolled along.

Special unicycles and other novelty cycles work well with clowning, such as, midget unicycles, off-centered wheel unicycles, feet wheel unicycles, animal saddle (such as horse) unicycles, side zig-zag giraffe unicycles, off centered wheel bicycles, or half bicycles ridden on one wheel. A handlebar unit can be used in combination with a standard unicycle. A special bicycle that breaks apart into two unicycles can be highly effective. Most of these special cycles are not available in manufactured versions, but you can have them custom built or construct your own. I recommend my how-to manual, *How To Build Unicycles and Artistic Bicycles*, Solipaz Publishing Company.

Other Ideas

The basic ingredients of clowning on unicycles have been covered here, but this is only the beginning. There are hundreds of ways to put them together. A good way to get ideas is to study unicycling clown performers and to read some of the publications produced by various companies and organizations. See Appendix A for a list of organizations and publications.

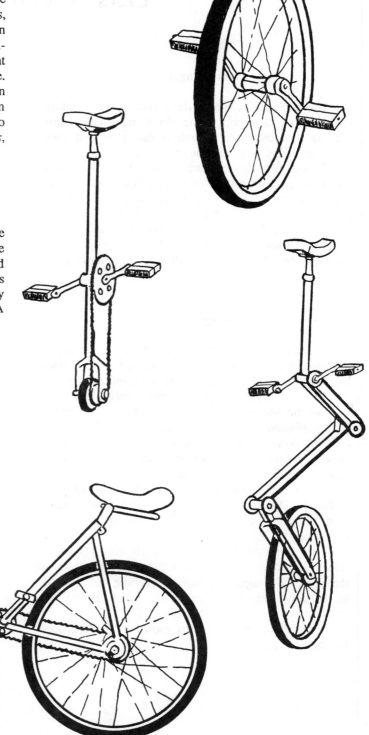

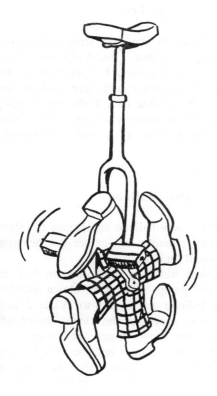

CLASSIC CLOWN GAGS

It's Magic

The audience is shown three hats and a gumdrop resting on a table top. The clown magician claims that he will make the gumdrop disappear and then reappear under any hat the audience desires.

A volunteer chooses one of the hats. The clown sticks the gum drop into his mouth, licks his lips, and says "Yummy." He then picks up the chosen hat and places it on top of his head and says "The gum drop has disappeared and is now under the hat."

The clown can make the gumdrop reappear momentarily by opening his mouth before swallowing the candy.

Noisy Chair

Two chairs are in front of the audience. A clown is sitting in one of the chairs as a second clown comes by. "Mind if I sit here?" the newcomer asks.

"No, go right ahead" the first replies.

As the second clown starts to sit in the chair a loud explosion occurs and he jumps up with a fright. Looking down at the chair he sees nothing. The other clown looking in another direction appears to be unaware anything has happened.

Again he starts to sit down when a loud bang is heard. This is repeated about three times. Each time the first clown takes no notice of the events occurring.

One last time the second clown attempts to sit down. Bending over he moves his posterior towards the chair but stops just before reaching it. Just as he does he sees the other clown stick an inflated balloon on the seat of his chair.

Now discovered, the first clown runs off chased by the second.

A Mind Of Its Own

One end of a long thread is attached to a clown's hat and the other end is held by an assistant hiding off stage. As the clown walks in front of the audience his hat appears to fall on the ground.

The clown picks it up and carefully places it back on his head. The assistant pulls the string causing the hat to fall off again. This is repeated several times. Finally the hat jumps off the clown's head and "runs" away with the clown in hot pursuit.

For My Girl

Stilt walker is carrying a package. With a look of joy he exclaims, "This is a present for my girl friend." Opening the box he pulls out a pair of six-foot long stockings.

Leap Frog

Two clowns begin to play leap frog, each taking turns jumping over the other. Suddenly one clown stops as he is about to leap over his companion. He looks at his friend bent over with rear sticking up. His eyes roll and he smiles then kicks the bending clown in the seat of the pants and runs. The kicked clown falls forward turning a complete sumersault.

The Balloon

A clown takes a new balloon and begins to inflate it. He blows into it harder and harder but manages only to get a small bubble.

A second clown walks by and offers to help by lending him a tire pump. The first clown attaches the pump to the balloon and begins to inflate it with ease. The job is so easy that the clown smiles and pumps as the balloon grows bigger and bigger.

Finally the balloon explodes and the clown jumps high in the air with fright. Now angry, he picks up the pump and begins chasing the second clown.

CHAPTER 16

CREATING YOUR OWN COMEDY ACT

Have you ever enjoyed a good comic routine by a comedian, magician, or other entertainer and wondered where he got his material? How does a successful entertainer come up with a good script? One of the most common concerns for new clowns, and others entering the entertainment field, is how to go about creating an original act.

To listen to some of the successful entertainers today, such as Bill Cosby, you might think that they just sit down and spontaneously produce a brilliant script. That is far from the truth. The creation of a new routine doesn't just happen; it is the result of careful planning, writing, revising, and practice.

A script for a comic routine will start off as a rough idea and gradually be molded and revised into a cohesive, humorous act. Most anyone with the desire can write a script if given some guidelines. The success of the script depends on the effort you put into it and on your ability to make things funny.

BACKGROUND MATERIAL

Before you even make your first attempt at writing a clown script, go out and observe some professional entertainers. Watch clowns if you can, but also see what jugglers, magicians, stand-up comics, and others do during their acts. Ask yourself these questions:

How do they get laughs? How do they present their show to make it entertaining? What elements are present that add to the show's effectiveness? What types of verbal and physical comedy do they use?

Watching successful performers and analyzing their techniques will provide you with insights that you can incorporate into your own shows. This doesn't mean that you copy another person's act; rather you pick up elements that helped make their act successful. These include the types of props, music, assistants, lighting, visibility, and audience participation techniques—in brief, many of the elements which make up good showmanship.

Keep a journal and record the things you learn and observe. A journal can provide a wealth of information, jokes, and ideas as you write new scripts for your own clown act. We'll discuss journals in more detail later in this chapter.

Be careful never to copy or plagiarize another performer's act word for word. No performer can become a success by copying somebody else's material. All successful entertainers use original material. Many do borrow jokes and ideas, and that's OK, as long as they change them to fit their own style and personality. In this way the joke becomes personalized and original.

I highly recommend that you subscribe to some of the periodicals listed in Appendix A. They can provide you with ideas and new material which you can adapt for your own use. They also offer invaluable instruction from experienced professionals to make your own shows

better. *Laugh-Makers* magazine, in particular, is the best source of information I have seen for helping clowns, magicians, jugglers, and other family entertainers.

GETTING STARTED

The first question most people ask when attempting to write a new routine is "Where do I begin?" The possibilities are so numerous that if you don't make some simple decisions at the beginning, you will needlessly waste time just thinking of a place to start.

Without question, the most difficult part of writing a clown script, or any script for that matter, is finding a suitable starting point. Once a start is made, the rest of the routine is relatively easy. Thoughts and ideas will come to you automatically as your creative juices begin to flow. Your initial ideas will evolve and grow. New ideas, situations, and jokes will constantly surface. Some of these will be incorporated into the script while others will be modified or rejected.

The First Three Steps

A suitable starting point can best be found by asking yourself "who?", "how?", and "what?" Before attempting to write any new script you must have answers to these questions, each of which is discussed below.

Who is the audience? The first thing you must decide is who the audience will be and what is expected of you. Clowns perform for a wide variety of audiences in many different places. The physical location may play an important part in the type of show you give. An act that works well for a large staged show, perhaps combining unicycles and juggling, may not be appropriate for a small home birthday party.

Routines designed for walk-arounds such as those used in malls and other business promotions, are short and snappy. This type of presentation works well to attract people for the sponsoring company, but is not good for a seated audience such as a school show.

Another consideration is the type of audience. Many schools, clubs, church groups, and businesses hire clowns for parties, picnics, and other special occasions. A show suitable for one audience may not be effective with another. A presentation for elderly patients at a hospital, for example, may be different from one performed at a child's birthday party.

How is the act presented? The second decision you must make is the type of clown skills you will use. Will it be a puppet routine? A juggling act? Will it include magic, stilt walking, or mime?

Once you have made that decision, you will need to pin it down even further. If you decide to use puppets, will you use hand puppets, stick puppets, or ventriloquism? If you are going to juggle, what props will you use—balls, clubs, stuffed animals, or cigar boxes?

Answer these questions the best you can. As you will see later, you may change your mind about the type of props chosen. The important thing is to gather as much information as you can before you start to write your script.

What is it about? After defining who your audience is and how the act will be presented, you need to decide what it will be about. Choosing a theme or plot will focus your energy on a specific topic, providing a nucleus on which to build, thus avoiding unnecessary wanderings.

The choice of topics is endless. Themes can be comical or serious. Serious topics can be presented in an entertaining way and still teach a lesson. These include topics on bicycle safety, substance abuse, good nutrition, dental health, and the like. This type of presentation is popular for school shows. Many churches also use clowns to teach religious ethics—love for others, sharing, and respect for parents.

The longer the show will be, the more detailed the plot must be. School show presentations and other staged shows need well developed plots.

For walk-arounds, parades, and other occasions where the clown will perform for only a few minutes at most, the plot must be very simple. Short routines are commonly composed of just a few jokes or tricks. The theme may be little more than the clown presenting his skills (or apparent lack of skill). He doesn't have time to develop a detailed plot. Just linking a few jokes through magic, stilt walking, or some other skill is sufficient.

WRITING THE SCRIPT

After deciding who the audience is, how the act will be presented, and what it's about, you are ready to begin the actual writing of the script. Go to the library, a quiet place in your home, or any place where you won't be disturbed. You need to be undisturbed so your creative juices will not be interrupted once they start flowing. Take a pencil and paper, think about the decisions you made, and start brainstorming. How can the skill you choose be used with your theme?

Let me illustrate what I mean. One of my clown routines, "Monster Balls," provides a good example of a script developed by this procedure. The first decision I made was that the routine would be for a general

audience and would be performed on a stage. My next step was to choose a way to present the act. I wanted to make it a juggling routine, initially using three balls. The theme I chose was visiting a doctor.

Now that I had answered the three basic questions, the next step was to find a way to link a visit to the doctor with juggling. I came up with the idea of a juggler with a sick juggling ball. The routine would center around bringing the sick ball to the doctor's office for an examination. The more I toyed with this idea, the more things I dreamed up, until I had worked out a complete routine.

The routine started with the juggler demonstrating to the doctor why he felt the ball was sick. The most obvious difference was that the ailing ball was a sickly green color while the other two balls were a bright, healthy red. When juggling, the green ball would always do something different from the other two. If the red balls went up, the green one would go down. The red would go one way, the green the other. When the juggler attempted to bounce the balls on the floor, the sick ball would manage to hit him in the head; it was totally out of control.

The doctor took the green ball and went through a series of comical medical treatments, which making it even sicker and even turned it into a monster before finally finding a cure. It proved to be a very funny routine.

Another of my acts, called "Huidiot the Magician," combined two skills, juggling and magic. In this routine a mixed-up juggler performs magic. The juggler comes up on stage carrying his suitcase of props. When he opens the suitcase, he finds to his dismay only magic props, having picked up some magician's suitcase by mistake. Not having time to exchange it, he attempts to juggle some of the magic props.

The juggler finds several items he could juggle, but they keep disappearing, multiplying, or fighting with him. The routine consists of a series of misadventures with uncooperative props, involving both magic and juggling.

Let's come back to you now. You're in a quiet room, pencil in hand and paper ready. With your central theme in mind, start by writing down anything that pops into your head. Make a game of it and have some fun. Fantasize in your mind how a good comedy routine would run. Make it as fun and ridiculous as you want, and let your thoughts flow freely.

Once you have started, you don't need to take too much time thinking about what to write down. Don't pressure yourself to think up something funny; let it come by itself.

Write everything down that comes to your mind. If you don't do this, you may forget ideas which could have been developed into a clever part of your routine. An idea may not sound good at first, yet later as you write your script, it may find a welcome spot. You will find that once you start writing, new ideas will start popping into your mind easily.

As you work the script in your mind and write it down, new ideas will emerge which will eventually require you to alter something you had previously written. The story may begin with you talking to a dog puppet, but as you proceed you may find situations in your story where a pig would work better. Make a note to change the dog to a pig, and continue.

Don't do any rewriting until after you complete the first rough draft of the script. The reason for this is so you won't disturb your creative train of thought. If your inspiration is flowing, don't stop it up by rewriting or correcting grammar. Take full advantage of the situation and write until you feel satisfied.

Once the first rough draft is finished, go back and make all the changes that came to mind as you were writing the script. If new ideas hit you, insert them where appropriate. After rewriting the script, it should be much improved over your first draft but still not complete.

Review the script again, making corrections, additions, or deletions. Improve the wording and grammar. Make any dialogue realistic and exciting. All writers and entertainers rewrite their works many times before achieving a finished product.

HOW TO WRITE FUNNY

When you're writing a comedy script, a few guidelines will help make what you write both entertaining and humorous. Your own natural sense of humor will play a big part in thinking up funny lines and situations, but the following guidelines will encourage creative thought and keep your material interesting.

Personalizing Your Script

As you write and revise your script, try to use contemporary subjects. Discuss subjects that kids are involved in today. Jokes and stories about people and subjects known to the audience are always more enjoyable than some unknown character or unfamiliar topic.

Make an effort to know what kids today like and how they think; learn what toys and games are popular. A joke or story using a Transformer will be far more interesting to a young audience than one about jacks or cat's cradle, which were popular games in earlier generations.

Sit down in front of the TV some Saturday morning and watch the cartoons and the commercials. The cartoons will show you the types of heroes kids admire and the commercials will show you the toys that are currently popular. Also, talk to kids and ask them what they like.

The more personalized you can make your script, the more the audience will enjoy it. For example, instead of a routine where you are riding in an airplane, use a bicycle or a skateboard. Rather than have a bird bounce off the windshield and fly away, have a bug smash into your forehead. Kids can relate to things like this.

If the audience consists of one particular group (church, company, school, club, etc.), adopt some jokes specifically for that group. Turn a generic joke into a personalized one and the audience will think you are extraordinarily clever.

Using a person or subject known to the audience in a joke magnifies its humorous appeal. If I told a joke about some unknown man named Jones but changed his name to a popular hero, school official, or classmate, the excitement and laughter would be far greater. We'd much rather laugh at one of our buddies' humorous mistakes or misfortunes than a stranger's. Take this joke for instance: "They laughed when they saw me sit down at the piano with both hands tied behind my back. They didn't know I played by ear." That was the original joke. To personalize it simply add the name of one of the people in the audience. "They laughed when they saw *Miss Winthrop* sit down at the piano . . . "

If you're giving a school show presentation, use the principal's name in some of your patter or in a joke. Mention physical features of the school, the lunchroom or playground, things that are familiar to the kids. Watch Bob Hope give a show. He always says some things about the location or the people, and they love it. Be careful not to criticize or embarrass anyone— make the jokes fun for all.

Personalizing your patter works great with birthday parties. You know the name of the guest of honor, so use it in your show. Since most birthday parties are small, use the names of other kids as well. We all like to hear our own names, and the children will

Keystone Cops (1913).

love the personal attention. It makes the group feel special because the performer has gone out of his way to create special jokes just for them. Not only will the kids get a kick out of it but you will impress the parents as well.

Exaggeration

"The only way I'll ever be as trim as Sylvester Stallone is if he swallows a steel-belted tire."

What's so funny about this statement? It makes an ridiculously exaggerated conclusion which comes across totally unexpectedly.

Exaggeration is sometimes the easiest way to make something ordinary become funny. Take whichever topic you are exploring and imagine what would happen if you carried it to a ridiculous conclusion. Take parts of your topic and distort them out of perspective. Think about your subject and envision an absurd picture as a result. Doing this will lead your thoughts into unexplored channels, creating new material and bits of humor. Train your mind to "think bizarre"; use your imagination and exaggerate.

Much of the humor clowns create uses exaggeration: exaggeration in movement, in speech, and in the use

of oversized or disproportioned props. Distorting the ordinary or familiar is funny. Reacting to sitting on a hot frying pan by grabbing the injured spot and running around in over-dramatized pain, with accompanying silly facial expressions, is much funnier than a simple "Ouch, that hurt."

An ordinary event can turn into a ridiculously funny episode by the simple use of exaggeration. Chasing a fly with a fly swatter is not particularly funny, but if the fly is very tiny and the fly swatter enormously large, you have a funny situation. Another example is trying to protect yourself from the rain by using a tiny umbrella with an unusually long handle. The combination of something reasonable (in this case using an umbrella to keep dry) with something unreasonable (an impractically designed umbrella) makes this scene amusing.

Conflict and Tension

Entering the room, Gus looked for a vacant chair and sat down. As he waited, he began to talk to the person beside him. "John, what do you do for a living?"

"I'm an auto mechanic."

"That's nice." Gus said.

Several other people were in the room listening to this conversation. They were bored. Let's start the conversation again, throwing in a twist.

"John, what do you do for a living?"

"I'm an auto mechanic."

"A mechanic! Why would you ever want to make a living doing that?"

"Well, because I like it and it pays good."

"It sure does pay good," Gus replied. "Too good. I don't see how you guys can get away with charging $30 to drain an oil pan. Don't you think anyone with half a brain could do most of the simple car maintenance you guys charge an arm and a leg for?"

Do you notice the difference in the two dialogues? In the first conversation there was no tension, no conflict, no unanswered questions. It was dull. In the second conversation the mechanic's job was ridiculed. He had to defend himself. Gus egged him on by supporting his statements and asking critical questions. Eventually the mechanic would criticize Gus. An argument might even follow leading to an exchange of punches. This conversation builds tension. You can bet that everybody in the room is listening intently.

When writing dialogue, include tension to interest the listener. It doesn't have to be caused by insults or criticism leading to a physical confrontation. It could be two people falling in love and each trying to make the other admit it. You can use personal, social, economic, physical, and mental problems as a catalyst to generate tension.

The use of conflict and tension in your skits, stories, and jokes creates interest, builds emotional involvement, and intensifies the audience's attention. Whether you're working on an entire skit or simply a single joke you can use conflict and tension. For a skit you will need a plot; this plot will require you to solve some type of problem, building the tension which is needed in order to carry the audience's interest from beginning to end. Individual jokes too, can make use of emotional involvement to enhance the humorous impact of the punch line.

Choose a subject or problem that will create tension for any specific audience, and with a clever turn of a phrase, puncture that tension and release laughter. Start the buildup of tension by hanging the story or joke on a common or recent hostility that everyone shares. Identify what causes the tension in the following short joke:

"I love work. It fascinates me. I can sit and watch it for hours."

The key phrase here is "I love work." Most people dislike work and believe others share the same feeling. A statement contrary to popular opinion creates conflict, and immediately the listeners become curious and suspicious. Suspense is intensified by the statement "It fascinates me." Then finally the punch line switches the thought around, giving a surprise, humorous release. Here is another example:

A policeman walks up to a man who is lighting up a cigar. "Say, you, if you're gonna smoke here you'll have to either put that thing out or go somewhere else."

Janet Tucker and Brian Tucker.

Immediately tension emerges because of the policeman's presence. We all become apprehensive when approached by a law enforcement officer, and we are curious whenever others attract their attention.

Tension can be created in a more direct manner by using hostility, such as insults or criticism.

"You're an ugly, bumbling, worthless, lazy, ignorant skunk."
"Well, nobody's perfect."

Everyone feels hostility toward some person, thing, or idea. For kids these feelings could be caused by mentioning a villain from popular cartoons and movies, homework, chores, taking a bath, brushing teeth, table manners, eating yucky food, or any of the numerous unpleasantries in a child's life.

Charlie Chaplin used unmotivated aggression such as pulling other men's beards and blowing into their bowls of soup. When he did things like this it was hilarious, being hostile yet innocent.

A verbal exchange can occur between two clowns or between a clown and a puppet. Ventriloquists often use the smart-aleck child character to generate tension. Read the following typical ventriloquist type dialogue, noticing how tension and conflict are used. The "V" stands for ventriloquist and the "P" for puppet.

V: I have a new hobby.

P: What's that? Girls?

V: Don't say that.

P: Why, is your wife listening?

V: No, I'm studying hypnotism.

P: At your age, you should study rheumatism.

V: I'm going to put you to sleep. Look me in the eye.

P: Which one?

V: OK just close your eyes . . . You have your eyes only half shut.

P: That's as far as I trust you.

V: Come on, look into my eyes . . . What do you see?

P: Stupidity.

V: You are getting sleepy—sleep, sleep. You are now drifting off into a deep, deep sleep.

P: I'm hungry.

V: Hungry?

P: I always have a snack before I go to sleep.

V: Pipe down. You are under my control. You will do everything I say. Raise your arm . . . now drop it. Good. Stick your hand into your pocket . . . Yes, that's right. Now lend me ten dollars.

P: That's going too far!

V: Hey, you're supposed to be hypnotized—are you trying to make a monkey out of me?

P: Why should I take the credit?

V: How long can someone live without brains?

P: I don't know. How old are you?

V: I want you to know that I'm not so dumb. I live by my wits.

P: Don't you get awfully hungry?

Surprise

Unquestionably the most important element in comedy is surprise; the punch line draws the laugh. A good comedian in telling a story creates an expectation which is suddenly reversed. This sharp contrast between a reasonable sequence of events and the surprise reversal makes us laugh.

A scene from one of Charlie Chaplin's films provides an excellent example of the use of surprise in creating good humor. We see the villain walking down a street. On the sidewalk in front of him, lies a discarded banana peel. Without noticing the peel he continues to walk toward it. The camera shifts swiftly back and forth from banana peel to approaching walker (tension builds). As he takes the final step onto the slippery skin, his foot stops in midair. Seeing the potential danger he jumps over it triumphantly—only to disappear into an open manhole.

In this scene if the villain would had stepped on the peel and fallen it would not have been a surprise and would not have been funny, but having him avoid the "obvious" slip, only to jump into the manhole creates the surprise and humor.

The problem with many jokes and gags is that they do not come across as a surprise. The comedian or clown unintentionally tips the audience off by telegraphing the surprise ending before it happens, thus diluting its humorous impact. If the audience knows or suspects what is going to happen, no one is surprised and there is little laughter.

Coming up with a surprise ending to a story or joke often takes a good deal of thought, trial and error, testing, and rewriting. Let's take beards as a topic and come up with a joke.

What's funny about beards? For one thing they're hairy, and hair gets in the way, as when eating. Our joke can build from this fact. We might say, "I dislike beards, the whiskers always get in the way." This statement may get many people nodding in agreement, but it is not particularly funny. We can improve it by using exaggeration. Change the statement "I dislike beards" to "Beards are stupid." This adds more feeling and increases the humorous potential, but still the joke lacks the element of surprise. Instead of using "Beards are stupid" let's turn it around by saying, "I love beards" or "I love my beard" to personalize it. Personalized jokes are always funnier. This statement can be reinforced and intensified by adding, "Do you notice how distinguished some men look in beards?" To connect more smoothly with the first part you can reword the ending "The whiskers always get in the way" by adding, "The only one thing I don't like about them . . ." This retains the idea that beards are a nuisance.

Finally we have "Do you notice how distinguished some men look in beards? I love my beard. The only thing I don't like about it is the hair."

We took an idea, reworked it, exaggerated and personalized it, and added an unexpected ending, thus creating a simple joke. Use these ideas as you write jokes for your script.

Wordplay

A careful choice of words and phrases can do wonders for a monologue or a dialogue. Read the following conversation between two kids.

"Hey John, look at my new bike!"

"Yes that is a nice bike, Steve. Say, what's this thing on the handlebars?"

"Oh that's a radio. I have that so I can listen to music as I ride."

"I see. Well, Steve, I have to go now. Good-bye."

"OK, bye."

By changing a few words and adding a few more descriptive ones the dialogue transforms into this:

"Hey Hurkie, take a look at my new set of wheels!"

"Zow-wee, Gilbert! That's one awesome looking racer. Say, what's this funny looking gizmo on the handlebars?"

"Oh, that's a high-speed, chrome-plated, ten-transistor radio. I have that so's I can catch some vibes as I'm truckin'."

"I've got to run now Gilbert. Keep the bugs out of your hair."

"OK, I'll talk at ya later."

Do you see the difference? The second dialogue says basically the same thing as the first, but it is much more colorful and interesting.

The names were changed from the bland John and Steve to the more interesting Hurkie and Gilbert. Notice also the use of descriptive phrases rather than simple words. "Bike" became a "set of wheels," "radio" turned into a "high-speed chrome-plated ten-transister radio," "thing" became a "funny looking gizmo," and "listen to music" changed to "catch some vibes."

The characters became more realistic and less formal than they were in the first dialogue. The use of slang such as "so's," "truckin'," and "ya" by one of the boys helped to give him a separate identity from the other.

The second conversation also brought out emotions more clearly. Such words as "zow-wee," "awesome," and "funny looking," gave the listener a clearer indication of how the speakers thought and felt. Conveying emotion is an important factor for building tension and increasing audience interest.

Other ways to make your dialogues and monologues more colorful is to add funny, goofy, or unusual words and sound effects.

Sound Effects. To encourage laughter, it may sometimes require you to say certain words in such a way as to make them sound different or silly. Changing your vocal tone to show emotion conveys thoughts and feelings. Vocal fluctuations are essential not only to good clowning but to any type of acting. How you say a particular word is just as important as the word itself. Put accent and character into the words by varying the speed at which you say them. A multisyllable word or phrase can be said unusually fast or slow or both; saying part slow and the rest fast makes ordinary words sound silly.

Varying the pitch will has similar effect. Start by talking with a high-pitched Shirley Temple type voice and end up with a low Hulk Hogan voice. Pee Wee Herman gets a lot of mileage out of the varying the tone of his voice.

Besides fluctuating tone and speed, add vocal sound effects. While talking about a cow make a moo or two. Let the wind blow, the car engine roar, and the victim scream. The kids will love it. These effects help open up a child's imagination and increase their interest in what you're saying.

Funny Talk. Unusual or funny words add flavor

A customer in a restaurant asks the waiter, "What have you got to eat?"

"We have belchofatti, tongue-jellock, barflish, slo lock, and grissely grits."

"Yuck!"

"We have yuck too. Would you like it steamed or fried?"

Using funny words can make an enormous difference in your speech. Find places in your script for offbeat or unexpected words and phrases. Use your imagination to make up funny sounding words. Use made up words like: badinko, pig-wabby, and bel fella. Need help dreaming up silly words? Look in your English dictionary, you'll find many *real* words which are just as funny sounding, such as medula punjabi, schnitzel, callithump, farkelberry, and eponym.

Substitute funny words for ordinary ones whenever

the opportunity presents itself. For example, when expressing excitement, anger, or surprise, use colorful speech. The following words sound a lot funnier than "Oh my!"

wham	zowie
gee-whizzy	lalapaluzza
gol-lie	cowie-zow
ugg	zip-whoopie
honk	whizzy sizzle

Many of the words we use every day are naturally funny. "Twinkie" is funny, it sounds a lot better than "Hostess Cupcake." Other funny words associated with food are:

banana	pickle
prune	turkey
meatball	tootsie roll
peanut	lollipop
noodle	jelly bean
egg	salami

Many common words can be replaced with more colorful words that have similar meanings. Instead of using the rather bland word "nose" substitute "schnozzle." The kids may not know what a schnozzle means, but if you point to your nose while saying the word, they will understand. Other terms used to describe the nose are:

beak	beezer
boko	proboscis
conk	smeller
sneezer	snoot
snout	snoop

Many words have synonyms like this that can be used effectively. The word "nonsense" for instance, can be described in dozens of ways, with many interesting words such as:

applesauce	balderdash
bunkum	fiddle-faddle
eyewash	flapdoodle
guff	hogwash
humbug	hooey
malarkey	horsefeathers
pish posh	meshuggass
twaddle	tommyrot
slipslop	whangdoodle

All of these words may not be listed in the dictionary, but you can find them in a thesaurus listed under "nonsense." A thesaurus is a most valuable reference tool for finding synonyms such as these.

Using ordinary words in unexpected places or in unusual combinations is also effective. Food, something all kids (and adults) love, lends itself to be combined into gourmet dishes such as frog jelly, pickle pie, spinach-cicles, and green greasy monkey fat. Such expressions are enough to turn any kid's stomach and make him groan and giggle at the same time.

Magicians have an excellent opportunity to use silly talk when they perform. Instead of using the typical "abracadabra" or "hocus pocus" use words such as jelly beans, hockey puck, birdseed, peanut butter, and underwear.

If you use any names in your script, make them unusual. Some examples are Willy William Wilson, Terry Berry, Luann Figwiggle, or Bertha Pimpernuckel. Some of the funniest names can be found in the phone book.

LETTING THE DUST SETTLE

After revising the script, set it aside for awhile without looking at it. In a few days, pick it up and reread it. Again make revisions if needed.

This break will let the dust settle and give your

mind time to clear so that you will look at your script more objectively. This is a standard practice with most all writers. The period of time they allow varies from author to author. Some will let a text sit for only a few days or weeks; others, such as James A. Michener, the author of *Hawaii* and other best sellers, set their manuscripts aside for a full year.

The reason for this break is that when a script is freshly written, it is seen in much the same way a mother views a newborn child—perfect in every way. Also we have become so familiar with the script and we know what it is supposed to say that we may overlook things that are not clear to someone else. Given a few days for the freshness to wear off, the script can be analyzed more critically.

All successful writers rewrite their manuscripts several times until they feel that the work cannot be improved. Although you may not need to be as particular when you write a clown script, you should review and revise as much as possible.

GETTING YOUR ACT TOGETHER

The next step is to physically act out what you have written. Study the lines until you have them memorized, then go through the script as you would during a rehearsal. Practice it without spectators, and just visualize the audience and their reactions.

As you practice, new ideas may come to you—ideas which will make the routine flow more smoothly, new jokes, ways to get more audience participation and involvement, and choosing the right props.

As you rehearse, the act will evolve toward its final state. Rough spots are smoothed out, your delivery flows better; facial expression, body movements and vocal tones are developed through physical practice.

The addition of physical comedy to the script makes ordinary jokes funnier. Study the chapters on mime and physical comedy and keep those ideas in mind when writing and acting out your script.

Trial Run

Once you have the routine down to a point where you feel happy with it and have it totally memorized and the timing set, you can present a preview show or trial run. If you're new at clowning, this show should be in front of family or friends, not a paying audience. You need to have some audience feedback before taking the routine out to the public.

This step is important especially for the inexperienced clown. You may experience unanticipated problems. A friendly audience could help find these spots without too much embarrassment or confusion. You'll be able to test your jokes to see whether you get laughs, smiles, groans, or stone-faced stares. You can see how well the audience responds to your action and instructions.

I recall an instance when I was performing a new magic trick with sponge balls. A six year old girl from the audience was helping me out. I asked her to open her hand and then acted as if I were going to give her a sponge ball to hold. As she did, I slipped two sponge balls into her hand. She took hold of both balls believing she had only one. I instructed her to keep a tight grip on the ball(s) and not to open her hand until I told her to do so.

My trick was to make a second ball appear mysteriously in her hand. Since this was a comedy routine I had planned it to look as if the trick was not working properly. I said the magic word, which was not supposed to work, and led into some comic patter.

I made the mistake of not reminding my new assistant to continue holding onto the ball(s) until I was

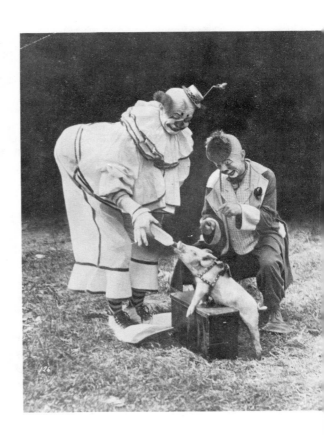

ready. When I said the fake magic word, she immediately opened her hand. Out popped the two sponge balls. Well, this looked like a good magic trick but it spoiled the rest of my routine. I learned from this experience and was able to correct my mistake for future shows.

The Final Step

The final step in creating your new act will be to change parts of it, incorporating those things you learn from your audience. You now have a semifinal act—semifinal because after you begin presenting it to audiences, you are likely to make additional changes. While your patter may sound funny to you, your jokes may fall flat. Keep eliminating the weakest lines and substituting stronger ones. In effect you will be fine-tuning the routine, making it even better.

BUILDING A STOREHOUSE OF KNOWLEDGE

Starting a Journal

I recommend strongly that you keep a journal. Get a notebook and write in it regularly. This could be a great source of information to you later, when you start writing a comedy act. Some people prefer to use a file of some sort in place of the   journal.

What type of things should you record? You may want to write about personal feelings, encounters with interesting people, unusual experiences, and new discoveries about life and how people act and interact with each other. You could include the highlights of a good television show or movie, interesting actors and plots, the type of props used, sound effects, and anything else that made the show entertaining.

You can also include any funny jokes or situations that you experience. Your journal can become a great sourcebook for jokes and gags. If you hear a good joke or make one up yourself, write it down. You may never know when it may prove useful.

A Sourcebook of Ideas

Your journal is the place where you will record sudden bursts of inspiration that can hit at any time.

Such thoughts need to be captured on paper immediately, before they are lost forever. You may want to carry a small note pad around with you for times like this. Believe me, you'll be glad you have something to write on while you're walking down the sidewalk, or sitting in a restaurant and a funny joke or idea hits.

A good habit to get into is spending a few minutes at the end of the day to write in your journal. This will force you to write something. Ideas recorded on a smaller note pad can be rewritten and expanded at this time. Don't get in the habit of throwing a bunch of small slips of paper containing your observations into a file. Organize and write them in your journal. Often I'll be in bed trying to sleep when a clever idea hits me. If I don't write it down then and there, I will have forgotten it by morning. Many other writers and entertainers experience the same thing.

"I get my best ideas in the middle of the night," says cartoonist Bil Keane. "If I wake up and think of something that I can develop into a cartoon, I grab a pencil and write down a few words. I don't wake my wife; I don't turn on the light. The next morning, I look and it says: 'Zup fmph fomph film.' At first I can't figure out what the words are, but when I get to the drawing board, the idea comes back to me."[1]

Creating New Routines

Sometimes a single thought, joke, or burst of creativity can lead to the development of an entire routine. The following short puppet dialogue was created as an afterthought from a single joke I told my wife. I recorded the one-liner in my journal and later built it into a funny little verbal exchange with a puppet character.

In the following dialogue "P" stands for puppet and the "V" for ventriloquist.

V: How are you doing today Hector?

P: Not too well. I've got a cold and my nose is all stuffed up.

V: That's too bad, have you taken anything to help you breathe easier?

P: No.

---

1 This is excerpted from an interview with Bil Keane, creator of *THE FAMILY CIRCUS* cartoon strip. It appears in *LAUGHING MATTERS* magazine, Volume III, #4 edited by Dr. Joel Goodman, Director, *The HUMOR Project*, 110 Spring St., Saratoga Springs, NY 12866.

V: Well I've got just the thing for you—squirt some of this up your nose and it will make you breathe easier (he pulls out a large can of decongestant spray).

P: Oh no, you're not sticking that up my nose.

V: Calm down Hector, this is a decongestant. It sprays into the nose and helps you to breathe easier.

P: How does that stuff make me breathe easier?

V: It shrinks your membranes—

P: No you don't! My brains are small enough, I don't want them shrunk any more.

V: No, no, settle down. I didn't say brains, I said membranes. Membranes are in your nose.

P: You mean I've got brains in my nose?

V: No, knucklehead—

P: What! First you say I have brains in my nose and now I have knuckles in my head?

V: No, you're not letting me finish. Membranes are part of your nose. They are different from brains and when you catch a cold they swell up, making it hard to breathe. This stuff I have will shrink the membranes so you can breathe easier.

P: Well, why didn't you say that in the first place? Give me a snort.

V: OK here goes . . . There, how do you feel?

P: HICCUP!

V: What was that, Hector?

P: Hiccup . . . what's in that stuffff? (Talking as if drunk.)

V: Let's see, it says here . . . mmmm . . . among other things, alcohol.

P: Alcohol! Hiccup . . . how dry I am (starting to sing).

V: Maybe I gave you a little too much.

P: (Still singing.) How wet I'll be . . . hiccup . . . if I don't find the bathroo—

V: That's enough, Hector (clapping hand over puppet's mouth). Take a nap until you sober up.

This routine had its start one day when I had a cold and my nose was stuffed up. I had been having a hard time breathing so my wife suggested, "Why don't you try a decongestant? It will shrink your membranes." I replied jokingly, "But I don't want my brains shrunk!" Using just that simple verbal exchange as a nucleus, I was able to create this dialogue.

Using that single joke as a starting point I was able to define my other parameters: who, how, and what. Since the joke used an exchange of words, I would have to use an assistant or partner. I chose a puppet as my partner and decided to use ventriloquism for his voice.

The theme was evident from the joke; one of us would have a terrible cold. I also decided this would be a good routine for a child's birthday party or staged show. I now had my three starting parameters and a ready made joke. The rest of the routine was built from there.

Don't underestimate the usefulness of a journal; it is one of the most important tools a entertainer or writer can have. You may feel a little unsure of yourself when you first start to write but you will soon see the wisdom of it.

One final point about keeping a journal. It does no good to write in your journal, even if you record the most amusing and enlightening subjects, if you don't read it. Reread your journal often so that you can remember what you have recorded. Clever jokes and interesting ideas if not reviewed, stay where they are—on the page unused.

CHAPTER 17

FUNNY BUSINESS

CLOWNING AS A PROFESSION

Once you have obtained a clown costume, acquired a unique clown face and personality, and developed some basic clown skills, what's next—joining the Ringling Brothers Circus? Not hardly. Running away to join a circus may sound like an exciting adventure, but few clowns find employment that way.

In the minds of many people, clowns are circus performers and anyone who is a clown works for the circus. But this is far from true; circus clowns make up only a small fraction of the working clowns in the world. Most clowns are employed around their own hometowns. They find lucrative ways of making a living as clowns while enjoying a stable family life.

Many benefits are open to those who pursue a career as a clown or a family entertainer and a part-time or full-time career in clowning can be very rewarding. What other jobs will pay whatever you request (within reason!), permit you to work for whomever you wish, and allow you the discretion of working when you want to? To top off these advantages, the best point of clowning is that it makes people laugh and forget their worries for a while. Quite an accomplishment, wouldn't you say?

While clowning does provide many wonderful benefits, it is a real job with many obligations and responsibilities, such as insurance, expenses, punctuality, and the need to perform whether you are ill, in pain, or under stress. Remember, clowning is a *job* that requires

you to be a "professional" at all costs—the show must go on!

Clowns often earn a living performing for birthday parties, picnics, carnivals, TV commercials, and other events. Theaters, balloon delivery services, and some advertising companies also hire clowns. The main job of a clown is to bring laughter, sometimes in conjunction with a goal, such as attracting more customers to a store or shopping center.

Jobs are available for clowns everywhere if you know where to look, from typical parties to the more exotic cruise ships.

Why Clown?

Some clowns derive their entire income from clowning. Others prefer to hold on to their "normal" job and to clown in their spare time, either as a hobby or as a means of earning extra cash. Many churches sponsor clown groups to help spread the good word with a smile or to lend a helping hand. Visiting hospitals and old folks' homes are some of the many charitable activities in which clowns can become involved.

Clowning is an activity that can be performed equally well by either men or women. It is not limited to any particular age, religion, or race. Many retired people get into the business as a means of supplementing Social Security benefits or simply to keep active and have fun. Younger folks get into it for enjoyment, satisfaction, and extra income.

When you work as an independent entertainer, you essentially become your own boss. Unlike employees with other types of jobs, clowns have a great degree of control over where and when they work and who they work for, which offers a sense of independence. You need to satisfy your clients but you have your own freedom to accept whatever jobs you want, set your own price, and take time off whenever you want.

Obviously clowns with many clients will have greater demands on their time, but they can pick and choose the most profitable or convenient jobs.

The biggest advantage to clowning is not the money nor who you work for, but the fact that you are in a profession that is both fun and satisfying. True success in any vocation is not measured by the amount of money you can make but by how much you enjoy what you are doing. If you make $100,000 a year but hate your job and dread going to work each morning, is that really success? It's not to me. I prefer to wake up each morning happy to be alive and excited about each day's activities.

The Professional

What is a professional clown? What is an amateur or a semi-pro? These terms asre used more to describe the performer's professionalism rather than how much money is earned.

A clown can be professional in appearance and action, yet not charge for his or her services. Many work in churches, visit hospitals, and participate in parades and other activities without charging a cent. They would still be considered professional clowns because of the way they conduct themselves.

On the other hand there are novice clowns or people who aren't really clowns at all, but who put on a costume and play the part for a few bucks, handing out sales literature or small gifts at business promotions. Many (not all) of those who do this are "amateurs" in the full sense of the word, even though they are paid for their services. Their knowledge of real clowning and performing is often limited.

Clowns vary greatly in skill and knowledge. They also carry on a wide range of activities, both nonprofit and profitable. A professional clown is a person who takes pride in his or her clowning and has developed the skills and talents consistent with that of true professionalism, no matter how much work is actually done for hire.

Flexibility

Don't let the idea that you are only a clown stop you from participating in some particular job. Clowns have many different skills, all of which can be used in different ways to produce income.

A clown is an actor who portrays an exaggerated comic character, but he can also be a magician, juggler, unicyclist, puppeteer, artist, dancer, or musician. Just because you own a clown costume doesn't mean you're limited strictly to clowning. You may find many opportunities to depart from the painted-face clown and perform as a comic juggler, magician, or ventriloquist. You may put your artistic talents to work by making balloon animals, character drawings, or by face painting. At times you may have opportunities to use any of these talents in nontraditional clown activities to make a buck.

What I'm trying to tell you here is to be flexible and not to limit yourself. Often you may be able to convince a potential employer to use a clown in place of some other gimmick he was considering. For example, what if a store owner called you to pass out flyers in a bunny costume for an Easter sale and you didn't have the needed costume? Instead of telling the owner that you couldn't do it, wouldn't it be better to convince him that the presence of a clown making white bunny balloons for the children would be just as effective? It would accomplish the goal of making people smile, while bringing more business into the store. You have turned what could have been a negative situation into a positive one, to the benefit of all. The store owner has something unique to offer the public, and the kids get to take something home for free.

You may be asked to dress or act in some manner other than the clown character you have developed for yourself. If you have the ability to do more than hand out balloons or being "just a clown," by all means do it. Let the store manager know you stilt walk or play a guitar; a jolly juggling giant or minstrel may appeal to him more than an ordinary clown. Maybe a magician, wizard, or mystic would satisfy his needs; any of these a magic clown can portray simply by wearing a different costume. Use your imagination to create new jobs.

As a clown you should possess some skills that help to distinguish your character, be it puppetry, unicycling, balancing or whatever. These skills give you an opportunity to make extra cash in more ways than a strictly as a clown character. As a juggler, for example, you can advertise yourself in several different ways and use your skills to generate income from a variety of sources. As a clown who can juggle, you have a unique talent to help sell your clown act to potential clients. If they want an entertainer but not particularly a clown, you can still interest them as a comic juggler. This will appeal to many of the older age groups who might consider that the clown character too childish for their activity. Office and adult parties, nightclubs, casinos, trade shows, TV commercials, theme parks, college shows, and cruise ships may all prefer the juggler over that of the clown. The jokes and other material may be much the same as you use as a clown but because you're wearing a different costume (jester's suit, tuxedo, etc.) you appeal to a different group.

INCOME AS A PERFORMING ARTIST

Clowning and Money

What can you expect to earn as a clown or family entertainer? Clowning can be a very profitable part-time job or a satisfying career. Typically you can expect to make $50 for a single show or as much as $400 if you're highly skilled.

Actually there is no upper limit to the amount you can make. Clowns are performing artists, just as actors or vocalists are. Many clowns get jobs working in TV commercials and some star in their own shows, usually on local networks. Fred Allen and W.C. Fields began their careers as clown jugglers.

We can only imagine the amount of money that successful movie and TV comedians make. Well known magicians such as Doug Henning, David Copperfield, Harry Blackstone and others make many thousands of dollars for their shows. Although you may never reach the heights of success these performers have, you can still make clowning a satisfying and rewarding profession.

Even though the payment for a single show may sound good and tempting, being a full-time entertainer is a hard business. Much traveling is required, and the hours are inconsistent. As your own boss, you must pay all your own expenses, insurance, and social

Ed: Where do all the bugs go during the winter?
Fred: Search me.
Ed: No, thanks. I just wanted to know.

security tax, to which employers contribute in other kinds of jobs. You get no paid vacations, sick leave, or retirement benefits. Also, the work can be very sporadic. Unlike a 9-to-5 job, you are paid only for the shows you give. Weekly income can be terribly variable, $1000 one week, $300 the next.

Weekends attract the greatest number of bookings simply because that's when people are most available. Jobs on weekdays are significantly fewer and harder to obtain. Lesser paying jobs may be accepted to keep income flowing in.

For these reasons most clowns and other family entertainers find part-time clowning most suitable. They can keep the stability and security of their "regular" jobs and still enjoy the excitement and extra income of show business.

Many college students have worked their way through school as magicians or clowns. Retirees find it an excellent way to spend their time and supplement their income. Many people who start out part-time, as most do, fall in love with the profession and quit their ordinary jobs to go into show biz full-time.

As a part-time way of earning extra money, clowning is hard to beat. Compared to other part-time jobs it has many advantages. Few jobs will pay as well for the amount of work performed. Sixty or seventy dollars an hour is not unreasonable to expect from a single show. Take birthday parties, for example, your involvement may only last 60 minutes, or about a dollar a minute. Sounds good, doesn't it?

Although this sounds like a lot, the amount earned per hour drops drastically if you add the time you spend putting on makeup and wardrobe and traveling to the event. The total time spent for going to a party may double. But on the other hand, most other jobs don't pay employees for dressing or for driving to and from work either. Whether or not you include the time you spend at these things, earning $50, $70, $90 or more to attend a party is still a lucrative part-time business.

Setting Your Rates

How much should you charge for your services? Prices vary from one area to another and fluctuate with economic conditions. You can get a handle on the prices charged in your own area by calling a local theatrical or entertainment agency or even individual entertainers and asking them what they charge. You can find them by looking in the *Yellow Pages* under "clowns," "magicians," "entertainers," or "theatrical agencies."

Rates will vary depending on the event (party, school show, picnic, etc.), its length, and possibly the type of show (magic, puppetry, comedy juggling, etc.). For a child's birthday party, $50 to $150 for a 30 to 90 minute show is typical. The price varyies with the length of the show, degree of skill, and reputation of the entertainer.

PUBLICITY KITS

As an independent entertainer you will need to contact many potential clients and convince them that hiring you will satisfy their needs. To promote yourself in a businesslike manner and to show clients that you are a professional, you will need what is known as a publicity kit—a sales tool which describes you and your show.

In any situation where you solicit a business or organization to use your services, leave a copy of your publicity kit with them so that they can check your qualifications and keep your name on file for future occasions.

Your publicity kit, in a sense, is a glorified resume. It should include pictures, letters of recommendation, newspaper clippings, and copies of published articles about you. Mention any awards or honors received, membership in professional organizations, schooling or training, any special or unusual effects you use, flyers describing specific shows, and anything else that may help convince a client to hire you.

Two of the biggest selling points in your publicity kit are testimonials and letters of recommendation. They give you credibility and show that other clients have been pleased with your work. If you've done a good job for one client and he was pleased with your performance, don't be afraid to ask for a letter of recommendation. The worst that can happen is that he'll say no. On the other hand, you may end up with a valuable recommendation.

Letterhead

One of the first things you must do, whether you are clowning full or part-time, is to have some stationery and envelopes printed with your business name. Becoming a professional clown is a business, and like any other business you need business cards and stationery in order to present yourself in a professional manner.

What type of letterhead would be suitable for a clown? If you have a company name such as "The Funny Company" or "CLOWNS-R-US," you can use that. If you don't have a company name, you can simply use your stage name along with your given name: "John Smith, Sparky the Clown." Adding a distinctive or descriptive logo also helps.

Design a letterhead that describes your specific talents or use something that illustrates your clown character. Tooter the Clown, for example, may use a picture of a horn on his letterhead. What type of letterhead would describe you?

Cover Letter

On your letterhead stationary, write a letter to your prospective client. Introduce yourself and state exactly what type of job you are asking for. Make it read like a personal letter, not like an ad. Be brief and to the point; the other materials in your packet will give the details.

To motivate him to look over your material soon after he receives it, make sure to say that you will call in a few days. When you call, he will be primed for your sale's pitch, and the job of selling him on your show will be easier.

Folder

All the material you will send should be neatly contained inside a folder. This folder will be the fir thing your prospective client sees, so it's important to make it attractive.

Folders used by entertainers come in a variety of styles and colors. It's best to have some printed up especially for you with your name, logo, and perhaps even a picture on the cover. Glossy paper and full color will give it a professional look, but will also greatly increase the printing expenses. Your printer or a graphic artist will be able to help you design a suitable folder.

ADVERTISING

Many full-time professional clowns saturate the media market with ads in newspapers, shopping papers, the *Yellow Pages*, radio, mailed flyers, and business cards. Where does the part-time clown advertise and how much can he afford to spend? Perhaps the most important first step in making yourself known is the business card. This card will be a reminder and a source of information about you to your potential customers. A speedy print shop can crank out 500 cards for about twenty dollars if the design is simple. One booking would pay for this initial investment. Another investment that is very important is a telephone answering machine. The cost (depending on the style) could run you about one hundred dollars, but consider it money well spent. Nothing is so annoying as trying to get hold of someone by telephone and never finding anyone at home. The mother who is trying to book a birthday party for her child will give up and look for another clown.

My favorite form of advertising is the shopping papers. From time to time they will offer free ad space so they can increase the size of the publication and increase the size of their distribution area. These small papers, which are found in grocery stores and convenience outlets, charge very little for ads in comparison to the local newspapers. With an investment of five to seven dollars, an ambitious entertainer may take in three or more shows.

Mailing flyers can be profitable if done in a well thought out manner. One area to investigate is the service offered that enables dozens of companies the opportunity to combine together into a package that will be mailed to a specific area in a town. Usually they will guarantee that no other business similar to yours will be promoted in the same mailing. Homemakers actually look forward to receiving these packages because they often contain store coupons. You should decide what to feature; should you give a five-dollar-off coupon or perhaps offer two shows for the price of one? Personally, I offer free balloons to be given out at the party in addition to the regular magic show. Be sure to note what neighborhoods the coupon packages are going to be distributed in—it wouldn't do you any good if they are circulated in areas where the people can't afford your services.

Personal flyers printed up by you and distributed at shopping centers and businesses are another way of bringing your message to the public. Newspapers are also useful in letting the general public know where and how to contact entertainers. Holidays such as Christmas, Easter, and Halloween, are excellent times to advertise holiday characters or services. Newspapers are also a great source of information regarding grand openings and special events. However, by the time the event is noted in print it, may be too late to include you in the budget planning.

Many performers prefer the *Yellow Pages*, and this continues to be the most popular way of informing the public of your services. In my case, however, I feel that the added expense is not needed. In the past I had to make a decision on whether to purchase an ad or to rely on my then present techniques. Listening to my fellow performers complain about having too much work and consequently having to give much of it away, I decided not to advertise in the *Yellow Pages* and to rely on the overflow from the others. It must have worked because I have had several hundred shows per year for the past several years—more than enough for me! The decision is yours, but you should carefully investigate before making such a large financial investment as the *Yellow Pages*. I have met some entertainers who swear by the *Yellow Pages*. If you are after quick and steady bookings and can afford the ad and extra phone charges, then by all means invest your money there.

My favorite and most successful technique for getting information out about me is by word of mouth. I firmly believe there is nothing better than a satisfied customer who is enthusiastic and willing to give out your name and phone number!

THE TELEPHONE SALE

When the phone rings, whether your two-year-old just spit up on you or your mother-in-law just moved out of the state, you should always answer the phone in a calm, friendly voice.

Doctor: Your cough sounds a lot better today.
Patient: It should, I've been practicing all night.

One of the first things I ask is "How did you find out about me?" This gives me useful information for future reference, even if the customer chooses not to hire me. Usually the caller wants to know what my service includes and more important, how much it will cost. I try to talk about the cost after I've had the chance to give them my "pitch." I may begin by explaining who I am and what I do for a living. I may tell them how many shows I perform yearly and mention several of the best-known shows which they may have heard of or read about in the papers. This establishes my credibility as a professional. Once the initial questions are answered I may try to book the show without discussing the price fully. This gives them a feeling of obligation. Information, such as the child's name and age, makes the conversation more personal and tends to clinch the deal. When I do discuss the fee, I make sure it is understood and state whether or not it must be paid in advance.

From time to time a customer may call and say that he or she has a certain amount to spend. If this amount is not within my price range and if I cannot persuade them to pay more, I will refer them to one of my fellow performers whose fee does fall within their range. My primary goal is to satisfy the customer, whether it will be me providing the services or another. If the customer must check with a spouse before accepting my services, I ask if I can hold the date open and phone them later. This increases my chances for booking the show.

I do retain a degree of flexibility regarding pricing. I charge less to come into a home and entertain as a magician than as a clown—it takes me less time to dress and undress. Also, I can eliminate the service of giving each child an animal balloon or perhaps shorten the show a bit. I will give in a little in order to satisfy the customer, but not so much as to underbid my fellow entainers or deprive myself of potential earnings.

Once the show is booked, I record all the necessary information such as time, place, directions, names of persons to be called on to assist in the show, stage, microphones, mileage (always plan on arriving ahead of time to allow for delays), tolls, and expenses. This detailed information assists me with my yearly taxes as well as providing prospective business for the next year.

ACQUIRING NEW BUSINESS

As I mentioned before, newspapers are an excellent source for gathering information on grand openings. Day care centers sometimes have available lists of other centers, along with phone numbers and addresses: these are great when it comes to mailing flyers and making phone calls.

I record each performance on a 3 x 5 card and file it monthly for use next year. Several months ahead of time I pull the cards and drop a flyer or make a phone call to the previous customer. A clown in Atlanta named John Cooper "Shortee" has a wonderful system which he calls his "fan club." At each birthday party where "Shortee" performs, he hands out a form for each child to fill in and mail back to him. This gives him a mailing list. He also includes a party planner for Mom to assist her in the preparation of the next birthday party. This technique has given John many new customers and many repeats of old business. He makes customers feel special with the extra attention he gives them. If you're interested in learning more about the details of this technique, write to SMILE-MAKERS, P.O. Box 341, Forest Park, Georgia, 30051-0341.

If you enthusiastically pursue new business, you will be rewarded. What does it cost to stop at a store on the way home from a birthday party and introduce yourself to the owner or manager? When a sharp entertainer sees an "Opening Soon" sign, he should take the time to investigate and drop off a card and/or a photo.

A great source of new business that I use is a booking agency. Basically, the agency will search for work for entertainers and charges them a 15% commission. This is a wonderful opportunity to gain new business and be protected by the agency's contract as well. This eliminates the need for the entertainer to worry about collecting the fee. Caution is needed in regards to quoting your price to the agency. Keep in mind that if you perform a show for a set fee, th agency will often deduct 15% from that, although som agencies will add it on. It may be difficult at firs to get an agency to hire you, so give them a call, o better yet, drop by and invite them to see you in actio at a public show. Let them know who they woul be recommending.

CHAPTER 18

JOBS FOR CLOWNS

TYPES OF WORK

Let's take a closer look at the types of jobs available to clowns and family entertainers. A booking agent or event planner may be the source of any of the following jobs, but you can also book them directly with a client yourself. A contract for one job can lead to another. A company which hires you for their picnic may later ask you to work at the company fair. Often guests or customers of your client will ask you to perform for their child's birthday or for another company. Doing a good job wherever you happen to work and being courteous to everyone you meet will open the door for many future bookings.

Birthday Parties

Most clowns begin their professional career by performing at birthday parties, and for many clowns this lucrative field remains their main source of income.

Clowns usually spend 45 to 90 minutes at a birthday party. About half of this time can be a formal show where everyone sits down to watch. The rest of your time at the party should be spent in interaction with the children. You may want to lead the kids in singing "Happy Birthday" and help serve the cake. You may do face painting, make balloon figures, or lead games. Some clowns provide the equipment for Pin The Nose On The Clown or Bean Bag Toss games.

Because birthday parties are the way most clowns get their start in the profession, Chapter Nineteen explains in detail how to set up and operate a birthday party business.

Banquets

Clubs, church groups, and other organizations often have banquets which include entertainment. You may start a banquet engagement by greeting people or by table hopping before the meal is served, but normally you are expected to do a show afterwards. You will be only part of the event. There probably will be some announcements or awards. Plan a show that will run 20 to 30 minutes and don't go over your scheduled length, especially if it's a banquet for a youth group on a school night. Be prepared to shorten your show if the evening's program runs over.

You may perform on an elevated stage, but more frequently you will perform on the floor with an audience seated at tables, which means you must keep props up high to make them visible. Magic tricks that can be held in your hands are preferable to ones that must sit on a stand.

Some caterers will refer their clients to entertainers. Another way to get banquet leads is to check the newspaper for stories about banquets that have just been held. Contact the people who planned that banquet. People often belong to more than one organization and may be involved in planning another banquet soon, or will keep you in mind for next year.

Blue and Gold Banquets. Every Cub Scout group holds a Blue and Gold Banquet in February to commemorate the anniversary of scouting. Families attend the banquet with the majority of the kids ranging from eight to eleven years old. Entertainment is usually part of the celebration.

You can do your regular banquet show, but should theme part of it to Cub Scouting by using scout symbols or a blue and yellow (gold) color scheme. You can change a prop's decoration by making a temporary cover for it. Copies of scout symbols are available from your local scout office.

The scout office is your source of contacts. Leave your business cards and flyers there in October or November when groups start considering their entertainment.

Company Picnics

Expect to perform for two or three hours when you do a company picnic. You start by greeting the arriving guests and doing walk-arounds. At some point you will present a half hour show that must be performable under outdoor conditions. You may also be expected to help organize and run the picnic games. Clowns who do many picnics sometimes supply gunny sacks, ropes, and other game props. Many clients expect a picnic clown to supply and distribute helium balloons. Balloon sculpture and face painting are also frequently part of a picnic package.

Large companies sometimes hire a caterer or event planner who books the entertainment. Private parks specializing in company picnics sometimes hire an entertainer to handle all their events. You can book picnics directly by contacting the manager or personnel director of each company.

Restaurants

Restaurants hire clowns to greet the guests and entertain them while they're waiting for a table or food. Usually you table hop, going from table to table doing short routines. Try not to let one group monopolize your time, preventing you from entertaining everyone. You must stay out of the way of people serving food and clearing tables in a narrow space so you're limited to props you can carry in a pocket or a small bag. Puppetry, ventriloquism, close-up magic, balloon sculp-

ture, and small sight gags paired with comic patter work well in restaurants.

Contact the manager to get a booking. Restaurant engagements are usually for an extended period to allow word-of-mouth publicity to build. Restaurants can't pay as much per hour as some clients, but some of them will allow you to carry a small container for tips. Table hopping is a good way to make contacts for higher paying jobs, but ask people to call you, don't discuss other bookings on the restaurant's time. If you would like to learn more about table hopping, Magic, Inc. publishes a small book by Bruce Posgate titled *Table Hopping.*

Restaurants also use clowns to promote the use of their banquet room for birthday parties. Whether or not you are hired to table hop at a restaurant, you may

Gene "Cousin Otto" Lee

be able to arrange with the manager to handle entertainment at all the birthday parties he schedules. These engagements consist of a 20 or 30 minute show, which can be supplemented by meet and greet activities or handing out balloon animals or other gifts.

Store Promotions

Stores that are having grand openings frequently hire clowns for the event. Commonly other promotions involving the clown are used in order to have something to advertise, to attract attention, and to generate goodwill. Many store managers mistakenly think of clowns solely as somebody to hand out helium balloons because they're unaware of what's possible. You can meet that expectation or convince them to do something different. You can perform scheduled shows on a stage or in a roped off area of the parking lot, but more often you will be continually performing short routines or shows on the walkway in front of the store. Choose props that don't have to be reset between performances. After each show, announce that you are there courtesy of the store and ask your audience to stop inside to thank the manager.

Some store chains book an entertainer to travel to each of their stores, but most often the managers of individual stores book entertainment for their own promotions.

If you make it known in your advertising materials that you're available for this type of work, clients will call you. To increase your business you may contact them first and suggest they use your services to promote their opening. Look for stores that are prepared to open up business. You've made the initial contact and have given them your name for future reference. Your contact may be just the thing to convince them that a clown is what they need.

Malls

Malls provide a lot of business for clowns and other family entertainers. Clowns can work for an individual store in a mall or for the entire mall. Mall performances fall into four types: walk-around, atmosphere, stage shows, and character breakfasts.

Walk-arounds, also known as strolling, is walking through the mall shaking hands, doing short routines, and interacting with the public.

Atmosphere performing includes strolling and interacting with the public, plus performing unannounced

shows 10 to 20 minutes long at various locations. The goal is to create a friendly, festive atmosphere and to attract people to some of the stores away from the center court without blocking doorways or distracting the shoppers for too long. When working alone, you do a show, stroll until you see another good spot, and repeat your show. When appearing with a group, you perform alternate sets, rotating among designated performance locations.

A *stage show* is performed according to an announced schedule, usually in the center court. Most malls have a platform and sound system you can use, but many performers supply their own equipment to meet their specific needs. Anything else you need, like a backdrop, you may have to supply. If you don't use a backdrop, be sure that being seen from behind won't give away your routines. Also, some malls are multistoried, with balconies overlooking the center court, so you need to choose routines that can be viewed from above. Generally mall shows last from 25 to 40 minutes. Your show should be long enough and entertaining enough to be worth coming to see, but not so long that it prevents people from making purchases.

A *character breakfast* is held for a special event such as Christmas or Easter, and takes place before the stores open. This is a catered breakfast for small children and their parents where a fee is charged. You start off by table hopping, and you may help with the drawing of door prizes. After everyone has eaten, you present a stage show concluding with the introduction, or magical production, of Santa or the Easter Bunny.

Malls provide an excellent source of revenue for clowns. In contrast to many other jobs like parties and banquets, which last only an hour or two, when you are hired to work at a mall, you will be booked for much of the day. Although you may not earn as much per hour as at some of these other events, you earn more overall because you are paid for working a full day (5 to 8 hours).

You can expect to be paid anywhere from $100 to $400 a day for mall work. The price varies with the type of work you do; less is paid for strolling than for the staged shows. You may be hired to stroll the mall for the day or to set up and perform four scheduled

Teacher: Why are you late!
Student: Sorry, It was late when I started from home.
Teacher: Then why didn't you start early?
Student: But teacher—by that time it was too late to start early.

shows. You may even combine the two by strolling between the shows. You may suggest this option, and of course charge more for the combined service.

Mall work also provides you with opportunities for promoting yourself, getting publicity, and making additional bookings. Customers, individual store managers and owners, and mall employees frequently will ask, "Do you do birthday parties?"

The mall hires performers to attract attention, promote goodwill, and attract customers. Any mall using the services of an entertainer will promote the event in the local newspaper, giving you greater exposure. Your picture may be included in their ads. You may even have a short feature written about you in the shoppers' news. Some of this material may be suitable for your publicity kit.

If you do a good job, you will have a strong chance for repeat business. The mall officials will become familiar with your work and will know what to expect from you. Repeat business can be your ace in the hole. It will save a substantial amount of your time because you won't have to dig up new business.

Most every mall has a marketing director or promotions manager, whose job is to keep something going at the mall every weekend. The job includes planning holiday events and decorations, publishing and distributing the monthly shoppers' news, and hiring entertainers for promotional purposes.

How do you get a booking at a mall? The mall's marketing director will not thumb through the phone book to look you up. You must contact him. Your first step is to find out who the director is and how to get hold of him. Published directories contain this information, contact your city library or Chamber of Commerce to get a copy.

Give the director a call and introduce yourself. Find out if he uses entertainers for promotions and explain that you would like to send him some information about yourself for his files. Avoid going into a sales pitch unless he encourages it.

Promptly send him a copy of your publicity kit containing pictures, newspaper clippings, letters of recommendation, and so forth. Include a cover letter explaining who you are and why you're sending the material.

Wait seven to ten days to allow the material to reach him and to give him time to look through it. Then call him up and make your sales pitch, or set up an appointment to visit with him in person.

You probably won't get an immediate booking, but you will have made a valuable contact. The director plans events four to six months in advance. When your

service's are needed, the impression you made and the material in his files will work for you in landing that next job. Send him a reminder every three to six months to let him know you're still available.

All mall performances are booked by that mall's marketing director. The marketing director is your boss, but each store manager is also partly your client because the stores contribute to the mall's promotional budget. Between shows, move around the mall and greet the store employees so they get a chance to see what their money has gone for. After each show ask the audience to thank the store managers for providing your show.

Many malls have a policy specifically prohibiting entertainers from accepting tips. Malls pay you well to generate goodwill for them, so if you're offered a tip, graciously decline, explaining that you are there courtesy of the mall.

Carnivals and Fairs

Fairs, carnivals, and festivals use clowns for walk-around, atmosphere, and stage entertainment, and also sometimes for supervising organized children's games. Most fairs have a stage for entertainment, including performances by local amateur groups. Many clowns who tour fairs provide their own stage or performance area because they can do more shows and receive a higher fee.

An option to working directly for the fair is to work for one of the exhibitors at their booth or to become an exhibitor yourself. Some clowns will rent a booth and then charge a fee for face painting, balloon sculpture, or photo buttons. Others use a booth to demonstrate what they do and to distribute promotional material, using the booth to obtain bookings for the rest of the year, instead of as a direct source of revenue.

Entertainment is booked by each individual fair, but most fairs belong to a regional association which holds an annual convention, including a showcase for acts. You can work at your local fair, or if you wish to travel, book a series of fairs and stay in their campgrounds. The staff of your local fairground can give you information on booking their fair and on the

A peanut sat on a railroad track;
His heart was all-a-flutter.
A train came speeding down the track.
Toot! Toot! Peanunt butter.

Mauri "Binkie" Norris

regional association, or you can contact the Chamber of Commerce. You can find detailed listings of festivals and fairs throughout the country from the following books: *Chase's Annual Events*, published annually by Contemporary Books and from the *Directory of North American Fairs and Expositions*, published annually by Amusement Business, Box 24970, Nashville, TN 37202.

Many fairs and parks allow street performers and strolling vendors to work without setting up a booth or paying a registration fee. The performer earns money solely by passing the hat through the audience. Although fairs and open air arts and crafts shows are popular places for this type of activity, you can perform wherever it's not prohibited by law. You can earn a good day's pay by giving several 15 to 20 minute shows in areas where there is a lot of passing traffic. In several of the larger cities in the United States and elsewhere, specific spots have become popular sites for weekend performers. For more information about street performing subscribe to *The Street Performer's Newsletter*, P.O. Box 570, Cambridge, MA 02238-0570

Trade Shows

A trade show is like a theme fair. Some are open to the public, like a home show, and others are open only to people in the industry so manufacturers can demonstrate their new products to distributors and retailers. Trade shows can be highly profitable and usually pay more than other clown jobs. A fee of $300 to $400 for working a trade show is not unusual.

Clowns are sometimes hired by the trade show's producer to provide overall entertainment. Individual exhibitors also hire clowns to attract attention to their booths either by distributing balloons and samples or by doing brief acts. Exhibitors book their entertainment directly or go through public relations firms that help them in planning their booth.

If you do a staged act, for which you would charge more for, you may be expected to tie your client's product into the entertainment in some way. By using the name of the company you're working for, you help accomplish their goal of advertising and name recognition. Use it several times and make them happy and consequently you'll increase your chances for working with them the following year.

Theme Parks

Theme parks are one of the few places where a variety performer can find steady work and regular pay. If you're interested in the excitement of places like Disneyland and are looking for steady work, good pay, long hours, hot sun, and lots of experience, you'll find theme parks right up your alley. Each year theme parks such as Disney World, Knott's Berry Farm, and Kings Island Park look for new talent to staff their shows.

Theme parks hire clowns for atmosphere entertainment and to give staged shows. They also use jugglers, magicians, musicians, unicyclists, trained animal acts, and other variety performers.

For atmosphere entertainment, park officials look for somebody who will make personal contact and interact with their guests. At a park you may spend much of your time entertaining people while they wait in line.

Theme parks also present elaborate stage shows that are produced by the park employees themselves or by an outside producer such as Mark Wilson or Paul Osgood, who cast the shows. Occasionally ads appear in trade papers announcing openings in these shows.

Salaries range from about $200 to $300 per week. One of the main benefits of working at theme parks is that they provide performers with the opportunity to gain a lot of experience. You will be expected to give five to eight shows a day, lasting 20 to 30 minutes each, six days a week. Performers also learn how to play to varyious sized audiences and to work with other performers and stagehands. Some have been able to use the knowledge they gained about putting shows together to get jobs after the park season as entertainment managers for nightclubs, parks, and other places which use live entertainment.

Like many other performing jobs, you get a theme park job by auditioning. The large theme parks hold auditions in several places throughout the United States and Canada. When you contact a park, find out when and where they will be auditioning in your area. Also find out whether the park will be looking for stage shows or strolling. Ask how much time you will have for your audition and find out whether you need to make an appointment or just to show up between specified hours.

Prepare a three to five minute routine and bring a one page resume or your publicity kit to the audition. Don't ask the auditioners what they want to see, just show them what you do. Prepare your best material; they want to hire the best performers they see. Be courteous and polite to everyone you meet and thank the auditioners for their time, a small thing for you to do, but auditioners look for people who get along well with others.

After seeing hundreds of variety artists audition, park officials will remember certain ones and are likely to offer them the jobs. You can help make your act memorable by following these suggestions. First be unique. If you're a clown magician you may be in competition with a dozen others. Do something special, use a different slant in your presentation to set it apart form the ordinary clown magic. This is best done, not by fancy tricks, but by emphasizing your own unique character. Let the personality of your clown be evident, matching it with appropriate tricks. If your name happens to be Yo-Yo the Clown, do some tricks and stunts with yo-yos. Freckles can use silks with red spots and other appropriately designed props. These spots (freckles) can disappear and reappear in different places. Use your character to make an impression so the auditioners will remember you.

You need not be an expert magician or juggler to land the job. The auditioners are more interested in your ability to entertain than in the tricks. Simple tricks, if made funny, are preferred over the more flashy stunts that lack good humor.

Working at theme parks isn't for everybody. It's hard work, but many performers love it and return year after year.

There are many theme parks of various sizes, the following list includes some of the largest.

Six Flags, Atlanta, GA

Produces shows for nine parks: Six Flags Over Georgia (Atlanta); Six Flags Over Texas (Arlington); Six Flags Over Great Adventure (Jackson, NJ); Six Flags Over Mid-America (Eureka, MO); Six Flags Magic Mountain (Valencia, CA); Six Flags Great America (Gurnee, IL); Astroworld (Houston, TX); Altoworld (Flint, MI); Atlantis (Hollywood, FL).

Audition tour starts in January. For more information, contact Show Operations (404)948-9290.

Kings Productions, Cincinnati, OH

Produces shows for six parks: Kings Island (Cincinnati, OH); Carowinds (Charlotte, NC); Kings Dominion (Richmond, VA); Great America (Santa Clara, CA); Canada's Wonderland (Toronto); Australia's Wonderland (Sydney).

Audition tour starts in January. For more information, contact Show Operations (513) 241-8989.

Busch Gardens Dark Continent, Tampa, FL

Auditions at the park on last Monday of each month. Contact the Entertainment Department (813) 988-5171.

Busch Old Country, Williamsburg, VA

Auditions in November and January. Contact the Entertainment Department (804) 253-3020.

Cedar Point, Sandusky, OH

Auditions in January. Contact the Live Shows Department (419) 626-0830.

Disneyland, Anaheim, CA

Auditions year-round in various cities. For more information write to Disneyland Entertainment Department, 1313 Harbor Blvd., Anaheim, CA 91201.

Disney World, Lake Buena Vista, FL

Auditions year-round in various cities. For more information write to Disney World, Magic Kingdom Entertainment Department, Box 40, Lake Buena Vista, FL 32830.

> Taken to the dentist for a checkup, young Johnny was told he'd have to have a filling.
> "Now, Johnny," asked the dentist, "what kind of filling would you like for that tooth?"
> "Chocolate, please," replied Johnny promptly.

Geauga Lake Park, Aurora, OH

Auditions in January. Contact the Entertainment Department (216) 562-7131.

Knott's Berry Farm, Buena Park, CA

Auditions when openings become available. Contact the Entertainment Department (714) 827-1776.

Opryland, Nashville, TN

Auditions begin in November and continue as needed. Contact the Talent Agency (615) 889-6600.

Worlds of Fun, Kansas City, MO

Auditions in January. Contact the Show Productions Department (816) 454-4545.

School Shows

Most of your work as a clown or family entertainer will be done on the weekends, when people are free to shop or attend parties, fairs, and picnics. During the summer months, when school is out, there is an increased number of opportunities during the week to attend activities without conflict. But during the winter months far fewer weekday engagements are available. School shows, however, are one thing that you can do. Next to trade shows, schools usually pay the highest fees for visiting entertainers. For many children's entertainers this has become their bread and butter. Those who have established themselves have as many as 300 to 400 school show bookings a year, frequently performing at two or more schools a day.

Prices range from $100 to $300 per show. Often the assembly hall is not large enough to accommodate all the children in the school, so two or more shows are scheduled one right after the other. A full day at school, giving three or four shows, can net the per-

A man rushed off a train and ran up to a little boy standing on the platform.

"We've only got a short stop here," he said. "Here's a quarter. Go in that lunchroom and get me a sandwich, will you? And here's another quarter. Get a sandwich for yourself, too."

The boy was gone so long the man began to get nervous. Just as the conductor hollered "All Aboard!" the kid dashed out of the lunchroom and ran over to the man.

"Here's your quarter," he said. "They only had one sandwich."

former $400 to $600.

To do school shows you must have a well organized act which will last 40 to 50 minutes. Many schools prefer that the shows contain some theme from which the children can learn. A sampling of some of the themes you might consider are: keeping your country beautiful (don't be a litterbug), bicycle and traffic safety, water safety, substance abuse, personal hygiene, good nutrition, and fire safety. The show should be fun and entertaining, yet teach something beneficial.

Much of the same material you would use for any other staged show will work well as long as you tie it in with the theme. You need not get heavily into the subject in question, but do use it wherever you can.

An alternative to an assembly show is a PTA fund raiser after school for both the children and their parents. The PTA sells tickets, and you receive a percentage of the proceeds.

School shows are booked by the principal or PTA president. In some regions, an annual showcase is held for school entertainers, where school officials can go and review available programs. Here they have a chance to see a sample of your talents. Some school districts have rules governing entertainers, and may require an audition. The PTA president of your local school can give you information for your area.

Any and all public schools within driving distance are candidates for you. Give them a call, find out who schedules the assembly programs, and talk to him. Tell him who you are and that you'll send him some material for his files. Send a copy of your publicity kit and a cover letter briefly describing your show. Call him back after he has had time to look over the material and discuss the possibility of a booking.

There are three times in the year when most schools plan their assembly schedule and make bookings. The first is from late August to mid-September, when the fall schedule is arranged. The next is just after the Christmas holidays in January, when the spring program is organized. Some schools get a head start on the new school year and make bookings in May for the following fall.

Once you're booked, be sure to send a card in the mail several days in advance or call the day before the event to remind them that you're coming. Arrive at least 30 minutes before the show is to begin, whether you need that much time to set up or not. School officials tend to get nervous when the star of the show doesn't appear until ten minutes before show time.

Be polite and courteous to school officials, teachers, and students. Clean up any mess you make on the stage. Doing these things will leave them with a good impression and will increase your chances of a return

Circus World Museum, Baraboo, Wisconsin

visit. You might even consider sending the school a thank you card to show your appreciation.

For a detailed look at school shows, an excellent source is David Ginn's *School Show Presentations,* sold in three volumes and accompanied by cassette tapes of his shows. He covers not only how to organize this type of show but also how to work with children, and provides details of some of the routines he actually uses. These books are available in your local magic shop or by writing David Ginn, 5687 Williams Rd., Norcross, GA 30093.

Library Shows

Libraries provide another source of income for clowns and family entertainers. Library directors frequently hire storytellers, puppeteers, magicians, and others to give shows as part of their summer reading program. For those who work school shows, library shows offer an excellent opportunity for summer bookings.

Libraries hire storytellers and others to entertain children primarily to teach the value of reading and to ignite a spark of curiosity so that children will use the library's services. For this reason library shows should channel the youngsters toward exploring the many stories and instructional books available in the library.

In keeping with this theme you can ask the librarian to pull all books on magic, clowning, and other variety and circus arts and make them available for checkout after the show.

A good way to wrap up a library show is to explain to the kids that most magicians get their start in their youth by reading books on magic. Explain that books are also available for puppetry, clowning, juggling, and other arts. Have these books on display and ready for the kids to examine and check out if they wish.

If your presentation centers around some particular theme, you may encourage the children to read books on that subject. The themes you might choose could be westerns, mysteries, adventure, biographies, science, how-to, humor.

To locate all the libraries in your area, contact your State Board of Education. They have the names and addresses of all the libraries in the state. Contact the library director as you would a school principal, with phone calls and letters.

Museums, parks, and ranches are other places where you might try to sell your services. As with library and school shows, you need an act with a theme that fits the environment and satisfies the sponsor's needs. A museum of relics from the American Western era would naturally want your show to center around a western topic.

The Circus

As a child, did you ever dream of what it would be like to run away and join the circus? The excitement of circus life has thrilled many people. Clowns are stereotyped as circus performers, and in the past most clowns were, but today few clowns are engaged in this type of work. In comparison to other forms of work, the circus is unique. Circus clowns work as part of a team with other clowns and circus hands, clowning being only one part of their responsibilities. Depending on the show, the clowns may be expected to help set up equipment and tear it down, drive a truck, or do publicity appearances. Actual clowning may be a small percentage of their job.

Circus clown acts tend to be short, and often are used to fill rigging breaks between other acts. The show's producing clown decides which acts will be presented and provides any special props that are needed. Individual clowns are expected to provide their own makeup, costumes, and some walk-around props.

Although circus clowning can be hard work, many clowns are thrilled at the opportunity to join the circus just for the experience.

There are two ways to work in circuses: join a touring company or *spot date*. By joining a permanent touring company, you are put on a salary and travel along with the circus. Circus clown salaries tend to be at the low end of both the circus and the clown pay scales. Some shows provide meals and a bunk in a dormitory trailer. Selling coloring books, programs, or balloons on commission is a much sought after benefit which allows some clowns to more than double their income.

Spot dating, the other way to work in circuses, is working for a producer who has contracted to put together a show of limited duration in one location. Sometimes a producing clown and individual clowns will be hired, but at other times a clown with a self-contained specialty act will be used. The pay scale for spot dating is higher, but you are paid only for those days on which you perform. Even if a producer agrees to use you for all the circus's spot dates, you will have long layoffs and many long trips. You are responsible for your own transportation, and must have a van or a trailer to live in.

When you see a circus, check at their road office for information on available openings and how to apply for the next season. *The Circus Report* is the trade paper used by most circuses and performers for ads about circus jobs.

> Ed: Why aren't you working today?
> Fred: The boss and I had a fight and he won't take back what he said.
> Ed: What did he say?
> Fred: You're fired.

Cruise Ships

Taking an all expenses paid cruise to exotic places and foreign lands can be an exciting experience. It can also be very rewarding financially. Depending on your experience and the type of people on the cruise, you can earn anywhere from $500 to $2000 a week.

Look in the travel section of your newspaper and call the entertainment directors of the cruise lines that are listed. Send them a copy of your publicity kit and a brief description of your show(s). Follow this up with another call and make an appointment for an audition or ask if the director would like to view one of your videos.

For such assignments you may do better promoting your juggling, ventriloquism, or magic show rather than (or in addition to) your clown act. Most employers who book entertainment for cruises want material for any age group. The fact that you can present variety in your show will help convince the director to use your services. You will be expected to have three or more complete 30 minute shows. Since you will be seeing many of the same people, they won't want to hear the same jokes twice. Using a lot of audience participation is both fun and passes the time. You may even try to teach audience members to make balloon figures or do magic tricks which will ad variety.

Working on a cruise ship can be fun, with plenty of food and leisure time, but you will be expected to dress well, be conscious of your manners, and be courteous to everyone. Performers who have not lived up to expectations have been put off in ports before the end of their contracts.

Other Jobs For Family Entertainers

In addition to cruise ships, a talented entertainer can work in the college circuit, nightclubs, and casinos. These places may not fit the clown character, but a clown who has skills that can be used outside the clown role has a tremendous opportunity to perform as a variety artist such as a juggler, magician, ventriloquist, or stand-up comic.

This chapter does not cover all the possible places where clowns and family entertainers can find work, but only the most common and readily available forms of employment. From time to time you will get requests to entertain at bar mitzvahs, do a TV commercial, or appear at some other special event not mentioned here.

NON-PERFORMING JOBS

Teaching

Although clowns are performing artists and make a living entertaining people, they can do other types of activities to earn a handsome income.

The teaching of clowning and other clown skills such as magic, unicycling, mine, and juggling is becoming increasingly popular. Many universities and colleges are now offering courses in these subjects, taught by working clowns. Most large colleges already have theatrical arts departments and courses in mime and acting.

Individual clowns are opening their own clown schools or sponsoring annual or semiannual workshops and conferences to teach their skills.

City parks and recreation departments, the YMCA, and health clubs all hire people on occasion to teach activities such as juggling and unicycling. Approach these organizations directly and asked if they are willing to sponsor such activities. They can pay you a set fee, or you can take a percentage of the registration paid by the students. Registration fees of $5 to $20 are typical.

I work as an independent instructor for a local community education organization, teaching three courses related to clowning. I'm paid according to the number of students who sign up for the classes. These classes are perhaps more aptly described as miniclasses or seminars. The total classroom time varies from 90 minutes to three hours. Attendance at these classes is variable, but I can receive anywhere from $20 to $100 an hour for actual class time. For a part-time job, that's hard to top.

Some innovative people have managed to make teaching certain clown skills a full-time profession. Juggling, for example, has been taught successfully at school assemblies. These workshops are designed to teach children hand-eye coordination while enjoying a physical activity.

Classes are smaller than the schoolwide assembles for obvious reasons. Trying to teach 200 kids to juggle all at the same time can be a hair-raising experience

Patient: What do you charge for extracting a tooth?
Dentist: Twenty dollars.
Patient: What! For only two seconds' work?
Dentist: Well, if you wish, I can extract it very slowly.

(although if you're bald you may want to try it). Limiting the class to 90 participants at a time or by grade level has worked successfully. All the students in the school can be taught in a series of classes in the course of a day, with a fee of $50 or so per class.

There is no limit on age, anyone from first graders to adults can be taught to juggle. Because of their physical development, younger children have difficulty in learning to juggle bean bags and balls, but they can learn to juggle scarves which gives them a sense of accomplishment.

The teaching of juggling at elementary, junior high, and high schools is a new idea in most parts of the country, but in some areas it has been working for several years with great success.

If you would like further information about how to teach juggling in schools, contact The Juggling Institute, 7506J Olympic View Drive, Edmonds, WA 98020. They offer a course in which they will teach you everything you need to know in order to set up this type of operation in your own area.

Arts and Crafts

Rather than earning money as a performing artist, you can make a substantial income as a non-performing artist or craftsperson. At art fairs, festivals, parks, zoos, and carnivals you can sell balloon animals or helium balloons, make caricature drawings, and do face and hand painting, all of which are very popular. Selling these items while dressed as a clown gives a novel twist that attracts both attention and customers.

Many clowns and crafts people have found local festivals and fairs an ideal way to earn extra income. To find the dates and locations of fairs and festivals in your area, contact your local Chamber of Commerce. Call the person in charge of each event and check on any permits or fees which may be required. At many of these events you will be allowed to roam the grounds or set up a booth without paying a fee. Some may require a registration fee. Some fair organizers screen each applicant and even require a demonstration of skill or a sample of their work before allowing them to register, so check with the fair officials before setting up shop.

Face Painting. Face and hand painting has rapidly become popular for both clowns and non-clowns. Prices vary from $1 to $10, depending on the complexity of the design. The pictures can vary from a simple flower painted on the cheek or the back of the hand to

Calumet Clowns face painting at Lake County Sidewalk Semi-Circus Griffith, Indiana.

elaborate designs using both cheeks or even a full clown face.

At present there are few good sources on this subject. If you have a desire to learn more, get a copy of the book *Art of Face Painting* by Donald and Patricia Gonsalves.

Selling Balloons. Making balloon animals is considered a standard clown skill. Often clowns make animals and other figures as giveaways at parties and business promotions. In these cases the clown is being paid to entertain or attract business and the balloons are just an added benefit. But balloons themselves can be used as a means for financial gain.

Balloon creations are typically sold at fairs and other places for one dollar each. This is a tremendous profit since each balloon costs only three or four cents.

The balloonologists I have seen at fairs have always been surrounded by kids eager to buy one. Taking only a minute or so to make each animal for a constant stream of kids, these clowns can rake in a bundle.

Easy visibility is a key to success in this endeavor. Dressed in a colorful costume and makeup, a clown is easily spotted. The addition of a noise from a small bicycle horn will help make customers aware of your presence and keep business booming.

The most successful balloonologist I've seen wore a pair of stilts. Set up above the crowd he was easily visible. When he made the balloon figures, everybody could see what he was doing and consequently he had a continuous line of excited kids waiting to purchase his balloons and a fat pocketbook at the end of the day.

Armed with a hand pump, or a good set of lungs, and $12 worth of balloons, an eight-hour day (with breaks) can bring in $400. This may not be possible at all fairs, but I've seen it done where I live, so I know it's possible.

Caricature Drawing. People get a kick out of seeing an artist draw funny portraits or caricatures of them and will pay $2 to $10 each for them. Drawing caricatures does not take much artistic skill, only a little practice and preparation. You can design a half dozen body positions such as a surfer, bike rider, muscle man, and bathing beauty. Use them repeatedly with different customers. Just match the customer to any one of the preplanned body positions, leaving only the head with which to be creative.

Because the caricature is supposed to be exaggerated and humorous, accuracy is not essential. Drawing features which describe your model, such as nose shape, hair style, eyeglasses, whiskers, etc. will make your picture identifiable.

Believe me, anybody with any amount of drawing ability at all can do this and do it well if they practice. If you have any desire to try this, I suggest reading the book *How to Draw Caricatures* by Lenn Redman, which can be obtained from your local library or bookstore.

A boy ran by a man standing on the curb. Five minutes later the boy rushed by again. After this had happened a half-dozen times, the man stopped him and asked, "What's the idea, Sonny? What's the rush?" The boy looked up very indignantly and shouted, "I'm running away from home!"

"Oh," said the man. "But you've gone around this same block at least five times."

"I know it!" shouted the boy over his shoulder as he started running agin. "My mom won't let me cross the street."

Juggling Lessons and Supplies. You can set up a booth and give juggling lessons and sell balls, bean bags, and scarves. This has been popular at Renaissance Festivals which are held yearly throughout the United States, but any fair or carnival would be a good place.

Juggling is a fascinating skill most everyone likes to watch and would like to learn. The excitement of learning how to juggle from a real clown can encourage a lot of people to try it, just to see if they have what it takes. For a fee, customers could be taught with balls that you supply, or you can sell the balls with a free juggling lesson.

I have found that children under the age of about nine have a difficult time learning to juggle three objects. Most kids, however, can learn to juggle using special juggling scarves. These scarves are very light and float slowly to the ground, giving the student plenty of time to catch them and toss them back into the air. They're also a lot of fun to play with while learning to juggle. Get a bunch of kids (or adults) tossing scarves around, and you have a humorous riot which everyone enjoys.

The biggest problem with scarves is that the slightest breeze will carry them off, forcing the student to reach out or even run after them. If you are in a building or some place where there is no wind, you might consider selling scarves. Scarves made especially for juggling can be purchased at local magic shops or from juggling suppliers such as Brian Dube' and Jugglebug. Their addresses can be found in Appendix B.

Novelty bean bags add to the people's desire to purchase the props and try their hand at juggling. Chasley, Inc. sells a line of unusual bean bags in the shape of penguins, bears, pigs, whales, dinosaurs, scotties, cats, stars, and salad—yes salad: cucumbers, carrots, and tomatoes. Their address is also listed in Appendix B.

Barber: Well, son, how would you like your hair cut?

Small Boy: Just like my Dad's, and be sure to leave that little round hole on the top where his head comes through.

CHAPTER 19

HOW TO BE A BIRTHDAY PARTY CLOWN

Take one youngster who is nearing his birthday, sprinkle his home with lots of friends, add a dash of food, entertainment, games and gifts and what do you have? . . . An exciting, fun filled birthday party!

Who doesn't like parties? Parties are fun whether you're a guest or the main attraction. As a birthday party entertainer, you have a unique opportunity to visit and enjoy many parties (and get paid for it). The entertainment portion is often the highlight of the festivities for the guests and makes a party memorable. You, as the performer, are the center of attraction, the star of the show, a celebrity. Sounds exciting doesn't it?

One of the great pleasures of being a clown or other family entertainer is the chance to be in the spotlight. The kids respond to you, and laugh at your jokes, which gives most performers a psychological high. Self-esteem and pride are by-products of clowning. These feelings are hard to describe, but you'll know what I'm talking about when you see kids become wide-eyed with excitement at your presence and hear them giggle uncontrollably at your jokes.

Parties provide an ideal way for beginners to polish performing skills and learn how to handle an audience, and test material, while gaining practical experience. Because audiences are usually small, you also build self-confidence. As a birthday party clown, you learn how kids react and how to control them. You learn what kids like and don't like, improving both your entertaining skills and your show.

Working at birthday parties also introduces you to the business aspects of the entertainment field—how to sell yourself, talk to potential clients, and keep records and time schedules. It builds your reputation, giving you exposure and opening the door to activities other than birthday parties. I get invitations to work at office parties, picnics, ranches, give demonstrations, and attend other types of children's gatherings. Some of the opportunities, I never realized even existed.

Some clowns enjoy working parties so much, that is all they do, and they make a decent living at it. You can expect to make anywhere from $50 to $300 for each party. The prices depend on the area of the country, the type of show, and your degree of skill. Obviously a stilt walker who rides a unicycle, juggles, and performs magic at the same time will demand a higher fee than a clown who just tells jokes and hands out balloons.

When you first start out, you may be hesitant or unsure of yourself and your material. You might want to give your first couple of shows for free just to see what it's like and to get some experience.

The first party is always the hardest. If you have a friend who has a child with an approaching birthday, offer to entertain for free. Your friend would probably love the idea of getting a free clown, and you'll get some valuable experience without the pressure of having to give a polished performance.

PLANNING THE SHOW

When you start performing for a fee, you technically become a professional. As a professional clown you are expected not only to look the part but to act the part as well. To give a performance worthy of the title "clown" and the fee you are paid, it is best to present a well planned, rehearsed, and tested show.

I know some entertainers who view birthday parties as an easy way to make a few bucks. They go to the party with little preparation, tell a few canned jokes, show a few tricks, and generally goof around with the kids, acting almost as one of the guests.

This type of activity may work fine for preschoolers, but for children age five and older, a prepared show is professionally the standard type of entertainment, and what parents usually expect.

For the beginner, having a well prepared show will eliminate those butterflies that many novices experience. I recall how nervous (and excited) I was the first few times I went "on stage." I worried about how well I would be received and whether my presence would help make the party a success. Once I started into my rehearsed material and began to get a few laughs, I forgot about these apprehensions and hammed up my act to the fullest, making the show fun for the guests and satisfying for me.

Birthday party shows usually run between 20 and 40 minutes and are supplemented with greeting the kids, passing out giveaways, playing games, and other activities.

Practice your show to perfection. Be able to perform all your tricks flawlessly and coordinate your patter for greatest effect. Kids can be unmercifully honest; if they see how you did a magic trick, they will be quick to tell you. Likewise, if your jokes aren't funny they will let you know it, either by word or by action. It's a tad bit discouraging when in the middle of a show one of the kids says "Let's do something else."

Audience response, even if negative, is valuable to you. The feedback you receive gives an indication of what the kids like and don't like. Your shows should continue to evolve: add new jokes, cut material which doesn't prove effective, improve timing. As you gain more experience with a new show and make modifications, it will take on the character of a polished performance.

Once you are comfortable and confident with one show and get a good response, you can start working out a second one. As your business increases, you will want to have the second show ready. Use it for repeat customers or for parties of kids who had been guests at one of your previous shows. A happy party guest telling his mother what a wonderful clown you are is excellent advertising and results in many additional bookings. The child is likely to have many of the same friends who attended the first party, so you need something new for them. Kids love to get attention, and will shout out your punchlines and make other comments such as "I've seen that before," often spoiling the surprise of your tricks and jokes. Having a second show eliminates this problem.

Most of your requests for parties will come from parents of children age four to nine. As kids get older, parents feel that their children are outgrowing clowns. Family entertainers billed as jugglers, magicians, and such tend to pick up more of the older kids' parties because they are not restricted to the clown image, even though the material presented could be the same. For clowns, teenage parties are rare, as are adult parties. However a family entertainer has a greater chance of being asked to do parties for these older groups.

On some occasions you will be asked to entertain for children four years old or less. Children this age are too young to appreciate magic, juggling, and other traditional clown skills. Shows that may be a big success with a group of seven-year-olds may be a miserable flop with a bunch of two-year-olds.

If you're asked to entertain at a party of preschoolers, in most cases your prepared show will not go over well. Some entertainers explain to parents that their shows are designed for older children, and will not accept such jobs.

Even though very young children will not appreciate many of the jokes or tricks that a clown ordinarily does, you can still entertain them. I would suggest that if you get booked for such a party, you leave your show at home and do something else. I find that telling stories, using hand puppets, and playing games with the kids while acting silly work best. The parents can go into another room and relax while you "play" with the kids.

DRUMMING UP BUSINESS

You've planned out a show, rehearsed it, and are ready to knock the socks off an audience, now what do you do? Sit at the phone and anxiously wait for people to call, or go door to door like an Avon lady? How do you let the word out that you're available for birthday parties? Obviously you must advertise if anyone is to know your services are available.

Once you've begun to do shows you will get calls from referrals, but even then you will need a constant form of advertising working for you. The following are the methods most often used.

Newspapers

One of the most useful tools businesses use to let their existence be known is by advertising in the local newspaper. Entertainers can also take advantage of this medium.

There are two types of newspaper ads: display and classified. Display ads usually contain pictures or drawings, and are very expensive. Several hundred dollars for a few inches of space is not uncommon with large circulation papers. At these prices display ads often are not cost effective.

Classified ads are composed of straight type with no graphics or variation in lettering style, but are much less expensive. The biggest drawback with classifieds is that fewer people see them. Usually people do not even read them unless they're looking for something specific. Most of us think of these ads as a way to sell cars, boats, and real estate, not to find a clown. For these reasons advertising in big city newspapers is generally unproductive.

That doesn't mean all newspaper advertising is a waste of time. If you live in a small community, the local paper may be effective. In large cities there are often small papers which are circulated to only select areas. These may be cost effective for you. Advertising rates in these smaller papers may even be low enough for you to run a display ad, which will be seen by many more people than a classified ad. You may want to try it at least once in your area to see what type of response you get. It may prove an effective means for getting you business.

Bulletin Boards

A 3 x 5 card placed on bulletin boards at launderettes, drugstores, beauty shops, and other places provides you with an excellent way to advertise. Except for the cost of the cards, it's essentially free.

It also announces your services to those who are most likely to call you—namely mothers. Women usually do business at places with bulletin boards and will see your notice.

A typical card might read:

BIRTHDAY PARTY CLOWN
Juggling — Magic — Balloons
All Ages — Reasonable Prices
Call Joyce "Buttons" Jones 123-4567

This ad will bring you some calls, but you could do much better. Your card will be on a bulletin board, possibly lost among a mass of others, each card competing for the readers' attention. If yours isn't noticed, then it's doing no good. If you can design your card so as to grab people's attention, your response rate will soar.

How do you make your ad stand out? You must make it unique. You're a clown and that's unique. So let your ad reflect your service. For starters, add color. Bright cheery colors will draw attention. Use colored ink or colored cards. Add a small drawing or picture. Advertisers know the value of using pictures in their ads. People usually focus on an illustration before reading anything. If you have a picture on your card, people will look at it first. It could be a simple drawing, a cute rubber stamp impression, or even a professionally printed photo or other illustration. Use a picture which describes what you do: a clown, balloons, a unicycle, a juggler, even your own picture in clown makeup. Keep the picture simple and leave room for your message. A picture of yourself is a great way to show yourself as a professional. A print shop can make one or two hundred of these, with colored ink for under $45. This is a worthwhile expense; a single booking will pay for the cost.

A unique card will stand out, and people will read it first. Many people give bulletin boards only a passing glance, but an eye-catching card will be read and will earn jobs for you.

What about the words you use? The example I gave is a good ad. The heading BIRTHDAY PARTY

CLOWN is brief and to the point. The first sentence or title should always be short, descriptive, and interesting. Avoid such sentences as "Do you need a clown for your child's birthday party?" It's too long. Keep the message short and sweet. Other good examples are "Liven Up Your Party," "Comic Juggler," "Crazy Clown," "Magic Clown."

To add interest, mention some of the things you do at your parties: juggling, magic, puppets, balloons, games, and prizes.

Using your clown name gives you an identity and tells customers that you're not simply a generic clown but a professional entertainer. You can add other incentives such as reasonable prices, all ages, any location, day or night, special weekend rates.

These are some of the things a good ad contains. Being a clown, you have an image as a comedian and a person with a creative personality. You can use this image to turn good ads into fantastic ads. By making your ads different, you tell the reader that you're special and will be a bucket of fun at a party. Let me give you some examples.

PARENTS. Be amazed, amused, and confused at your next birthday party with the delightful comedy of Buttons the Magic Clown. Call . . .

FOR SALE. An afternoon of spellbinding entertainment for your next birthday party. Call Buttons the Magic Clown . . .

FOR SALE. One slightly used clown to entertain at your child's birthday party. Cheap! Call . . .

HELP WANTED. One birthday child and several friends to join Buttons the Clown at your birthday party. Call . . .

FOUND. One crazy juggler who can turn your child's birthday party into a fun-filled adventure. Call . . .

FOUND. One disappearing rabbit, two clown shoes, and one hilariously mixed-up magician who will entertain at your party. Call Buttons the Magic Clown.

All these ads have an element of humor. They begin like ordinary ads but than describe something totally different. Being creative like this in your ads lets the readers know that you're funny.

This same approach isn't limited just to cards on bulletin boards but can be used in newspaper ads, and flyers.

The Yellow Pages

Putting your name in the *Yellow Pages* is probably the best way to get new business. When a mother wants a clown for her child's birthday, where does she go? The first place parents look is the phone book. Placing your name in the *Yellow Pages* will bring you a bountiful supply of callers and business. It will cost you some, but is worth it. Check with your local phone company for rates. Phone books usually come out only once a year, so you may have to wait a while before your name appears. Having to wait may be beneficial because it gives beginners a chance to test the water before committing to a listing that will remain in the phone book for an entire year.

You might consider adding the words "children's parties" to let readers know your specialty. If you don't, you'll get a lot of calls for other types of shows or activities.

In large cities several different phone books may be published. Each community or suburb may have its own book. I have found that for the cost, it isn't worth advertising in these other books. A single ad in the major city directory is enough. People who live in the suburbs will receive both phone books anyway and most people will look in the large directory first.

Entertainment Agencies

Booking agencies are described on page 184. These agencies do a lot of advertising and have their foot in a lot of doors, which is helpful for many performers. You can sign on with them as strictly a children's party entertainer if you like, but you may be asked to audition first or at least show that you've had some experience. Agencies must protect their reputation, and may not be too responsive to raw beginners.

As a birthday party clown, you can do just as well without an agency. Your own advertising methods will

Johnny, at breakfast: "Dad, today is Lincoln's birthday. He was a great man, wasn't he?

Pop, always eager to teach his young son a lesson: "Yes, Son, indeed he was. And mind you," he added pompously, "when Abraham Lincoln was *your* age, he was out splitting rails."

"Yes, Dad, I know," retorted Johnny. "And when he was *your* age, he was President of the United States."

bring you plenty of customers and leave you free to arrange your own shows.

Restaurants

Many restaurants have banquet rooms or side areas for large groups or parties. Contact the owner or manager and interest him in letting you entertain at parties in his restaurant. Such an arrangement will cost him almost nothing and may provide him with additional business.

Parties like this are easy for restaurants because they must be scheduled in advance, giving the cooks and servers plenty of time to prepare. The same food is served to all the guests and is paid on a single tab.

The price the restaurant charges covers the food and your fee, which is added to theirs. Your presence does not cost the owner a cent but it serves as an incentive for parents to hold a party at his place of business. These advantages have been recognized by many restaurant owners so inquire about a package deal which would involve your services.

Restaurant work is basically the same as a home party. You can do your normal show as long as there is room enough. Depending on the size of the area, you may have to modify some of your regular material.

Sometimes the parents will rent a banquet room at a restaurant and then ask you to come there to entertain. Such an assignment will give you an opportunity to talk to the owner afterward. He has just received some business, highlighted by your performance, and the profits of this party are fresh in his mind. Inquire about setting up a joint agreement for future parties.

Spreading the Word Yourself

The first type of advertising you should do, and definitely the cheapest, is word of mouth. Tell others what you do and ask them to spread the word. If you do a good job for one client, she will tell others and more business will follow. Print up some business cards and pass them out as often as you can. This will serve as a nice reminder.

Some entertainers go a step further and have signs painted on their cars or vans. Wherever you drive, your wheels serve as an advertisment. This is a good way to publicize yourself and get some business, but it has one major drawback. A van with your stage name and number printed on it has a "show biz" appearance. Many people equate this with expensive electrical equipment and other things of value, as a result vans are repeatedly broken into. I have heard this story often from those who use this form of advertising. If you decide to try this, consider yourself forewarned.

BOOKING THE PARTY

The Telephone

The word is out, your show is ready, and you now begin to receive inquires. The phone call will be your first contact with your customer. During this time you must collect all pertinent information and convince the caller to hire you. Ninety percent of the time the child's mother will be the one who calls.

What do you say after you've answered the phone? At first you may feel somewhat self conscious, don't let it show, speak with confidence and with a "smile." A clown is supposed to be cheery and friendly, so let it show in your voice without sounding corny or fake.

One of the first questions she will ask is "How much will it cost?" Avoid answering this question until you have explained to her what she will get from you, and has had a chance to get to know you. A simple price quote often scares potential customers away because they don't realize what they are getting. You are more than just a funny person dressed in a clown suit. You are an entertainer, a performing artist who has planned a spectacular show with gifts and games to make her child's party a memorable experience.

When you speak with a customer on the phone, it's best to take immediate control of the conversation by asking questions. If she asks you for a price, respond by saying something like, "Before I can answer that, I need some information about your party." Ask for the location, time, and the date. This is really all you need to know to figure the price (and to determine if you are available at that time), but continue with questions such as name and age of the birthday child,

---

Shingles were coming loose on Mr. Rustmore's house, and he complained of the leaks.

"Why don't you mend the roof? asked the neighbor next door.

"I can't today—it's pouring rain."

"Well, why don't you mend it in dry weather? Mr. Rustmore replied "It don't leak then."

number of guests, which room will the show be in, or will it be outside? Asking these additional questions shows your interest in the child and the customer feels she will get a custom tailored show. I feel getting the child's name is important. By asking for this information, you are telling the parent that you're interested in the child. It's also helpful to know who the guest of honor is when you enter the party. I feel that it shows a lack of respect to arrive and have to ask, "Whose birthday party is this?"

Often the caller will begin the conversation by telling how she found out about you—through a friend, neighbor, or a giveaway with your name on it brought home by a child. Take note of this because it will help you evaluate which promotional materials are bringing you the most business. If the caller doesn't volunteer this information, ask her where she found out about you.

Have an appointment book or calendar and a map ready by the phone. When she tells you the time and date, check your schedule and see if you're available. If you're busy at that time, ask if she has already sent out the invitations (surprisingly many parents will do this before giving you a call). If she has, tell her you're unavailable at that time and refer her to another clown, if possible.

If she hasn't sent the invitations, try to have the time changed so that you can attend. Most people will be willing to modify their original plans to accommodate you.

If she doesn't have a firm time already planned, suggest a time for her that will work best for you. I find that I can get more business and save time by careful planning. Divide your day into blocks of one and a half or two hours, starting at about 11:00 A.M. If possible, schedule the first party at this time, the next at 12:30, followed by 2:00, 3:30, and 5:00, one right after the other. This will save you the problem of having one show at noon and waiting until 4:00 for the next.

Use the map to locate the area of town the caller lives. This will be important in figuring what price you charge. I've divided the city I live into three areas.

Area 1 is the closest to me, and includes any place that I can drive to in under 30 minutes. Area 2 requires one way travel time of 30 to 60 minutes, and area 3 is any place beyond that. I charge those living in area 1 my normal fee for a basic party. If the client lives in area 2, I add on $10, if she lives in area 3, I add $20. It takes a full hour to drive from one end of my city to the other, and I get calls from all over town. A two-hour round trip drive can take up a big chunk of time, so I feel charging extra is justified.

Beside the price, another often asked question is "What will you do?" Understandably, mothers want to know what they will be getting for their money.

Your answer should convince her that you're the person she's looking for. You should think about the answer to this question in detail beforehand so that when asked, you can give a brief description that will interest her. This sales talk should convince her that you are a professional and that she will get her money's worth. Make it sparkle, but be honest. My description goes something like this:

"I come in full clown costume so that when I arrive the kids will know that they're in for a wonderful time. The first thing I do is to give _____(child's name) a special greeting, letting her know that I have been invited to your home to entertain her and her friends. Since the party is in her honor, I try to emphasize the birthday child and make it a special occasion for her.

"After greeting the rest of the guests, I lead into a combined show of comedy juggling and magic. This show will continue for 35 minutes. The material I present is designed for children in your child's age group and has been proved to be very successful. I also include some special material designed especially for your child.

"At the end of the show, I give each child a balloon animal and a puzzle to take home as a souvenir. This way you don't have to worry about the extra expense of buying the customary party gifts. Your daughter _____ (child's name) will also receive these, plus another special gift just for her."

The extra gift I give to the birthday child is an autographed photo with my name and phone number printed on it. It is inexpensive, and serves as a special reminder of my presence at her party and the good time she had. Parents like to see their children get preferential treatment—especially if they're paying for it. Hinting at the attention you will give their child will go a long way in convincing them to hire you.

When you arrive, make it a point to give the birthday child a special greeting. If you use any volunteers during your show, make sure the guest of honor has a chance to participate. Customize a few

---

As he paid his hotel bill the departing guest turned and yelled to the bellboy, "Quick, boy, run up to room 999 and see if I left my brief case and overcoat. Hurry up, because I've just got six minutes to catch my train."

Four minutes later the bellboy was back, all out of breath. "Yes, sir," he reported, "they're up there."

Felix Adler

jokes, using the birthday child's name; don't make jokes about her, but use her name in a story. Make the party special for the birthday child by acknowledging her in these ways.

Parents will love you for giving their child this special attention. It makes your show look custom-made and unique. You will also increase your chance for repeat business with her and new business from references.

There are three major parts to most children's birthday parties: the present opening, cake and ice cream eating, and the entertainment or games. As the clown, you will be in charge of the entertainment part of the party. Whether or not you include games along with your show is up to you.

My shows lasts about 30 minutes; I spend another 10 or 15 minutes greeting the kids and handing out balloon animals. Altogether I spend approximately 45 minutes at the party, and then leave. Occasionally I will remain another 30 minutes or so, supervising party games (which I charge extra for).

Normally I do not stay for the present opening or cake eating. The food and gift opening are entertainment in themselves and don't need my presence. In fact, the kids become so engrossed in these activities that they don't care if the clown is there or not.

Some birthday party clowns do participate in these activities and take on the role of a supervisor. I'd rather avoid this hectic time, with kids struggling over the new toys and eating their share of the goodies. I would rather keep my image as an entertainer and leave the supervisory role to the parents.

Often the hostess will invite you to share in the gift opening and eating. To avoid any problem, let her know while you're on the phone that you will be coming only for the show (and games if that's part of the agreement) and then will leave. You can explain, since you're an authority on the subject, that your presence during those two activities is not needed.

Most parties begin with games or entertainment and end with cake and presents. I suggest that you recommend this schedule to your caller. Arrange to make your entrance at least 30 minutes after the party is scheduled to begin, so that most, if not all, of the children will be present before you arrive.

I do not recommend opening the gifts before the entertainment because it creates too much of a distraction. You may find yourself frequently interrupted by the noise from some of the toys or from kids fighting over them.

The gift opening is usually the highlight for the birthday child, and ideally should be saved for last. Once the presents are opened, the new owner will be absorbed in the gifts, and other things lose interest.

Some clowns like to stay after giving their prepared show to supervise a few games and other activities. Musical games and contests can be loads of fun for the kids and will keep them occupied while mom and dad relax or prepare the refreshments. This extra service will take up another 30 or 45 minutes. I recommend never staying longer than 90 minutes. Leave while they're still having fun and enjoying your presence.

Setting Your Fees

After asking the caller your questions, showing interest in her child, giving her your sales talk, and calculating what to charge, you can bring up the price. She now knows what she will get and who you are. By now you should be a friend to her, rather than simply a voice on the phone.

What you charge may depend on several factors. The primary consideration in pricing your show is determined by the area of the country in which you do business. The price of a party in Beverly Hills, California would be much more than in Flat Lick, Kentucky. If you have no idea what the local standard is, call up a few clowns listed in the phone book and ask them what they charge. Their answers will serve as your yardstick.

You may well charge more then one price, depending on what you do. Avoid having too many different prices or it gets confusing. I have two different methods for pricing. The first is determined by the distance I am required to travel to reach the party. I start with a base price of $60 for a 30 minute show and a few minutes greeting and passing out party favors. I check my map; if the party is in area 1, I charge $60; in area 2, $70; and in area 3, $80.

Some parents like more than just a show, and are willing to pay extra for supervising some party games for another 30 to 45 minutes. Games are usually self-entertaining, and if you have a handful of fun games, just being your normal wacky self and goofing with the kids can be effective. I usually charge only an additional 10 to 20 dollars for this service. Since I'm already in costume and at the party, it doesn't require much more effort to handle the games.

If you enjoy supervising the games and receiving the extra cash, you may make the games a part of your standard party package and charge whatever is appropriate. If after telling the parent your price on the phone, you hear a gasp for air and the phone drop, you can safely reason she was a little surprised. Hopefully your sales talk will have cushioned the blow somewhat, and she will still be interested.

If the price you quote doesn't bother her and if she schedules you to come for the party, you've sold a full party package. If she begins to hesitate, you may want to mention that your prices are typical of those charged by other clowns and are in fact cheaper than most because you're not using a theatrical agent or an entertainment service. If she's still reluctant to schedule your service, you can offer her a discount party plan (she may even suggest it). You can then come down on your price by eliminating the games and the extra $20.

Even if $60 is more than she had expected, it will sound reasonable compared to $80. Emphasize that at the reduced price she will still receive the show, the party favors, and the special recognition for her child.

I strongly recommend that you stick to your price schedule and not make special concessions. Some parents will try to get you to lower your price for them. Unless you have a good reason, don't do it. You will find that most parents will go ahead and book you even though you won't lower your price. If you start giving people a break, they will spread the word and others will expect it too. Callers may question why you are

A boy was down on his hands and knees looking for something on the sidewalk when a policeman approached.

"What are you doing?" said the cop.

"I lost a silver dollar on Third Avenue," was the answer.

"But this is Fourth Avenue," the cop pointed out. "If you lost the dollar on Third Avenue, why are you looking for it on Fourth?"

"Becaue there's more light here," said the boy.

charging them more than their neighbor. To them it looks as if you're jacking up the price, and they will resent it. Avoid this problem and stick with your ordinary price schedule. Then, if you're questioned by someone who was referred to you, you have a legitimate reason for the price differences. Explain that prices vary by area and even by which party package they want (with or without games).

Information Cards

You may find it convenient to use what I call an information card. These cards contain a pretyped list of the important questions I ask, such as name, address, and phone number.

I keep a stack of these cards near the phone. When a potential client calls, I can pull out a card and fill it in during our conversation. I can take the card to the party so I have all pertinent information at my fingertips. The card also serves as a permanent reference that can be filed in a card box. The following year, a month or so before the child's birthday, I can call the parents and inquire about another party. Even if the person who calls doesn't use my services, I can save the card and inquire with them the following year. I then send out a letter reintroducing myself, including a more detailed description of myself and my qualifications, talents, special citations, and recommendations. I also enclose a printed picture. I leave out the price out so they will have to call for that information, giving me a chance to talk to them in person.

Cards are filed by date, not by name. I can either give the parents a personal call or send a letter to let them know I'm alive and available if they decide to have a party and need entertainment.

The front of the information card contains all the specifics on the price charged, location, time, and names. The back can be used for detailed directions to the party or any other bits of information I care to remember. It is a convenient place to note which party I gave, #1 (bumbling juggling) or #2 (juggling/magic). If I'm booked for a return visit I know what show I've already given them.

INFORMATION CARD

NAME: Mary Brown
ADDRESS: 643 Fifth St. / area 2
PHONE: 123-4567
DATE: Sat. Aug. 14
TIME: 12:00 (leave home at 11:15)
STAGE: living room
REFERENCE: Yellow Pages
NO. OF GUESTS: 15
CHILD'S NAME: Sandra
PARTY PACKAGE: show/games
FEE: $85 ($60 show, $10 area 2, $15 games)

Ask where you will be giving your show. Most often the family or living room is used, but the show can be on the porch or in the back yard as well. Depending on the type of show you give, location may be important. Some rooms can become very crowded when 20 wiggly kids stacked inside.

If you have tricks that require a lot of elbow room a tight space may cause some problems. One mother told me I would have plenty of room outside on her roofless porch. When I got there to do my juggling act, I found out why the porch was roofless. A large shady tree with lots of low branches shadowed the area. I ended up doing my show while juggling between the limbs.

Reconfirm the date and time, and mark it on your calender. Get directions to the party location, if necessary and make sure the phone number is correct. At times as you are driving to the party you will find yourself lost. No matter how accurate your map may be, the directions you received may not be accurate, or a street sign may be down. If you find that you're going to be late, give the parents a call. A mother cooped up in a house with 20 screaming, jumping kids may be going out of her mind. She will appreciate your call and won't be angry at you when you finally arrive. In all cases, allow a little extra time to get to the party and give a call if you find you're going to be late.

Since the party will most likely be scheduled several days in advance, it's a good policy to call the day before or on the morning of the party to confirm your engagement and to assure the parents that you will be there as scheduled. Events can alter previously made

plans: people get sick, change their minds, or have emergencies. Calling first will let you know if the party is still on as planned, if not, the call will save you a needless trip and preparation.

AT THE PARTY

Arrive at the party in full costume. Live up to your image as a clown; never put on pieces of your makeup in front of the kids, or you will appear as just a person dressed up like a clown and not a real clown. Give yourself plenty of time in case you're delayed or lost. Work out all details over the phone so that when you reach the party you can get right to work.

Once you've reached the party, one of the first things you should do is greet the birthday child and give her that special recognition that she deserves and that parents love.

Ask the hostess (or host) to lead you to the area where you will be performing. Most often the kids will be scattered throughout the house as you enter. The word will spread that "There's a clown in the living room." Greet the rest of the kids.

A few short jokes or gags help break the ice and let the kids know they're in for a fun time. Typically you will spend just a few minutes with the greeting, until all the children have gathered. Sometimes the hostess will ask you to wait for a late guest or two. In this case you will need to have something planned to entertain them before getting into your "prepared" material.

What do you do in cases like this? . . . Anything you feel comfortable with: have the children play some simple games, show them some close-up magic tricks, show them how to make hats or other things with folded newspaper. Simple games such as Simon Says or Follow the Leader can be fun and can eat up the spare minutes. Whatever you do should be brief. You shouldn't be expected to wait any longer then 10 or 15 minutes.

Whether you have another party scheduled or not, tell the hostess that you can wait a few minutes but no longer because you have other appointments you must honor. You don't want your 45 minute booking

Ed: What were all your chickens doing out in front of your house early this morning?
Fred: They heard some men were going to lay a sidewalk and they wanted to see how it was done.

dragging out to 90 minutes; you're not being paid for this extra time. Explain to her that you'll be happy to wait a few minutes but you have a limited amount of time and will have to start the show soon. If you bring this to her attention, usually she will not insist that you wait more than the amount of time you've allowed.

If you explain to the hostess on the phone beforehand that you must stick to the time schedule you have agreed on, you will rarely have problems. She will understand your position and the show will proceed without undue delay.

Let the Show Begin

When you begin your show, have all the kids come into the room and sit down. Encourage them to remain in their seats and to be still. Kids at birthday parties are wiggly and full of energy, so you need to get their attention and interest from the very start. Show them that you're taking control of the party by having them all participate in a simple opening activity. By having them do this, you are establishing your role as the leader. Use audience participation techniques similar to those discussed in Chapter Six.

Promising to give them a reward for behaving will help encourage them. Tell them that those who sit still and smile will be chosen to be your personal helpers later on. Note that I don't ask them to be quiet, only to be still and smile. It seems contradictory to tell them to be quiet and then try to make them shout with laughter, but when you tell them to smile, you're telling them to behave, yet to feel free to laugh and giggle. Besides, it's hard to talk and smile at the same time.

You can also use a balloon animal as an incentive, promising to give one to all of those who remain in their seats. (Of course you will eventually give one to everybody, but they don't know that.) You might even make an animal and put it aside so that they can see it throughout the show as a constant reminder. You may have to remind them from time to time by pointing to the balloon and asking them to settle down. Never be harsh! You have been invited to come into the home to entertain, not to discipline, and if you follow these steps you should have few problems.

At the end of your show, give the balloon to the best behaved child and say, "All of the rest of you have been so good I think I'll give each of you a balloon." Don't leave anyone out, even if they were overly energized during your show.

PROPS

Most birthday shows will be in the living room or family room. I strongly recommend that you avoid any tricks or gags which will make a mess. Spilled milk or flour on the rug will not make a happy hostess, nor will she appreciate cleaning confetti and other scraps of paper off the floor.

If you perform a trick that requires the tearing of paper or some other trick which will create trash, store it in your case or prop bag and discard it later. One mother commented to me about a magician (or magic clown) who had left a mess and a bad impression. He lost the chance of returning and of any referrals she might have given.

Most any type of show will require you to carry props. The most convenient way to do this is in a prop bag or case. Any type of portable container which can be closed up to keep curiosity seekers out will work.

A suitcase table is an ideal way to carry props, especially if you do magic. It converts into a table that can be used in your show, and provides a convenient way to get to your props without digging through piles of gadgets. The contents of the case are kept out of sight yet are easy to locate. When the show is over, you put the props on the bottom, fold down the top and wheel the case out to your car.

Bruce Fife as "Dr. Dropo".

The props you use should be small, for the most part—no trick guillotines, sword boxes, chain saws, or torches. Shows are usually performed in small (and at times overcrowded) rooms, so close-up magic tricks and other small props work best. Since the audience is usually small and near the performer, hand held props are easily seen by all.

PARTY FAVORS

Giving party favors or souvenirs to the guests has become a custom at birthday parties. As the host or hostess, the parents are responsible for providing these gifts to all the kids. When the entertainer takes over this responsibility it not only relieves the parents of this duty, but allows the clown to enjoy several benefits. Promising the kids a gift if they behave allows you to keep them under control. Giving a souvenir or a gift to all the kids also makes a good ending to your show. All kids love receiving presents; giving them something will make your show more fun and end it with a bang.

Gift giving also allows the performer to relax a bit. Making balloon animals or paper creations can eat up spare minutes, giving you more time with the kids without having to memorize or rehearse additional material.

Although giving out presents may cost you a little, it's worth it. Keep the gift inexpensive, and whatever it is have your name and phone number printed on it. This will remind the kids of the fun they had and will let the parents know who you are and how to contact you if they ever plan a party. A child coming home and telling her parents that a funny clown was at the party is an excellent referral for future parties. The gift provides a way for these parents to know who you are and how to contact you.

What type of gift should you give? The most common gifts are balloon animals, but there are many other inexpensive gifts that would be just as good. Let's look at some of the most popular types.

Balloon Animals

I believe balloons are an ideal gift. They cost only a few cents each, and *kids love them!* Some children's entertainers have commented that everybody gives balloon animals, suggesting that children get bored with the same type of gift. But how often do kids go to

parties—a couple of times a year perhaps? I've never seen a child disappointed at receiving one. Most children never get tired of them. My own kids have seen me make hundreds of the rubbery creatures and have walked away with armloads, only to come back begging for more. They never tire of them, no matter how often they get them.

You don't have to be a skilled artist to make balloon animals, nor do you need to make a different animal for each child. If all you can make is a simple dog (which anyone can learn to do with a few minutes' practice) then give them all dogs. Using different colored balloons will add variety.

Blowing up 25 balloons can wear out even the best set of lungs, especially the hard-to-inflate pencil balloons used in making balloon animals. Few people have the natural lung power to blow these balloons up when they first attempt it. You will have to practice and gradually build up your strength in order to inflate them without complete exhaustion. As a beginner your lung power may not be up to full strength, but don't be discouraged. You can still inflate 25 balloons by using a small hand held balloon pump (obtainable from magic dealers or wherever balloons are sold).

Some clowns feel unprofessional using a pump, but I use one and I don't feel it hurts my presentation at all. The kids still jump with excitement no matter where the air came from. I can easily fill 25, 30, or more balloons without the slightest strain on my lungs.

If you prefer, you might even consider making up a dozen or two animals in your leisure time before going to the party and handing them out when it's time. Still I feel you should make the first few from scratch (with or without a pump) just so the kids can have the thrill of seeing how you transform an ordinary balloon into a lovable figure.

You don't have to limit yourself just to animals. You can make balloon toys, hats, and games. Even balloon puppets combined with ventriloquism, can be used with pleasing results. *Dewey's Balloon and Clown Notebook* is one of a series of books written by Ralph Dewey, which shows many figures and toys that can be made from balloons.

Warning—do not give balloons to very young children. Kids under the age of three or four like to stick

Ed: The horn on my car doesn't work.
Fred: Is it broken?
Ed: No, it's just indifferent.
Fred: What do you mean, indifferent?
Ed: It just doesn't give a hoot.

things in their mouths. If the balloon pops, this can be dangerous. A scrap of balloon put in the mouth and cause the child to choke and even suffocate. Although toddlers like balloons, it's best to save them for the older kids.

For more information on balloons, see Chapter Nine.

Paper Games and Puzzles

I usually give balloon animals as a gift, but I also like to give a second gift that I can easily print my name and phone number on. A sheet of paper or a small booklet of games, puzzles, or brain teasers works well. This way everyone at the party will know who I am; so will their parents when they take the gift home. Your expense is the cost of the paper and printing, which amounts to only a few cents each if you buy in large quantities.

You can have an artist make a coloring book taken from pictures of you in costume. This would be an excellent way to promote yourself. A single sheet or a short booklet with dot-to-dot drawings, mazes, cross word puzzles, jokes, and magic tricks can make an excellent gift. (See Chapter 20 for other examples.)

Paper toys can also be made with much the same success as balloon figures. You can do this yourself, or have everyone make their own as you show them how. Kids always take pride in something they make themselves and will be sure to show it to their parents. Paper hats, airplanes, and puppets are a few easily made items. You may find some intriguing creations and ideas in books on origami or paper airplanes.

Bookstore Clerk: Here's a new book called *How to Help Your Husband Get Ahead.*
New Wife: Oh, no thank you. My husband already has one.

Doris: What did you get that little silver medal for?
Daisy: For singing.
Doris: What did you get the big gold medal for?
Daisy: For stopping.

Ed: Did your mother ever lift weights?
Fred: Why do you think that?
Ed: How else could she have raised a big dumbell like you?

Photographs

A black and white autographed photo of yourself is another excellent gift. Have your name and number printed on it and use it as the special gift just for the birthday child, or you can give one to each of the guests.

I like to give the guest of honor a special gift just for her (along with the other gifts). Receiving something that no one else gets makes her feel important and makes the parents happy because you show her special attention.

Use a studio photo and look as professional as you can. A studio photo is expensive, but it can serve you for several years. You can also use it in other promotional materials.

Handing out actual photographs can be expensive. Rather than using a real photograph, you can have copies (halftones) of the photo printed for a reasonable price. Have the printer use glossy paper and it will look just like a photo. Don't forget to have your name and phone number printed on it.

The old saying "A picture is worth a thousand words" is true. The children who receive your picture will remember you longer. Parents will be able to see the funny clown their child was talking about, giving them a longer lasting impression and an increased chance of remembering you when their child has a birthday.

I recommend that you autograph each picture. Autographs give the picture a personal touch and increase the chance that the child will get it home and keep it around for a while. I prefer to autograph each picture personally rather then have the signature printed. The autographs can be done beforehand with a simple such as "Best Wishes, Fumbles the Clown."

You could also make the photo more personal by waiting until the party and asking for each child's name. Write something like "Keep smiling Jennifer, Fumbles the Clown."

Toys and Candy

Balloon animals are a favorite giveaway for most clowns, but you certainly can use your imagination and try other things. If you do magic, an appropriate gift would be an inexpensive magic trick or puzzle. If you buy them in large quantities at wholesale prices, the cost can be minimal. Whatever you choose, keep the cost low.

Richard "Snowflake" Snowberg

Some of the cheapest toys are balloons—not pencil balloons which are used to make animals, but spinners, rockets, and other novelty balloons. They are inflated, then turned lose to fly or spin. They are reusable and kids love them.

Another interesting toy is the "talking tapes," a thin strip of plastic which carries a recorded message. You make it talk by running your fingernail down the length of the tape. The messages include "I love you," "Happy birthday," "Happy anniversary," and others. These toys fascinate kids because they can mysteriously produce a human sounding voice.

Candy and other treats are enjoyable and can make an inexpensive giveaway, but you should check with your hostess before giving this type of gift. Some kids are restricted from certain foods either for health reasons or simply because the parents don't want to dig candy out of the rug after the party.

Small lollipops and such are easy to carry and are appreciated by the children but once eaten, they're gone. There's nothing to take home to show mom, and let her know who you are. If you want to give candy, consider combining it with another more permanent gift with your promotional material printed on it.

Balloons are fun, but don't use them just because everyone else does. Use your imagination and find something different. The more unique the gift, the greater the chance it will be kept by the recipient as a reminder of the fun he or she had with you.

GETTING PAID

How do you collect your payment? As with any service, it is customary for the customer to make payment immediately following the work. You should collect your fee after you've finished your party activities and just before you leave.

As the American Express commerical says, "Don't leave home without it." You're asking for trouble if you leave with only a promise that payment will be sent to you. Payment may not be forthcoming for a variety of reasons: forgetfulness, busy schedules, and even outright deception. If you don't get paid before you leave, you may have a hard time collecting.

Often the hostess will be ready with your payment as soon as you finish. If you explain beforehand that you need to be paid as soon as you finish, most people will try to accommodate you. You may have to track her down in the kitchen or some other part of the house and tell her you're ready for payment. You might even tell her that you would appreciate it if she got the check ready as you make balloon animals or hand out your party favors.

At times the hostess will be in a frenzy, shovelling out ice cream as rowdy kids eagerly bear down on her. She may try to put you off and suggest sending payment it to you later. Don't let her. You've explained to her (or should have) on the phone when payment was to be made. Insist that you receive it then, and explain you can't stay because you have an appointment elsewhere. This will help motivate her to pull herself away from the children and complete her part of the arrangement. Be firm, but remain friendly.

When you leave the party, you will be richer both in your pocketbook and in spirit. The thrill and fun of making kids laugh and getting paid to do it is a unique experience. It has its trials on occasion, but the benefits more than compensate for them.

Ed: How do you like my new car? Doesn't it ride smooth?
Fred: It's a nice car but you race around these mountain curves so fast I get scared!
Ed: Then why don't you do what I do when we make a sharp curve?
Fred: What's that?
Ed: I close my eyes.

CLASSIC CLOWN GAGS

One Dollar Pickup

A clown casually walking along notices a dollar lying on the ground. He looks both ways to see if anyone is watching then bends over to pick it up. As he reaches for the money an unknown hand slaps him on the seat of his pants. He jumps up, turns around, but sees nobody. Again he bends over to grab the dollar and again is slapped. This is repeated several times.

The mysterious hand is a padded glove which has been attached to a long stick. A second clown hiding nearby uses the stick on anyone who attempts to pickup the dollar.

Talk Talk Talk

One clown is endlessly talking to another clown. The second clown is tired of listening and tells him to shut up. But the first clown continues to jabber away.

Feed up, the second clown tells him to shut up and places his hand over the talker's mouth. When the hand is removed, the teeth come with it—still chattering.

Long Underwear

A clown noticing that his underwear is sticking out of one of his sleeves tries to push it backup out of sight. But it keep coming back out. Frustrated be begins to pull on it. As he does it comes down over his hand. He pulls more. The more he pulls the longer it gets. Soon a couple of yards of sleeve is hanging from his arm. One last pull brings the rest of the garment out.

Mind Reader

A clown claims his companion can read minds. To prove this statement a few members of the audience are asked to come up to assist them.

The mind reader sits in a chair which faces sideways so that the audience can see only one side of his face. A blindfold is then tired around his eyes.

The first volunteer form the audience is instructed to stand a few feet in front of the mind reading clown. The volunteer is instructed by the other clown to hold up any number of fingers he chooses and that his friend will correctly call out that number.

The volunteer holds up two fingers (or any amount he chooses). The clown sitting down begins to concentrate and read the volunteer's mind. The other clown standing behind him hits him twice on the head with a rolled up newspaper. Then he asks his seated companion what the number is. He answers "two."

Two more volunteers in turn are given the chance to test the mind reader's power. They indicate their chosen number with their fingers and the blindfolded clown gives the correct answer each time after being hit over the head with the newspaper.

Standing clown asks audience if they believe now that his friend is a mind reader. They say "No" and he confesses it was a trick and has his companion stand up and reveal their secret. He stands up to show an eye hole cut in the far side of the blindfold.

The Hat

A clown wearing a hat slips and falls onto the floor. He gets up and goes over to retrieve his hat. As he bends down to pick up the hat it jumps away from him. He reaches for it again and it leaps away. Each time he tries to pick it up it jumps out of reach.

What is really happening is that as the clown steps toward the hat he gives it a kick. Timing is important to make this look good. The clown must begin reaching down for the hat as he makes the last step which delivers the kick.

After chasing the hat around for awhile he tries to sneak up on it. Slowly he creeps toward it. Suddenly he leaps, coming down on the hat with his whole body. The hat is crushed.

CHAPTER 20

BEING LOVED, BEING REMEMBERED, AND BEING BOOKED!

Hi! I'm Hal Diamond, the magician. Why, you ask is a magician contributing to this—a clown book? The answer is simple, I've worked with hundreds of clowns—and from the perspective of a "non-clown," it's quite easy to see which clown characterizations work and which do not, which clowns work steadily and which do not, and which clowns are lovingly remembered and which clowns people don't even care to remember.

My performing credentials span a wide range of performing arenas: the Kennedy Center, the White House, the National Press Club, the Smithsonian Institution, several casinos in Atlantic City, including Trump Plaza and Caesar's, the National Air and Space Museum, the U.S. House of Representatives, hundreds of schools, shopping centers, banquets, military bases, TV shows, recreation departments, and literally thousands of company picnics and parties. In twenty years, if you keep busy, you can play many places, and you learn what it takes to be remembered and loved.

BEING LOVED AND REMEMBERED

Don't be a "generic" clown—be somebody! If you've got a name—and you better have—make sure the audience remembers it!

Many clowns who are excellent performers will remain known to their audiences simply as "the clown." No matter how successful they are in the art of clowning, how many people they make laugh, or how great they were; they failed to make their name stick! Writing as a talent agent, I assure you that you can't book an act if it doesn't have a name!

Let me give some examples drawn from clowns I have met in the last two decades. Some I remember because they were very good, others because they were not.

I've encountered several clowns named "Jingles." A cute and popular name for a clown. The one I remember best performed at the Touchdown Club in Washington, D.C. about ten years ago. Why do I remember this particular Jingles? Because he jingled— *he really jingled.* Dozens and dozens of bells of all sizes and colors were sewn all over his costume. He even wore a large gold styrofoam bell for a hat! Every step he took, every hand he shook, reinforced his name, "Jingles." He was an excellent clown with an excellent marketing gimmick. I'm convinced that everyone, young and old, who met Jingles remembered him.

A few weeks ago I met a wonderful clown named "Sparkles" (another popular name) at a large promotion for the National Gas Company. Sparkles had everything going for him—talent, personality, etc.—but he just didn't sparkle. He was attired very nicely in pink and baby blue. What a difference a liberal dose of sequins,

Hal Diamond

rhinestones, and tinsel would have made! Or a nose that glittered! Kids love sparkling things. Imagine Sparkles dressed like Liberace extending his hand for a handshake, and there on each finger is a giant, dazzling, diamond ring. I assure you, he would be remembered!

"Buttons" is another common clown name. The best "Buttons" I ever met was covered with buttons of all shapes and sizes—both the sewing variety and the pin-backed type with pictures and sayings on the front. Children of all ages enjoyed inspecting Buttons. He even wore buttons from foreign countries. Before a performance, if a person, organization, or company sent Buttons a button, he would wear it and let people search for it. To top it off, Buttons produced a large jar of buttons out of his pocket and conducted an impromptu "Guess the Number of Buttons in Button's Jar" game. The great thing about it was, that everyone was a winner! No matter what number kids guessed—three hundred and twenty-nine, ten, seventeen thousand six hundred and fifty-two—Buttons always said, "Close enough for a prize!" The prize, as you might guess, was a free button with Button's picture and advertising on it! Buttons was fun, Buttons was creative, and Buttons was booked a lot!

Peace, promise, and love are all wrapped up in the name "Rainbow," which I'm sure is why so many clowns choose it. Most Rainbows capitalize on the potential of the name and dress accordingly. I have seen some wear gloves with each finger a different color; another had a rainbow painted across his fore-head. A particularly enterprising Rainbow set up a table and did face painting, providing rainbows for everyone to wear and enjoy—and everyone wanted one!

Sometimes in the desire to be popular, funny, or the center of attention, a person can overdo it and clowns are no different! I remember the following types very well—and, I also remember very well *not* to book or recommend them!

"Confetti," with one of the greatest clown names I've ever heard, had a great deal going for her—costume, makeup, and enthusiasm. The thing that killed everyone's love for Confetti was her behavior! She ran around, darting in and out among people, honking a loud horn, throwing handfuls of computer confetti in their faces and letting out a hideous death laugh. She was truly frightening! She would have been perfect in a feline movie. I only saw her "work" a cocktail party once, but what a lesson in how to lose friends and influence people the wrong way. Dale Carnegie would have died! Just like Confetti's clowning career did.

"Buzzer," another misguided merrymaker, had a great idea but failed to play it right. His makeup and outfit were a splashy mix of lightning bolts in hot colors. His downfall was shaking hands, because every time he reached out and took someone's hand, a loud—very loud—buzzer went off, followed by Buzzer letting out a piercing scream and shaking his entire body as if he had been electrocuted. Needless to say, every victim was scared out of his wits! The one evening I worked with Buzzer, I heard dozens of screams, saw several spilt drinks, and witnessed an elderly gentleman fall to the floor and grab his chest! Just imagine! It was funny, in a morbid sort of way, watching Buzzer set up his innocent victims for the kill. Buzzer had a very short-lived career. I am convinced that if he had continued, one day his kin would have had to drag the river to find his body.

Another clown, Thumper, went around thumping folks over the head with a large sponge mallet. Doing it to other clowns is one thing, but doing it to guests at a party is another. Thumper was a real pain to have around. So naturally, Thumper wasn't around long.

> Doris: What is the best way to prevent infection caused by biting insects?
> Daisy: Don't bite any.

Despite what most magic catalogues and ads say, people really don't like being tricked or fooled—not to mention being the brunt of practical jokes. People like being entertained.

PROMOTING YOURSELF AND GETTING BOOKED

Now that I've expressed some of my likes and dislikes about clowns, let me suggest some ways I have used in the magic business to promote my act which can also work for clowns.

It's most important for folks in an audience to know your name and know how to get in touch with you so they can book you for future events.

Make sure you wear your name. Sew it on your hat or sleeve, stencil it on the back of your outfit, your cases, or stitch it on your bag of tricks. Of course, wear a button with your name on it. The name badges that contain chasing lights instantly draw attention and captivate both young and old.

I am convinced that if you want to be booked, you must be in the telephone book (listed under "clowns"), have your own business cards, get listed with local booking agents and party planners, and give something away—not something edible, but something your audience can take home and keep. Recently I have seen clowns at picnics and parties slapping round, fluorescent stickers on kids that read, "I've been kissed by a clown!" It's a cute idea, but totally worthless other than just giving the clown something to do. For about the same amout of money, you can go to any print shop and have a personalized message printed on the same hot pink stickers. The following messages would be much more fun and much more commercially productive: "I've been hugged by Snuggles the Clown," "I shook hands with Shakey," "I ♥ Chuckles the Clown." Be sure to include your phone number and area code. Your complete address is not that important. In twenty years of performing, I've had few written requests for bookings; the telephone is king!

The amateur performer will foolishly give away lollipops or bubble gum—something that is of momentary satisfaction and quickly forgotten. The more seasoned pro will think of more creative and long-lasting giveaways. The following items have served me very well in promoting my magic show. If you select one or two and personalize them, they will work very well for you also.

One of the greatest giveaways of all time, *the mystery dollar bill,* is valued by children and is a super handout at adult shows for "those of you that may have a boy or girl at home who would enjoy performing their own magic tricks." It's easy to hand out, fits in a purse or wallet, and is inexpensive to produce. Everyone wins! Get your basic dollar bill pattern from artist Ed Harris (5901 Drew Avenue S., Minneapolis, MN 55401; phone 612-922-4021), then personalize it as I have done and have it printed on green paper. Because of the size, you can print two to a page and cut the page in half. For less than ten dollars you can have several thousand bills.

All performers are in demand around the major "kid" holidays—Halloween, Christmas, and Easter. At each type of party the host organization (service club, church, recreation department, etc.) usually will give the children a packet of goodies to take home. It may be a trick-or-treat bag, a Christmas stocking, or an assortment of Easter candy. When you are engaged to perform for these events, announce that you'll be pleased to donate in advance a free game, puzzle sheet, or mystery dollar that can be placed in the goody bag ahead of time so it's in there when the child receives it from Santa or whoever. No one has ever refused to do this—they love it—and look at it as something extra that you're giving them, which you are! You're getting a little something extra too—some great advertising!

For Halloween I give out the *Cryptic Crosswords* puzzle. I stamp or type my advertising message in the space above the title and have it duplicated on orange stock paper. I give away a similar *Magic Toy Search*

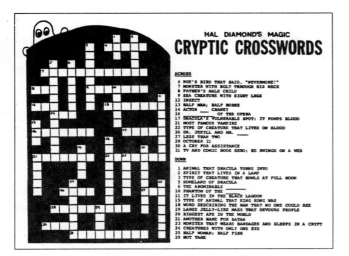

for Christmas and a *Find the Rabbits* for Easter. Because I do many repeat shows, I have two designs for each holiday so I can alternate them every year. Just try using the same handout two years in a row. Kids may not know how to add one plus one, but they'll remember you gave them the same game last year!

The *Magician's Assistant Diploma* has been around for years and is as popular as ever because it makes every child who receives one feel very important. Personalize yours as I have mine. If you do a show

and want to make the diploma more official looking, take two pieces of red or blue ribbon and attach them to the lower left corner over the seal. Stick on a shiny gold notary seal available from most stationery stores. If you do birthday shows, make one with the birthday child's name on it (spelled correctly) ahead of time to · give to the guest of honor. It will be cherished, prized,

and remembered, and so will you!

If you perform at schools, camps, or recreation departments, the *Color the Magician Poster* is very good. It is educational and keeps the little folks busy after the show (the teachers will thank you!). It's also something the kids can take home, show mom, and tape up on the bedroom wall or attach to the refrigerator door. Call artist Ed Harris and have him tailor a coloring poster just for you. A word of caution: sometimes I send the coloring pictures ahead of my shows, and it's always great to see these works of art decorating the halls when I come in. But never, NEVER get put in the position of judging which is the best. They're *all* wonderful!

The *Animal Hunt* is a fun and easy activity for kids. No directions are given because it's obvious even to the youngest student what you're supposed to do. Add your name, logo, phone, and advertising at the top, on each side of the clown's hat. If you wish to give a holiday theme this one, it's so simple to do. Just add a happy Jack-o'-lantern, Christmas tree, or Easter egg. Run the Animal Hunt on colored stock; I perfer a bright canary yellow, which shows up well and is very attractive.

For older children and adults, try the *Crazy Intelligence Test*, which contains nine funny, challenging puzzles. Place your advertising at the top or bottom and duplicate it. I choose blue paper because it appears more mature. When you hand out this one, people will start guessing right away. Don't be flustered. They'll also ask you immediately about the puzzles they can't figure out. Don't be tempted to give in and answer the questions. Smile and suggest that they consult someone else (thus showing your advertising to even

more people!). If they persist, tell them the answer so they can be a "genius" too. If after looking at the Crazy Intelligence Test, you can't figure out all nine puzzles, the answers are: Water on the Knee, Cutting a Lady in Two, Harry Houdini, Lost in the Stars or Lost in Space, Paradise, Deep in the Heart of Dixie, Split Level, Blooming Idiot, and Long Johns.

Some years ago during the first week of December, I mailed out a Christmas flyer to my clients from the past couple of years. This is a friendly way to wish them the best during the holidays—plus, it fills in those open dates. I have run the same flyer on the back of my giveaways from Thanksgiving through New Year's.

If you do birthday parties, how about giving the birthday child an *engraved pencil* which reads, "Happy Birthday from Chuckles, the Clown." Engraved pencils are very inexpensive if purchased by the thousands. Check with your local printer. Chances are he can't print pencils, but he will know who can do the job.

Postcards with your photo on them are a dynamite way to drop a line, especially as a thank you to the person who booked your show. If it's a birthday, send the postcard to the child. Children love to receive mail because they think it's a sign of growing up. And don't be mistaken and think nobody will read your card (and advertising) except the child. Your postcard will be prized and shown to parents, relatives, friends, and neighbors. For postcards and 8 x 10 photos, I recommend ABC Pictures, Inc., 1867 E. Florida St., Springfield, MO 65803; phone 417-869-9433. Write and ask for a price list and free samples.

Check out the *classified section* in your local weekly papers. If there is a classification for entertainers, it may be worth your investment to take out a small ad.

Young Soldier

Old Sea Captain

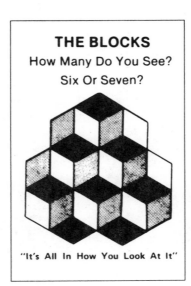

THE BLOCKS

How Many Do You See?

Six Or Seven?

"It's All In How You Look At It"

can you see both women ?

one young...one old

Be very brief. Just give your clown name, phone number, and what you're best at, such as "Children's Birthdays a Specialty."

I'm flabbergasted at the amazing number of clowns who don't have their own *business cards*. They are so inexpensive and easy to obtain. Call any quick print shop and you can usually get them in less than forty-eight hours. The price is usually a bargain. If you like a "gimmick card" you may want to place one of the designs illustrated here on the back of your business card. Because they are a type of mini-illusion that the recipient can show to others, they are rarely thrown away. Always keep some cards with you. Put some in your wallet, purse, car, jacket pocket, and of course, in your clown costume. Have them available so when someone asks if you do birthdays or company picnics you can say, "Oh yes! I love doing those. Here's my card!"

There are countless other items that you can hand out. The list is limited only by your own creativity and imagination. I believe anything that works for you is good, as long as it is in good taste. Some people say that taste is a matter of personal opinion. I don't buy that! Courtesy and politeness are always in style and appreciated. If you are a good entertainer, promote yourself well, and respect others, people will love you and reward you handsomely—what more could any clown ask for?

I'm always interested in promotional items other entertainers are using. Have a good one? Drop me a line—I'll be pleased to hear from you. Hal Diamond, P.O. Box 351, Kensington, MD 20895.

APPENDIX A

PUBLICATIONS AND ORGANIZATIONS

Backstage
Backstage Publications, Inc.
330 W. 42th Street
New York, NY 10036

The Christian Conjourer
Fellowship of Christian Magicians
Connersville, IN 47331

The Circus Report
525 Oak Street
El Cerrito, CA 94530

Clown Alley
International Shrine Clown Association
1122 Third Avenue
Rockford, IL 61108-3102

Clowning Around
World Clown Association
P.O. Box 1905
Allentown, PA 18105

Clowns International Newsletter
Clowns International
174, Stockbridge Road
Winchester, Hants. SO22 6RW
England

Genii
P.O. Box 36068
Los Angeles, CA 90036

Juggler's World
International Juggler's Association
Box 29
Kenmore, NY 14217

Kascade-European Juggling Magazine
Annastr. 7
D-6200 Wiesbaden
W. Germany

King Pole
Circus Fans' Association of Great Britain
43 Waterloo Lane
Skellingthorpe, Lincoln LN6 5SJ
England

Laugh-Makers
P.O. Box 160
Syracuse, NY 13215

The Linking Ring
International Brotherhood of Magicians
P.O. Box 227
Kenton, OH 43326

Magic Manuscript
6 West 32nd Street, 4th floor
New York, NY 10001

Mime Journal
Grand Valley State College
Performing Arts Center
Allendale, MI 49407

Mime News
National Mime Association
Pomona College Theater
Homes Hall, 6th & College
Claremont, CA 91711

MUM
Society of American Magicians
P.O. Box 368
Mango, FL 33550

The New Calliope
Clowns of America International
P.O. Box 75248
St. Paul, MN 55175

New Oracle
Society of American Ventriloquists
414 Oak Street
Baltimore, OH 43105

Newsy Vents
North American Association of Ventriloquists
P.O. Box 420
Littleton, CO 80160

New Tops Magazine
Abbott's Magic Mnfg. Co.
Colon, MI 49040

On One Wheel
Unicycling Society of America, Inc.
P.O. Box 40534
Redford, MI 48240

Puppetry Journal
Puppeteers of America
#5 Cricklewood Path
Pasadena, CA 91107

Street Performers Newsletter
c/o Stephen Baird
P.O. Box 570
Cambridge, MA 02238

Unicycling
International Unicycling Federation, Inc.
67 Lion Lane
Westbury, NY 11590

Unowheel™
Solipaz Publishing Company
P.O. Box 366
Lodi, CA 95241

White Tops
Circus Fans' Associations of America
Four Center Dr.
Camp Hill, PA 17011

In addition to the publications and organizations listed here, special mention should be made to The Clown Hall of Fame and Research Center, 212 East Walworth Avenue, Delavan, WI 53115. The center is dedicated to the preservation and advancement of clowning, operating a living museum with resident clown performers, conducting special events, and maintaining a national archive of clown artifacts and history.

APPENDIX B

SUPPLIERS

This is a partial list of some of the many suppliers and manufactures who sell clown props and related equipment through the mail. Most local fun shops and magic stores carry many of the same items sold by these mail order suppliers.

Artistic Clowns
P.O. Box 811
Mt. Clemens, MI 48046

Axtell Expressions
272 Dalton Street
Ventura, CA 93003

Balloon Box
St. James's Park
2416 Ravendale Court
Kissimmee, FL 32758

Books By Mail
P.O. Box 3128
Santa Ana, CA 92703

Brian Dube', Inc.
25 Park Place
New York, NY 10007

Chasley, Inc.
P.O. Box 19202
Seattle, WA 98109

The Circus Clowns
3556 Nicollet Ave.
Minneapolis, MN 55408

The Clown Factory
11705 Perrin Beitel #5
San Antonio, TX 78217

Dewey's Good News Balloons
1202 Wildwood Dr.
Deer Park, TX 77536

Freckles Clown Supplies
4560 Sussex Ave.
Jacksonville, FL 32210

The Funhouse Magic Shop
3535 Belair Road
Baltimore, MD 21213

Fun Technicians, Inc.
4782 Streets Drive
Syracuse, NY 13215

Hank Lee's Magic Factory
125 Lincoln Street
P.O. Box 1359
Boston, MA 02205

Hutch's Emporium
110 N. Main St.
Adrian, MI 49221

Ickle Pickle Products, Inc.
883 Somerton Ridge Drive
St. Louis, MO 63141

Java Publishing Co.
6510 Lehman Drive
Colorado Springs, CO 809·

Jenack Circus Corp.
67 Lion Lane
Westbury, NY 11590

Jugglebug
7506J Olympic View Dr.
Edmonds, WA 98020

Juggling Arts
612 Calpella Dr.
San Jose, CA 95136

LaRocks Fun & Magic Outlet
2123 Central Avenue
Charlotte, NC 28205

Looney Balloney's
9755 66th St. North
Pinellas Park, FL 33565

Lynch's
939 Howard
Dearborn, MI 48124

Magic City
15528 Illinois Ave
Paramount, CA 90723

Magic, Inc.
5082 N. Lincoln
Chicago, IL 60625

Maher Studios
Box 420
Littleton, CO 80160

Masters Costumes
5845 Leesburg Pike
Bailey's Crossroads, VA 22041

Mecca Magic, Inc.
49 Dodd Street
Bloomfield, NJ 07003

Morris Costumes
3108 Monroe Road
Charlotte, NC 28205

Morrissey Magic Ltd.
2882 Dufferin Street
Toronto, Ont. M6B 3S6
Canada

One Way Street, Inc.
Box 2398
Littleton, CO 80161

Spotlight Circus Products
Box 16441
Amsterdam 1001 RM.
Holland

Stevens Magic Emporium
3238 East Douglas
Wichita, KS 67208

Todd Smith Products
13401 Lake Shore Blvd.
Cleveland, OH 44120

Tony Blanco's Props Unlimit
P.O. Box 3440
Reno, NV 89505

Up Up and Away
Box 147 Main Street
Beallsville, PA 15313

Under the Big Top
1525A N. Placentia Ave.
Placentia, CA 92670

INDEX

KIDS SAY THE DARNDEST THINGS
by *Art Linkletter*

"I'm going to be a doctor."
"What would you do if I came to you with a broken arm?"
"Put it in a cast."
"What would you do if I had a stomach ache?"
"I'd give you a pill."
"And what if I had a hole in my head?"
"I'd put a cork in it."

A hilarious collection of priceless quotes by youngsters on all aspects of life from parents to pets. Illustrated by Charles Schultz. Hardcover. $5.98

DR. DROPO'S
BALLOON SCULPTURING FOR BEGINNERS
by *Bruce Fife*

In this entertaining book clown balloonologist Dr. Dropo provides step-by-step instruction for making several fascinating balloon animals, toys, and games. Includes: dog, giraffe, rabbit, frog, mouse, kangaroo, bee, swan, ladybug, squirrel, camel, bird, seal, Mr. Wrinkle, bubble baby, Captain Marvel, troll, Ziggy, Bubbles the clown, airplane, flyers, spinners, whistlers, Fearless Freddy Fly Fighter, pirate sword, a balloon gun that really works, and many others. A fun book to experience!

Comes complete with a package of pencil and apple modeling balloons, all you need to add is the air. Paperback. $6.50

VERY SPECIAL PEOPLE
by *Fredrick Drimmer*

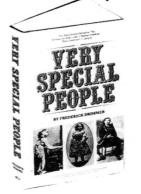

The Elephant Man . . . Hermaphrodites . . . Bearded Ladies . . . Missing Links . . . more than 65 rare photos and amazing facts about the most bizarre human oddities who ever lived!

The stories of their triumphs over physical imperfection are as inspiring as they are fascinating. An international super-seller! 375 pages, hardcover. $5.98

DR. DROPO'S
JUGGLING BUFFOONERY
by *Bruce Fife*

Here's a whole book jam-packed with comic juggling material written by clown juggler Dr. Dropo. Contains a introduction on how to juggle, how to manipulate cigar boxes, and do balancing comedy. Includes 25 complete comedy juggling routines, 106 pages. All funny.

Most all of the juggling tricks are simple and easy to learn, some routines don't even require any real juggling skill, relying strictly on comedy dialogue and mime. Paperback. $7.95.

"People who want to develop an act for birthday parties or street corners, but who don't know where to start, will find this book a blessing."—*Juggler's World magazine*

ORDER FORM

Please send me the following books:

_____ Copy (copies) of **KIDS SAY THE DARNDEST THINGS** $5.95 ea.
_____ Copy (copies) of **VERY SPECIAL PEOPLE** $5.98 ea.
_____ Copy (copies) of **DR. DROPO'S BALLOON SCULPTURING FOR BEGINNERS** $6.50 ea.
_____ Copy (copies) of **DR. DROPO'S JUGGLING BUFFOONERY** $7.95 ea.

Enclosed is my check or money order for $_____ including postage (please enclose $1 per book for postage).

(PLEASE PRINT CLEARLY)

NAME_____

ADDRESS_____

CITY AND STATE_____ ZIP_____

Mail to JAVA PUBLISHING COMPANY, Dept. A, 6510 Lehman Drive, Colorado Springs, CO 80918